THE CANINE CRITICS AGREE!

"A sweeping tale of epic pawportion!"

"FOUR paws!"

"Fetching!"

"A tour de fur!"

"One of the most waggish works in recent memory!"

"A tasty morsel of spiritual wisdom! I ate half this book before breakfast!"

"Bow WOW!"

"Magnifiscent! Sniff-worthy! Smells good too!"

"Provides as much pleasure as licking my nether regions!"

"From the very first woof, it made my head tilt!"

"Spell-bound by this hound!"

"An endless supply of treats for the soul!"

"A Magnum Barkus for our time!"

Also By William B. Miller

The Beer Drinker's Guide to God:
The Whole and Holy Truth About Lager, Loving, and Living

The Gospel According to Sam:
Animal Stories for the Soul

THE LAST

HOWLELUJAH

Tails from the Trail

by

WILLIAM B. MILLER

THE
HOWLELUJAH
PRESS

ISBN: 978-1-7357716-0-1 (Paperback)
ISBN: 978-1-7357716-1-8 (Audiobook)
ISBN: 978-1-7357716-2-5 (eBook)

Library of Congress Control Number: 2020919315

Front cover image by Diana Branton
Interior book design by Melissa S. Rabidoux
Photographs © Sea Light Studios unless otherwise credited

Printed by IngramSpark in the United States of America

First printing, 2020

For more information on our books or to invite William B. Miller to your event, please contact our Event Coordinator at the address or email below:

Howlelujah Press, Inc.
P.O. Box 4291
Covington, LA 70433

info@howlelujahpress.com
www.HowlelujahPress.com

For Wili.
And Waylon. And Sinbad. And Lili. And Mano. And…

TABLE OF CONTENTS

First Paw:
TO ALL THE DOGS I'VE LOVED BEFORE (AND AFTER)

Second Paw:
ON THE ROAD (AGAIN)

Third Paw:
HOWLELUJAH! HE IS RISEN! (INDEED)

Fourth Paw:
ROOM AT THE END

Has not God sent us a good messenger?

Saint Brendan the Navigator, 6th Century

THE LAST HOWLELUJAH

Tails from the Trail

INTRO**DOG**TION

All things bright and beautiful, all creatures great and small, all things wise and wonderful: the Lord God made them all.

Anglican hymn

This is a book about a dog. Or maybe it's a book about a boy and his dog. Then again, this is a book about God. Or perhaps it's a book about a boy and his God.

It's definitely a book about faith and faithfulness, healing and hope, and doubt and discovery. It's also a book about relationships, community, caring, and sharing. It's certainly about cancer, prayer, priorities, purpose, and meaning. It's absolutely a book about disappointments and detours, surprise and serendipity, and about welcoming the unexpected and venturing into the unknown—but not alone. It's positively a book about road trips, bonding with best friends, barbecue, beer, ball, and helping out when and where we can.

On one hand, this is a book about America, at least about what Americans might long for more than anything else during these challenging and divisive times—a period of turmoil in which canines more consistently exhibit a quality of character than our elected officials. On the other paw, it's a book for planet earth—another reminder that the Creator still has "the whole world in His hands," and that includes our animal friends.

The French writer, Francois-Anatole Thibault (whose literary agent must have told him he would be more marketable if he changed his name to Anatole France), once wrote a book about a nearsighted priest who mistakenly baptized a bunch of penguins who were then miraculously, though unfortunately, transformed into humans. The world was worse for it, reminding us that sometimes the animals get closer to realizing God's intention for creation than the humans do. The priest in the story suggests the all-too-pervasive reality that "nearsighted" religion—a way of believing that cannot see past itself, promotes its own self-interest, and fails to see the bigger picture—is always barking up the wrong spiritual tree. "Farsighted" religion, an approach that takes the long and broad view of the whole world as sacred, believes all of creation is worthy of respect and reverence, and sees over the fence and down the street and clear across the world. Now that's a perspective worthy of a thousand wags and a united shout of *Howlelujah!*

For a time, the writings of Anatole France were on the "no read" list, having been prohibited by certain nearsighted religious authorities. It was another sure sign that he wasn't far from the heart of God. But beyond penguin perceptions and banned books, Anatole France is credited with this delectable nugget of an observation: "Until one has loved an animal, a part of one's soul remains unawakened." Can I get a *paw*men? If there was ever a truer, more spiritually accurate statement about our relationship with the created order (as well as the doggone disorder), I'm still sniffing around to find it.

I've loved five dogs in my lifetime. Oops, make that six. Dammit. Seven. I admit that I have a problem, but I'm aware that they all have a purpose. Each one of them has awakened parts of my soul I didn't previously know existed. There was the original "King of the Terrier Trinity," my 82 lb. Airedale, Sam Houston. Born in Fort Worth and living out his dog days in the Texas capital, Sam's great adventure began with a Sunday morning fire when he was just a puppy, still trusting that life was always a big bowl of tasty treats, never-ending belly scratches, believing that all puppies and people were to be trusted, and that tragedies were something that happened to the dog down the street. Sam was home alone at my ex-girlfriend Rachel's apartment in Austin. She had accepted my invitation to visit my multicultural, eastside Austin Episcopal Church for a special presentation by the Root Wym'n Theatre Company. While she was away getting religion, Sam got way more than he wanted or deserved. A tragedy burst into Sam's previously pristine world as he was simply doing that thing that he did best—napping on Rachel's bed. There was a gas leak in the apartment, which caused a great explosion shattering all the windows and nearly knocking the "H" out of the nearby Whole Foods sign. Flames swept across the apartment and everything therein—including

Sam. Severely burned, Sam ran and hid in a closet under a pile of clothes as the flames threatened to engulf the entire building.

The neighbors heard Sam's cries and rather than run away from the danger, they ran toward it, and even into it. Although they weren't traditionally "religious," they were able to see beyond themselves and their own safety, practicing the essence of all real religion, and observing the most important commandment of all—love your neighbor as yourself (even if your neighbor has four legs and dog breath). They raced up the stairs, kicked in the door, scooped up Sam, and carried him to safety. Thanks to them, Sam got saved. He found religion in its purest form: kindness, compassion, and love. As my boss, Episcopal Presiding Bishop (and preacher at the royal wedding of Prince Harry and Meghan Markle), Michael Curry, likes to say, "If it's not about love, it's not about God!" Sam's salvation reminds us that it's all about love, which is all about God, and sometimes all about Dog.

Sam was severely burned in the fire, and we weren't sure he would survive. The fire inspector's official report came out the following week and, to add insult to injury, next to "cause of fire," it read, "dog turned on gas jet." Not only was Sam burned over 80% of his body, he was also officially accused of a felony (which sounds a lot like *feline-y*, Sam might add given his sense of humor even in the most dire of circumstances). Sam began to heal and the following Sunday, the neighbors threw Sam a big party where they elected him Austin's Mayor of Baylor Street. They unfurled giant banners from second story windows that read: "Get Well Sam!" and "Sam is INNOCENT!" His ears were burned so badly that they had to be amputated, so Sam became known throughout the city, and eventually throughout the world, as "The Fearless Earless Airedale."

Sam's salvation became the basis for my first book, *The Gospel According to Sam: Animal Stories for the Soul.* As Sam and I grew older and he began to mature spiritually, I started paying more attention to not only our life together but, as I traveled around the world, I also began to pay more attention to our animal friends and the adventures that accompanied our introductions. Before I knew it, I had an entire book of often furry, sometimes funny, stories. I realized along the way that to be a good writer one must cultivate the same quality that makes for a good Christian and, ultimately, a good person: *Awareness.* When we pay attention and actually notice what God's up to in the world, we'll gain unimaginable insights and become more enlightened. Combine such keen observation and mindfulness with a sense of deep gratitude, and one will always end up on the right, if not righteous, path.

The second member of the "Terrier Trinity" was Andrew "Jack" Jackson. An Okie with cow dog tendencies, Jack was a bundle of mischief wrapped in sacrificial love. In other words, he was damn-near perfect. In American history, Sam Houston and Andrew Jackson were good friends. In American *canine* history, Sam and Jack were *best* friends. Jack ended up with some pretty *paw*found stories of his own, even demonstrating toward the end of Sam's life just how far love will go. As it turns out, love will take us farther, higher, and deeper than we've ever gone before, to a better, more blessed, and more blissful place than we've ever known. I know such love because I know Jack.

The third member of the "Terrier Trinity" should've probably been demoted to the angelic realm given his questionable purity of breed. He was my Texawaiian poi dog (mutt) Nawiliwili "Wili" Nelson, so named after God's musical messenger whose theology is often purer than your average preacher. I never imagined I'd write another book about a dog. But then again, I never imagined that there'd ever be a dog like Wili.

Wili was a one-in-a-million dog. Those who knew him, or even knew of him, would agree. Or maybe his kind is more common than we think, and we're simply not paying attention. Wili was my son, my brother, my partner, my spiritual director, my inspiration, my best friend, and my playmate. He was my everything. Our adventure together lasted more than thirteen years. Even now, Wili seems to be directing a passion play that's changing the world for the better, improving the lives of his animal friends, and making the humans much more, well, human. Or is that divine? Rhymes with *canine*, you know!

Dogs don't seem to find me unless they have stories to share. Since I'm a storyteller of sorts and slightly more adept at the English language than they are (at least some of the time), these beastly bearers of tales with tails would always seem to show up whenever I thought I might be running out of inspirational material. Sinbad (an appropriately named dog for a priest), who came so-named, was Wili's special-needs brother. He appeared to us during Holy Week in the year of our Lord, 2013. It's called Holy Week because it includes all of those powerful and holy moments that occurred near the end of Jesus' life, from the triumphal entry into Jerusalem riding on a donkey (even Jesus chose an unlikely animal), all the way to the crucifixion, and finally culminating in a day of bunnies, I mean, resurrection. Sinbad's origin story, unbelievably, mirrored the events of the Passion of the Christ. His (almost) final days contained all the elements of the Way of the Cross—betrayal, beating, piercing, denial, abandonment, even near-death and unimaginable resurrection.

After Wili, Sinbad, and I moved to Louisiana in 2015, our sweet pit bull entered our life. Mahalia Jackson Queen Liliuokalani "Lili" (obviously, half New Orleanian and half Hawaiian) is originally from Las Vegas, where a significant road trip with Wili would end just a few years later. She'd been living in New Orleans for several years with a very loving human in a van on top of a parking garage. When an educational opportunity of a lifetime called her human overseas, Lili found her way across Lake Pontchartrain and into our home. Her joyful enthusiasm for life and walks, and her deep appreciation for pillows and couches, has inspired many. Lili also continues to teach others how inaccurate our stereotypes and assumptions so often are, whether we're talking prejudices about dog breeds or people. Like most pit bulls, Lili wouldn't survive a fight with a Chihuahua and needs a sedative to reassure her that an afternoon thunderstorm isn't going to take off her giant head. Lili says, *Give pits a chance!*

After Wili died on May 7, 2018, I was absolutely certain that Sinbad, Lili, and I would take a dog-breath breather and not adopt another anointed orphan for a long time. But people immediately began sending me photos of potential candidates. I've never enjoyed being set up on dates—with women *or* dogs—so that didn't go so well. A wonderful woman who runs a small rescue nearby even brought by two very nice critters, a yellow lab and a Basset hound, but they weren't my dogs and had not been sent by God or by Wili. Still, I was able to help find them good homes. And finding a good dog a good home is almost better than adopting one.

But less than eight weeks after Wili said aloha, a tough little puppy-dude wandered into a house my good friends were renovating in the "ruff" part of town as a gesture of not-for-profit kindness, and it quickly became obvious that *he* was the gesture of kindness who would command all *my* profits. Little Mano (Hawaiian for shark) "Professor Shorthair" Miller became our newest family member. Mano showed up the very day I started writing this book proving that timing is everything—in love and in life. He's a feisty bundle of boisterous bark and rambunctious bite. He came with an attitude of gratitude, a longing to be loved, and pellet gun wounds to his face. Give me a critter with scars, and I'm a sucker for their story every time. In fact, I'll help write the next chapter. I've already had to edit and update this introduction thanks to his unanticipated arrival. But that's okay—I've already had his balls removed, so we're even. Give or take.

But Wili is the star of this blessed epiphany. I used to introduce him by saying, "Pit bulls revere him, poodles want him, and cats want to be him." He's been called the Archbishop of Caninebury, the Doggy Lama, and the Pope of Pups. But more importantly, he was my companion on this journey, and he never left my side no matter where the adventure led.

In November of 2016, Wili was diagnosed with terminal cancer and given as few as three months to live. Not knowing how long he'd be with me, but believing that prayer and a *paws*itive outlook on life could better the odds, Wili and I plotted the Last Howlelujah Tour in the summer of 2017. Wili and I would eventually travel more than 5,000 miles. Together we made twenty-three appearances in eighteen cities, sharing Wili's story, reminding people what really matters in life, and raising funds for local animal welfare organizations. In some ways, it was the hardest two and a half weeks of my life. We drove as many as twelve hours a day, but my co-pilot didn't once check the GPS, and even napped through one of the exits we were supposed to take. And he didn't bother to lift a paw while I loaded and unloaded a mountain of dog toys, dog food, dog beds, dog meds, dog books, dog gifts, tour materials, banners, signs, and treats every single day, and sometimes three to four times a day. But while I spoke enthusiastically of Dog's love at each stop, Wili demonstrated what such theology looks like by working the entire room, greeting every person present whether or not they were in possession of barbecue, reminding us that every person matters, in Dog's eyes and in God's.

While on the surface it was exhausting, on a deeper level it was energizing. In fact, it was the best two-and-a-half weeks of my life. Wili and I were able to reconnect with old friends and make many new ones, do some good, help some animals, and bring together people who might not ordinarily be together, all while driving through the stunning landscape of America's southwest. Best of all, I was able to spend time with my best buddy—who just happened to be a dying dog. Most of the stories in this book are "Tails from the Trail" that reflect the many and marvelous moments that we shared with so many special people and pups on the Last Howlelujah Tour. Wili raised more than $14,000 for his animal friends, but his good work wouldn't end there. In fact, it wouldn't end even when his earthly life would.

Just after Wili and I returned from the tour, I left home for another journey. I was always worried about Wili when I traveled, but I always felt his presence with me, revealing great truths even from afar. I traveled to Wales to study with the great writer of Benedictine spirituality and Celtic Christianity, Esther Dewaal, a lovely and brilliant woman Wili referred to as Esther De*woof*. Esther hosted me in her guest cottage for a week, as she'd done for several other artists and writers over the years. Her pattern was to have dinner with her guest the first evening, a home-cooked Welsh feast prepared with her own hands, have an engaging conversation, and based on that conversation, she would discern the nature of the assignments she would be doling out for the week. There would be reading and writing in the days ahead, visits to Celtic historical sites, attending poetry events and candlelit evensongs in ancient cathedrals, and a pub crawl to her neighborhood watering hole where neighbors had been gathering since the 1200s. Throw in the creamery within walking distance that offered the best ice cream ever churned, pastoral hills dotted with happy cows, bleating sheep and friendly farmers, the cider distillery just an apple's throw up the hill, and it was perhaps as close to heaven as one could get without a dog being present (and some days Esther even provided a dog).

Our first evening together, after listening to a bit of my story, Esther's eyes locked on mine and seemed to say, *I'm on to you.* She gave me two reading assignments, *Beasts and Saints*, a book about saints and their relationships with animals, and *The Voyage of Saint Brendan the Navigator*, a tale about an adventurous Irish saint born in County Kerry in 484. Thought to be written in the 8th century, it tells the story of Saint Brendan's quest to find "The Blessed Isle"—also thought to be the Garden of Eden or Paradise—or maybe the world's largest dog park. I was pretty sure that I'd already discovered "The Blessed Isle" while living on the island of Kauai. And in Louisiana, I discovered it might actually be Avery Island, where Tabasco is distilled, saving the world from bland food since 1868.

In the story, after Saint Brendan sets off in a small boat with fourteen monks, an arrangement that sounds only slightly more desirable than setting off with fourteen baptized penguins, he asks his fellow, somewhat saintly, sailors, by a show of hands, how many trust God. Every hand goes up. Brendan, seeking certainty that he's in the company of only those of the greatest faith, asks the men again, and again, every hand goes up. So Brendan tells them since their faith is so strong, and since they fully believe that God will safely guide them, that the rudder and all of the oars are to be thrown overboard so that they have to rely on only the winds of the spirit to determine their course. The oars are tossed overboard. The rudder is tossed overboard. The monks contemplate throwing Brendan overboard, but change their minds. The sail is set, and the adventure begins.

But, like every quest of faith, it's part triumph and part disaster. It is one knot forward and two *nuts* back. But they learn a lot about trust and about salvation. When I came to the part of the story where they discover the first island, I believed they'd found the paradise they were looking for, whether they were aware of it or not. The weather isn't conducive to smooth sailing or soft landings, but after a few ill-fated attempts, the weather lifts and they discover a cove into which they sail. They disembark, climb to the top of a cliff, and look out over a place of great beauty, but seemingly without inhabitants. Initially disappointed, they spot a small figure in the distance coming toward them. Only when the figure gets closer, do they recognize that it is a dog. The dog walks directly up to Saint Brendan, takes one sniff, and kneels at his feet. Saint Brendan turns to his fellow voyagers and says, "Has not God sent us a good messenger? Follow him." They follow the dog (always a good idea) and the dog leads them to a special place where they find food, drink, and rest. They never come across a single human inhabitant, but the dog provides just what they need, and they are renewed for the journey ahead.

My entire life with Wili, I never felt like I was leading. Rather, I felt I was simply following the lead of someone closer to the heart of God than I'd ever be. He always took me to a place where I'd find sustenance and strength, where I was fed in every way for whatever adventure might be ahead. When we set off on the Last Howlelujah Tour we didn't know for sure that anyone would welcome us, feed us, contribute to our cause, or delight in our stories. But I trusted. And I learned to trust even more. I trusted God. And I trusted Dog. And so, together, we shared the greatest adventure of my life.

I concur with my Irish brother, Brendan: God has sent us the best messenger. *Follow him.*

First Paw:

TO ALL THE DOGS I'VE LOVED BEFORE (AND AFTER)

*If thy heart were right, then every creature would be a
mirror of life and a book of holy doctrine.
There is no creature so small and humble
but it reflects the goodness of God.*

Thomas à Kempis

GOD'S MESSENGER

You go out to my people as God's messengers…
we sanction all that is beautiful
in nature and in art to the service of God.

Queen Emma of Hawaii

My favorite prayer has long been, "Lord, help me to be the person my dog thinks that I am." But the longer I lived with Wili, the more I began to wonder if the prayer should be, "Lord, help me to be the person my dog already is."

When Wili and I set off on our Last Howlelujah Tour, a few folks mentioned that John Steinbeck had already written about a tour of America with a dog in *Travels with Charley*. There were a few similarities, but many more disparities in our respective tours. Steinbeck was in poor health, knew that it was likely his last opportunity to see America, and could have died along the way. We'd been told in November that Wili only had three months to live, so when we began our tour in June, we knew that he was also living on borrowed time. Steinbeck named his custom camper *Rocinante*, after Don Quixote's horse.

I named my Honda after Willie Nelson's constant companion, *Bud*, although I was tempted to name it after his guitar *Trigger* (after Roy Rogers' horse). Steinbeck's encounters along the way seemed to only depress his outlook on our country's future. Every one of our engagements always left us feeling hopeful for America. Steinbeck stayed in plush resorts and in million-dollar ranch houses. Wili and I stayed in cheap motels and spare bedrooms. Charley was a French poodle who belonged to Steinbeck's wife. Wili was a Texawaiian mutt who was mine all mine. But the most important distinction was that while John Steinbeck may have been a better writer than William Miller, Nawiliwili Nelson was a way better dog than Charley.

Wili was the best dog. From the moment I met him, he communicated God's love and truth in the simple language of one who'd come directly from the source of all truth and great love. Wili seemed to embody his friend, St. Francis, who may have said to "proclaim the gospel at all times. If necessary, use words." And while Wili rarely used words, he proclaimed the gospel—the good news of God's love for all creation—at all times. This Dog of God suggested a "World According to Wili" that celebrated the most important spiritual insights for all God's critters—human and animal alike.

Be Grateful

When the call came for me to move from my home state of Texas to the lovely island of Kauai, how could I not respond but with the words of the prophets of old: "Lord, here am I. Send me. *Please!*" I wasn't unlike the donkey in *Shrek*, prayerfully screaming at the top of my lungs during my devotional time "Pick me! Pick me! Pick me!" But no place is perfect—even the garden island of Kauai.

I left more than closed-toed shoes, neckties, and long pants behind on the Mainland. I also left my family and friends. Not long after I moved to paradise, my Texas veterinarian and her husband came to visit. I wanted to show these good friends sites that weren't on the typical tourist map of Kauai. So I took them to the Kauai Humane Society, one of the nicest such facilities in existence. All the animals on the island refer to it as a "Five Paw Resort."

As we were walking around the grounds of the facility, I saw a sign that stopped me in my tracks. I'd just written a book about my Airedale terrier, Sam, who'd recently passed on to the Great Boneyard, and little Jack, his brother who'd stayed behind in Texas with Rachel. I was missing both dogs terribly. So when I saw the word on the sign I couldn't believe my eyes: AIREDALE. How good of God to bring me all the way to Hawaii to gift me a purebred Airedale terrier—and from the pound no less!

I didn't realize it at the time, but on the island of Kauai any dog with facial hair is called an Airedale. And the dog that came running up to greet me definitely met that description. He had enough facial hair to costume the entire cast of *Planet of the Apes*. But other than that, he resembled an Airedale about as much as I resemble Margaret Thatcher. He was, perhaps, the goofiest-looking dog I'd ever seen. He had eyebrows like Einstein, a face that wouldn't get him any modeling gigs, an out-of-proportion tail that made him look like someone had played Pin the Snake on the Dog, a tongue that fell out of the side of his mouth and practically dropped down to the pavement, and an ear that got loose and flipped itself onto the top of his balding head. But he also possessed an eagerness and joy that seemed to melt the chain link fence that separated us. It certainly melted my heart especially when he pressed his entire body sideways against that fence so that we could pet the patches of fur that seemed to reach out to us from between the links.

We took him outside to the "meet and greet" area where he proceeded to have the time of his life playing with a plastic bottle. He would toss it into the air and then glance back to see if we were able to conceive of this most incredible of feats with this marvel of invention. He ran circles around us, jumped toward the heavens, and returned to rest his head against me. My vet did an impromptu exam and pronounced him physically healthy, but more importantly, psychologically sound. She said that whatever he'd been through in life, whatever hardship or abandonment he might have suffered, he'd already moved on. The humane society could only tell us that they'd found him wandering by the side of the road (apparently *On the Road Again*). My vet summed it up by saying, "He's just so happy to be alive. He's a keeper." Over the course of his thirteen years on earth, that attitude of gratitude was a constant. He gave thanks for everything. He lived out the prayer that asks for baptismal candidates to have the gift of joy and wonder in *all* of God's works. From the tiniest treat to the gentlest scratch, I knew that Wili was grateful.

Wili got his name by combining my original home and my new home—Texas and Hawaii. I realized early on that the port where the ships arrived on the island was called Nawiliwili Harbor. I'd also recently discovered my favorite island watering hole, the Nawiliwili Tavern, was owned by a member of my church, so I received a significant clergy discount every time I bellied up the bar (I, of course, reciprocated with free wine for him every Sunday). In fact, I'd recently been told that the owner of the only brewery on Kauai was also a member of my church. She paid a portion of her tithe each month in beer—to the priest. Tell ME there is no God! I was truly grateful, and, given these blessings of beverage and beast, I named my new critter Nawiliwili Nelson.

Love Your Neighbor

Like how so many of God's greatest blessings appear, Wili came into my life most unexpectedly. I wasn't prepared. I hadn't yet bought a house, so I was renting a condo without much of a yard. As soon as I brought Wili home, I called my landlord to see if he allowed dogs. I told him that I was asking for a friend. I also mentioned that, theoretically, this particular dog, who was most assuredly *not* sitting at my feet attempting to lick my toes off, and who'd definitely *not* already sniffed out every corner of the rental space and had perhaps peed on the parts he particularly liked, was still at the Canine Academy majoring in Manners. The landlord proceeded to utter three blasphemous words that put the terror back in terrier: "No dogs allowed!" I then asked the same question that the faithful have pondered for millennia as they've sought to do God's will only to be thwarted by uncooperative heathen: *now what?!*

As I was weighing my options there was a knock on my front door. Wili raced to the door to be the first to greet the woman who lived in the condo across the street, along with her adorable, adopted daughter. I'd heard the story from members of my new church about how this adoption was based on the African model of "it takes a village to raise a child." The mom, Connie, getting along in age, in poor health, and with limited income, had always wanted to adopt a daughter and give her a better life but couldn't afford to do so. I'd heard tales of extraordinary generosity and true community and how this child, Malia, was so welcomed and supported by everyone, that everywhere she turned there was an Auntie or Uncle who loved her as their own. I told Connie and Malia my tale of woe. I really had no idea what to do with Wili. Apparently, you need a village to raise a dog as well.

They told me how much they'd love for Wili to live with them while I searched for a suitable new home that allowed priests *and* pets. They shared how much they'd always wanted a dog but couldn't afford one. If I covered Wili's expenses he could live with them for free, and I could visit whenever I wanted. Perhaps because so many had been good neighbors to them, they were the best neighbors to Wili and me.

Wili moved in with them immediately. He was an excellent houseguest and endeared himself to both mother and daughter. Even long after Wili and I found a house with a big backyard,

Malia would ask, every Sunday at church, about her "cousin" Wili and Connie would inquire about her "favorite nephew." Malia would face many challenges in her life, but those challenges would never stop her from participating in the life of the community and offering her gifts to make a positive difference. That's the power of family and of the village that embraces and raises the child.

When Malia sang in our children's choir, she sang with the passion of Bizet's *Carmen*, the expressiveness of Aretha Franklin, and the sincerity of Patsy Cline. Whether she found the correct note was irrelevant. She conveyed with her facial expressions and full-body determination that she was going to "make a joyful noise unto the Lord" whether it blended with the other singers or not. When she danced in our hula ministry (yes, we had a hula ministry—you may now be jealous and never boast of your *quilt* ministry in quite the same way again) she danced with the fortitude of Ginger Rogers, the moves of Madonna, and the grace of Anna Pavlova. And even if she was a beat behind and her hand signals went left when they should've gone right, and even if her hips swayed when they should've pivoted, it mattered not. Her willingness to try, to put herself out there and risk embarrassment or failure, made her the star of the show time and again.

One Sunday I came up to Malia after church and said, "Malia, Wili said to tell you, *woof, woof, woof-woof, woof-woof-woof, woof.*" She put her hands on her hips, looked at me like she was in on the joke, and replied, "Father Bill, you know that I do *not* speak DOG!" But she did speak *of* God by her bravery, her compassion, and her consistency. She shared her living space with a strange new beast, gave him treats that must have seemed to him like a feast, and showed up when others didn't. She tried everything without fear of failure, even when failure was all but assured.

The time came when, because of limited financial and educational resources, Malia had to transfer from the private school she'd been attending to the public school in her neighborhood. Interestingly, it was the same school where just a few years prior Wili had attempted to take the second grade classroom hostage after he'd escaped from my church office. After only the first week in her new school, Malia was nominated for the Child of the Week award by a fellow student and was given a special certificate. Connie, who was always intentional about praising her for good behavior said, "Wow, Malia! That's quite an accomplishment to be named Child of the Week after only one week in the new school. You must be proud!" Malia assured her mom that it was "no big deal" because the little boy who'd nominated her had "one of those things on me—you know—a *squash*." In fact, she continued, there were at least three boys in her classroom who had *squashes* on her. And, if truth be told, she might have a *squash* on one of them, too. But it was too early in the game to show her cards. Her mom corrected her by saying, "Oh, Malia. I think the word you are looking for is *crush*. The little boys have a *crush* on you." Malia responded, "Well, I knew it was a word about getting run over."

Occasionally, "religion" and "religious" get confused, in both words and actions. From time to time, in the name of God, good Christian folks have confused loving their neighbor with running them over. We mistakenly think that God asks us to keep people out rather than welcome them in—to protect the village, rather than expand it. The essence of every religion and every authentic faith is the opposite of condemning, judging, tearing people apart, knocking them down, or running them out of town. It is, as Mr. Rogers, an authority on neighborhoods and on making every child a Child of the Week, often said, "We are loved into being." We are loved into being ourselves. We are loved into being what God calls us to be. When we love our neighbor as we love ourselves, the whole neighborhood improves—our neighbors *and* ourselves. We lift up, hold up, and stand up for those beloved by God, recognizing that each of us is adopted by God as God's own child. Whether we come from the orphanage, the pound, or a healthy traditional family, we all stand in need of a community of love and acceptance—a place where there's no judgment and thus no fear—where we can howl out of tune, fall on our faces, or dance with no rhythm at all. In this village, no one is ever viewed as an idiot, or anything less than our neighbor, beloved by God.

Live Aloha

Wili was a multi-talented dog. He understood three languages: Canine, English, and Hawaiian. His favorite Hawaiian word, which he spoke frequently, was probably the most important one. You may know it. You may have said it. But likely you don't know what it really means. "Aloha" is a combination of two words: "alo," which means face or coming face-to-face, and "ha," the breath of life. It's that animating force which gives us life. In the spiritual tradition, we might think of the *ha* as the image of God or the Holy Spirit. In the Polynesian tradition, when I draw near enough to you to feel your breath on my face or exchange breath with you, it's at that moment of unguarded intimacy that I look you in the eyes and recognize you as a child of God deserving of kindness, compassion, and love. It's seeing another like Wili saw me—even to pray that we might see in ourselves, and in each other, the person our dogs think that we really are.

Wili loved to get right up in my face and say *aloha*. He always said it like this, with an emphasis on the third syllable: Alo-*ha ha ha ha ha ha ha*. I called this phenomenon *Panting as Profound Expression of Divine Love* or *The Theology of Dog Breath*. Given the strength of his breath, or the particular part of his anatomy that he'd just licked manifested therein, it was occasionally difficult for me to acknowledge God's presence in his panting. But it was never difficult for Wili to discern God's presence in mine, regardless of what I'd had for lunch. Thus, we pray to be the person our dogs think that we are.

There's an old story about the difference between a dog and a cat that illustrates this Principle of Aloha—of seeing God's presence in ourselves and in others. The dog sees his master going to the store and returning with all kinds of food, toys, and treats, just for him. He thinks, given that his master has gone to so much trouble for a mere critter, and given that the master is motivated by such unconditional love and kindness that the master must be God. The cat sees his master doing the same generous good deeds for her, going to so much trouble for her, and thinks, given such kindness and love, that *she* must be God. Both dog and cat are theologically correct. When we experience *aloha* we recognize that God is good and must be our loving Creator, but also that we, too, contain the spirit of God and are part of God. Such a recognition will likely make us a bit humbler than the cat but no less sure of our self-worth.

When we live *aloha*, we see the beauty of every person and every creature, including ourselves. We recognize that each of us is a one-of-a-kind original. There was a lady in my church in Kauai who did many good things for other people. I cared for her and appreciated her a great deal. But she frequently said to Wili, "You are so ugly." While Wili may not have won any dog show awards except "Outstanding Eyebrows on the Island," which he won eight years running, he was quite the handsome beast. But his true beauty went beneath and beyond his fur. It was his spirit, his *ha*, his zest and love for life that made him the most beautiful creature I'd ever seen. Critical words never fazed Wili. It didn't change his awareness that he was special. When he posed for photos, he posed like a canine version of Zoolander! He was always feeling good because I believe he always thought he looked good! And he did. When you are beloved by God and you are aware of the blessing of this life, you cannot help but be beautiful. As the Velveteen Rabbit reminded us, being loved is to become more real. At that point, you will never be ugly to anyone except those who don't understand—themselves or God.

Aloha is a beautiful thing. It's a beautiful thing to know that God dwells within you. I know Malia believed that about herself. I believe Wili did, too. And because of the love I've experienced through loved ones like them, I believe it about myself, too.

God makes beautiful things, beautiful people, and beautiful creatures. We cannot be ugly if we are created by God and loved by God. When we love as we have been loved, the more beautiful we become. So, follow God's messenger, Saint Wili of Woofster. Be grateful. Love your neighbor as yourself. Live *aloha*. Become the person your dog already is.

SIN BAD, GOD GOOD

He ain't heavy, he's my brother.

The Hollies

Traditionally, it has been called *Moloka'i Pule O'O*, the island of powerful prayer. Indeed, life-changing moments of encounter with the Creator, prayerful pivots, and sacred shifts seem more commonplace in this sacred place. Picking your favorite Hawaiian island is a lot like picking your favorite dog—you can't go wrong with any of them. They are *all* among God's best work. But my place of pilgrimage for the last ten years has been Molokai the "friendly isle," and the most Hawaiian of all the islands. Molokai assumes a special page of honor in my ever-expanding Hawaii scrapbook. Even the Molokai Mule has become the official beverage of my backyard Tiki Bar.

Each year, I take a small group of pilgrims to this spiritually significant spot to follow in the footsteps of Father Damien, Mother Marianne, Brother Joseph, and others who've selflessly served their fellow humans. Father Damien was a highly celebrated Belgian priest and eventual saint who gave his life ministering to those with leprosy who'd been banished to the remote Kalaupapa peninsula. Mother Marianne Cope and Brother Joseph Dutton lived longer than Damien and never contracted the disease, but their long-haul commitment to loving those who were among the least and their compassionate gifts were no less heroic.

Molokai, where the first Polynesians settled in Hawaii, is a sacred place, not only because of its spectacular physical beauty, but also because of the beautiful souls who've inhabited its shores. These known and unknown saints alike loved unconditionally in their efforts to make suffering more bearable and an incurable disease-ravaged life more hopeful for those who often had no hope. In Celtic spirituality, another religious form that emerged from the islands that had been cut off from the "main" land but perhaps even more connected to the Creator, Molokai would be called a "thin place." That is, it's a place where the veil between earth and heaven is so thin you can reach out and touch the other side. Extraordinary things happen in such places.

There was a young, Jewish man who was an expert paddler from the island of Kauai. He'd been given the name Luke by his mother. Luke's grandfather, who'd been imprisoned in a Jewish concentration camp during the Holocaust, used to tease Luke's mother that she'd given him the biblical name of the only non-Jew among the apostles. In 2010, Luke planned to paddle with his outrigger canoe team in the Molokai Hoe, a demanding and treacherous 41-mile journey from

Molokai to Oahu across the Kaiwi Channel. Like the journey that took Father Damien from Belgium to Hawaii, and eventually to Molokai starting in 1864, this open-ocean race was not for the faint of heart or weak of soul. But Luke was a rare individual—an excellent paddler, an outrigger canoe builder, a committed crew member, and a fine human being.

Thirty minutes into the race, the time came for the crew's first ocean change, a sometimes-chaotic moment when several paddlers who'd been riding in the escort motorboat jump into the ocean to change places with crew members who'd been paddling at full steam. Those who'd been paddling roll out into the water, swim to the escort boat, and crawl in. A long, grueling journey requires trade-offs, a time of rest and renewal, a "Sabbath principle" that would serve us well in this race called life.

After Luke jumped into the water to assume the first spot in the canoe, a large wave lifted the escort boat and brought it down right on top of him. The boat's propeller left five large gashes across the back of Luke's body. Luke somehow swam to the surface and screamed for help. There was so much blood in the water the other paddlers feared that he'd been attacked by a shark, especially when they saw the severity of Luke's injuries. They feared he might die. And hearing the fear in the men's voices, so did Luke.

Miraculously, the propeller blades missed Luke's critical arteries, internal organs, and spinal cord by about an inch. Still, his wounds were so serious and deep that his spinal cord was exposed. The men were able to lift Luke back into the escort boat, but the odds of survival weren't in his favor.

The conditions were too perilous to attempt a helicopter rescue or a transfer to a larger, faster boat. The only option was to return to Molokai in the escort boat. Luke would later recall that during the one-hour trip back, the longest sixty minutes of his life, he thought he was going to die, but he wasn't afraid of death. He also remembered reflecting on his life's many blessings and being completely enveloped by a feeling of deep love.

After what seemed like an eternity, the boat finally arrived at Hale'o Lono Beach, and a helicopter life-flighted Luke to Maui General Hospital. Three surgeons worked simultaneously to repair the damage to his body, and less than twelve hours after suffering life-threatening injuries, Luke was able to call his mom and tell her not to worry. Luke also sent out a blog post that began with an apology because the potent painkillers he was on might make his thoughts incomprehensible.

As it turned out, his post-traumatic reflections were so poignant they were more powerful than the most potent painkiller. He expressed gratitude to all those who'd worked so hard to save his life, and emphasized that no one should be blamed for his accident, especially the escort boat driver who was more shaken up than Luke. He then reminded everyone how precious and unpredictable life is, that any one of us could die in an instant, and how important it is to be so mindful of such a possibility that we seize every opportunity to live life to the fullest, embracing completely every moment as a pure gift, and to love everyone with all we've got—especially our families and friends.

Not long after he was released from the hospital, Luke's

paddling community wanted to conduct a fundraiser to help defray his extensive medical costs. Luke agreed, but only if all the proceeds were donated to Project Pure, a non-profit organization that provided physically, mentally, and emotionally challenged individuals the opportunity to engage in water sports, particularly paddling outrigger canoes in the ocean. Luke had always been mindful of others, but after his near-death experience, he valued life so much more intensely that his heart began to break for the whole earth. In healing himself, he also responded to his calling to become a healer of others.

Luke moved back home to the island of Kauai to be with his fiancée, Sokchea, who shared an equally compelling story. The daughter of survivors of the horrific genocide in Cambodia, Sokchea was born in a refugee camp. After her family was granted political asylum in the United States, they moved to a public housing project in South Central Los Angeles. Sokchea shared Luke's commitment to making the world a better place. They lived off-grid, practiced vegetarianism, rescued animals, and adopted a completely sustainable lifestyle. Sokchea would later joke with friends saying, "I *would* fall in love with the only American who actually wants to live like a Cambodian." In Hawaii, such a lifestyle might be equated with the concept of *pono*, which means living in a way that's honorable, righteous, and balanced. It's a way of life our world deeply needs to reclaim.

One night, not far from Luke and Sokchea's home, I was home resting up for Holy Week which had begun that day with the Sunday of the Passion, also known as Palm Sunday.

Holy week retraces the last, most painful steps of Christ's journey—the Way of Sorrows and the Way of the Cross—and it's one of the most intense weeks for priests. That night, as Luke and Sokchea were returning home, they somehow spotted a tiny blur of an object in the distance. It turned out to be a very frightened creature cowering under a palm tree by the side of the road. He was so scared that he wouldn't look up, much less come to them. It appeared that the dog had been beaten and abandoned. His back legs didn't move, and he had a wound in his side that could have been from a wild boar attack or from the hand of a cruel human. It took them a long time and the offering of food, but he finally allowed them to get close. They lifted him up and gently placed him in the back seat of their car.

Their home being already at capacity with a menagerie of rescued beasts, they decided to take the scared, shy guy to the Kauai Humane Society—the same place where I'd adopted Wili six years earlier. Miraculously, the dog had an electronic chip that was encrypted with the name and phone number of his owner. But when they called, the man who answered the phone denied knowing him. "I do not know the dog." They asked again, and then a third time, but the man denied ever knowing the dog. I can't say for certain, but given the prevalence of roosters on the island of Kauai, I'm pretty sure the cock crowed after his third denial. Along with the owner's contact information, the chip also had record of the dog's name: Sinbad. That's Sin. Bad.

The people at the humane society examined Sinbad and determined that because he'd suffered such severe abuse, they would likely put him down and be done with him. He wasn't a young pup anymore, and the humane society had lots of young, healthy dogs who needed homes. Why should they keep an older animal that had issues and whose warranty had expired years ago, and who no one apparently wanted? They told Luke they'd give him until Friday to find Sinbad a home, but if no home was found, Sinbad would be put to death. On Friday. Sinbad would be put to death on Friday. During Holy Week. Sinbad would die on GOOD FRIDAY.

Let's review. A dog named Sinbad was found on Palm Sunday—the Sunday of the Passion—abandoned, beaten, and with a piercing wound in his side. He was denied three times by one who was supposed to be his faithful friend. He was sentenced to die on Good Friday. I have no idea why, but for some reason when Luke sent out an island-wide call for help, my name came up. Sometimes God sends clear clues even to the clueless like me.

Maundy Thursday is the day during Holy Week when Jesus shares a farewell meal with his faithful friends—friends who would turn out not to be so faithful. After the meal, Jesus took a towel and washed their feet—an act of unconditional love and selfless service meant to demonstrate everything Jesus stood for (and stooped for). I can still imagine Father Damien in the leper colony, stooping low to wash feet, bandage wounds, eating and drinking and praying with those who'd been abandoned and given up for dead. And I can still see Luke's friends hoisting his critically injured body into a small boat, hoping and praying that he would live, compressing his wounds with their own hands.

When Wili and I arrived, the woman at the humane society didn't seem too happy to see us. She insisted that there were plenty of dogs there more adoptable than Sinbad. I could've sworn I heard Wili growl in protest. Perhaps he was remembering his days at the same shelter when, for some good or bad reason, or for no reason at all, he'd been overlooked for too long. Wili and I took Sinbad outside. He was shy and sweet and spent most of his time cowering and trying to make himself as small as possible. The helper who worked there told us, "Yeah, that's Sinbad. He's a sweet guy, but he'll never amount to much of a dog. He can't really walk and he will definitely never run." At the sound of his name, Sinbad's tail began to slowly wag. Wili sniffed him and he sniffed back. Eventually Sinbad walked over to me and rested his big, sweet, perhaps somewhat hollow, but most sincere head on my lap.

Sinbad came home with us on Good Friday.

Good Friday has always been a bittersweet day. It's difficult to ponder death. Yet sometimes, when we get that close to death, we realize what life is all about. We recognize what is most important and we begin to live in a way that truly matters. On Good Friday, I'm fully present, but I'm also aware that Sunday is coming. Easter is that day when we finally confront sin. Sin is a way of disengaging from the One who made us, who knows us, and who loves us. Sin is a way of disengaging from our faithful friends and our truest selves. Sin is real and bad. Sin causes us to make poor and harmful choices that affect not just us but the whole world. Easter is the day when sin gets taken to the woodshed. It's that moment when we discover that sin may be bad, but it's not so powerful. And it's definitely not the last word about who we are, what we will become, or how we will live. On Easter, we recognize that even when all the evil powers of this world conspire to put people and pets down—literally and figuratively—there's an even more powerful force seeking to dispel them, overcome them, and defeat them in the name of Love. In this holy and sacred moment love wins and love stakes its claim on our future. Easter is the day of empty tombs and opened kennels, of fresh starts and new families, of real hope and even a dose of courage for those who have, for too long, cowered in fear. Miracles happen on Easter. But they often begin on Good Friday.

Wili and I brought Sinbad home on Good Friday. On Easter day, guess which previously defeated dog was delivered from sin and death? Guess who was running, jumping, leaping, and praising God in my backyard, shouting *Howlelujah*? Sin may be bad, but God is so good. And so was Sinbad—a good boy who finally got his chance to shine.

Wili accepted Sinbad with open paws. Although he's a sweet and gently abiding presence in our lives that never sought the spotlight, Sinbad's special needs have always been apparent. But such challenges have made us love him even more. Wili worked patiently with Sinbad to teach him what it means to be a dog. Wili never seemed to tire of Sinbad's inability to do as he did, and continued to try to show him the way, but Sinbad never quite figured out how to play. When a toy is tossed his way, he runs in the opposite direction. He knows something good is happening, he's just not sure how to embrace it or engage with it. When others are happy, Sinbad always wags his tail in solidarity, even if he doesn't completely understand. Sinbad has always assumed that doors are entered and exited only one way—at full speed! And if there's a screen door, he'll plow right through it. Many times over the years, Wili and I would awaken to the loud crash of a screen door being knocked off its track in the middle of the night. We'd look at each other knowing that Sinbad was definitely in the house. That's not bad theology. Sometimes to get home, to get to the place where we are most safe and most alive, might mean plowing right through every perceived obstacle. When God closes one door, perhaps he's just trying to tell us to go ahead and kick the S-O-B in!

I don't know why bad things happen to good people or to good dogs. I don't know why an extraordinary human being like Luke had been injured so severely in a paddling accident. I don't know why someone would be so mean to sweet Sinbad—hurting, abandoning, and denying him. I do believe that sometimes human beings make devastating decisions that create devastating results. Our poor choices often create many of our personal and global problems. I know that sin is bad, and evil is real, and even the best among us are capable, at times, of exhibiting attitudes and behaviors that are wrong. We pollute the world in ways that contribute to illness and disease. We refuse to pass laws that might protect our children and keep our communities safe. We fail to regulate things to make our world less dangerous, such as boat propeller protectors, a regulation Luke is passionate about. The scary truth is that we often bring suffering upon ourselves and our fellow human beings by what we have done and by what we have failed to do.

But I'm also keenly aware that sometimes random and terrible things happen to us and to those we love for no good reason at all. I don't believe the cliché that "everything happens for a reason." I don't believe that God is behind every unfortunate circumstance or terrible tragedy that occurs in the world in order to somehow make a point. I don't believe God is behind suffering as a way to punish those who don't measure up. Randomness is built into the universe in which we live. We take our chances every day. But, it's very much worth the gamble.

I also believe in redemption. I know that in our direst situations and in our darkest hours, God and good people can come together to work for good, as scripture suggests. What is painful can be poignant. What is tragic can be transformed. What is wounded can be healed. What we have messed up can be cleaned up. What has been broken can be mended. But true change begins with our awareness and confession that we have failed and fallen short, and that we have sinned badly. It's an imperfect world that God has entrusted to us, but it's also sacred, holy, and beautiful, even with its flaws.

I've always admired the way Wili loved and accepted Sinbad as his brother and as part of our family. He was never jealous that we opened our doors to another dog. I've also admired the way Sinbad has willingly loved and accepted us, as well. His imperfections have taught me so much about

God's complex world—about forgiveness, patience, kindness, and compassion. But you *can* teach an old dog, new tricks. Or at least teach him about trust, about near-death experiences, new beginnings, faithful friends, and hopeful futures.

Luke and Sokchea were married in 2011, and they now have two children. Finley is three and likes to throw eggs on the floor and ride her bike. That sounds like fun. Levi is one and enjoys cooling off in his tiny inflatable pool in paradise. That also sounds like fun. They have two dogs, Peanut and Piko, who, according to Luke, spend most of their time alternating between rolling in the mud and jumping on the couch. That, too, sounds like fun. Luke is a successful businessperson. Starting in college, he built what is now the largest manufacturer of outrigger canoes in America. His theory in founding the company is that part of America's problem is that we have forgotten how to build things. That's true. Whether we're talking about business, politics, religion, or life, we have become more skilled at tearing down, putting down, and standing in opposition than we have at stooping down, lifting up, and building up.

Luke decided to run for political office in 2018 and was elected to a position on the Kauai County Council. On his campaign website, he reflected on his wife's background as a refugee, which is not unlike the situation in which Sinbad found himself on that dark Sunday night of the Passion—alone, abandoned, and in danger. Luke suggests that Sokchea's direct experience with the horrific potential of humanity, as well as the transformative power of a welcoming community, have deeply affected both her and Luke's political perspectives.

Perhaps another way to put that important and profound observation is this: sin is bad and we are all flawed. But God is good and we are all created in God's image. A dog taught me that. A paddler reinforced its truth. You and I are blessed to have the free will to choose. I pray that we'll choose to do good.

IT'S A GIRL!

Everybody needs somebody.
Mahalia Jackson

There will always be a Hawaii as long as there is aloha and forgiveness.
Queen Liliuokalani

I always wanted a girl. It's just that I didn't expect her to be a pit bull. I expected her to be more like the little girls in my church who are so precious they sometimes make me want to get married and have babies—but not quite. Until recently, I valued the freedom to dip my toe into the shallow end of the dating pool even if my toe gets stubbed and I get snubbed. I reserved the right to remain single even if most of my evenings resembled the festive atmosphere of a gathering of comatose zombies on silent retreat at a convalescent center watching televised golf while preparing toast. Well, perhaps not *that* titillating.

As a priest, I have more than my share of critics. But apparently among the female demographic in my flock ages three to eleven, I can do no wrong. If I didn't have their occasional adoration and ongoing affection, I would likely have thrown in the stole long ago. It's important in life to have someone standing in your corner, cheering for you, writing you sweet somethings with colorful illustrations—especially if they're six years old.

On the island of Kauai, my biggest fan was a little four-year-old girl named Cooper. Cooper's dad, Ben, is a fellow priest, good friend, and frequent travel buddy. During a visit with Ben, Cooper, and their dogs, Bacon and Biscuit, who always made me hungry when I called them for a treat, we all settled onto the couch to watch an *Animal Planet* episode titled "I Was Prey," which made me want to title my next sermon "I Will Pray That I Am Not Prey!" Cooper was sitting so close to me that Ben asked her if she'd be more comfortable sitting with him on the floor. Leaning in even closer to me she replied, "No! I'm sittin' next to THIS!" For *this*, I'm eternally grateful. A few years later, Ben and Cooper would attend a gospel show at Padre's, my bar in Marfa, Texas. After the show, Cooper sidled up to the bar, ordered a virgin concoction, then handed me one of her prized possessions—a wild turkey feather. I thanked her for her beautiful and thoughtful gift by officially naming the virgin concoction she was drinking The Wild Turkey Feather.

The day I arrived at Christ Church in Covington, Louisiana, some adults were so unimpressed with me that they pummeled me from their pews with macadamia nuts and pineapples. But six-year-old, Macy, welcomed me by placing a rainbow-colored lei around my neck just before I began to preach my first sermon. After her initial greeting, she continued to write encouraging notes to me on the contribution envelopes with sentiments such as: "You're funny!" "I love church!" and "Put a lot of money in this envelope and return to me after the service if you ever want to see your dog again!" Oh, how I love her.

My good friend, seven-year-old, Piper, let me borrow her favorite stuffed animal, Cheetie the Cheetah, for the Sunday sermon in which I preached about a near-death experience on an African safari. The sermon was actually about a leopard, but their distinctions in spots are so insignificant no one knew the difference—except Piper. She allowed me to rename Cheetie the Cheetah, Larry the Leopard for that Sunday only, and I had to place him prominently on the pulpit as I shared stories about leaping leopards and leaps of faith. Piper reminds me frequently that the two of us will someday co-author a best-selling children's book. It will be titled, *Larry the Leopard, Cheetie the Cheetah, Pedro the Panther, Alan the Aardvark, and Steve, the Magic Squid*. Look out, literary world!

Then there is Savannah. Not a Sunday goes by that Savannah doesn't draw me the most beautiful pictures during my sermon. They are often thematically linked to the day's topic, and demonstrate a depth of understanding that eludes many adults. Savannah's father, a former college football player at North Carolina and a gastroenterologist who frequently threatens his friends with "free scopes," will often travel with me on what we tell her mommy are "spiritual pilgrimages." Thus far, her dad and I have been to a New Orleans Saints game in London, the hippest nightclub in Paris, a Cubs game at Wrigley Field, a brewery in Milwaukee, a beach in Hawaii, and recently, we started serving our Lord and Savior together on several mission trips to the French Quarter. Savannah's pictures occupy places of honor in my office. She'll often use the powerful symbols of a rainbow, a cross, and a heart. In other words, her theology more resembles God's intent than most evangelicals in America, whose priorities seem to have gotten lost. If we can ever get back to rainbows, hearts, and crosses, there may be hope for us yet.

There are so many other treasured gifts that I've received from my junior supporters. A blue-dyed Easter egg from Sophia was the only gift I received my first Easter, but it was all that I wanted or needed. Then there's Eliot's hand-painted letter "B," which is displayed prominently on my bookshelf and reminds me of my true identity—Boob, I mean Bill. Another bookshelf holds a painted sign that Eliot's older sister, Luci, made for me bearing my favorite Saint Irenaeus quote: "The glory of God is the human being fully alive!" All of these gifts bring me to a fuller, more aware, more alive, and more grateful place.

One of the most beautiful heart-opening gifts I've ever received was from six-year-old Camille. She was recently given The Gratitude Award by her first grade teacher who said that Camille was "always respectful and kind to everyone and lets everyone know that she appreciates them." Apparently she even appreciates her priest.

One Sunday morning, her family was running behind schedule trying to get out the door to church. As they were frantically getting ready to leave, Camille wandered back inside and showed her mom the tiniest, most delicate purple flower that she'd just picked from the front yard. She told her mother that she wanted to bring it to me at church. Her mom told me later that "it looked so tiny, even in her hand, and was so delicate, I thought there was no way it would survive the twenty-minute drive to church, much less the entire service."

But Camille took very good care of this exquisite gift. She held it carefully while they drove to church, cupped it in her hands throughout the service, and waited patiently while I greeted every single person as they left the church. She approached me, shyly held out her open palm to me and said, "Father Bill, my mom grows flowers, and the butterflies come, and I like them, and I thought that it would be nice if I gave one to you." *Nice* doesn't come close to describing the loveliness of her gesture. As I held the tiny flower, I thought of the William Blake poem that celebrates the curiosity and imagination that humans possess when we're able to see "heaven in a wildflower" and hold it as if holding "infinity in the palm of your hand." That morning I saw heaven. I held infinity. My heart opened wider than the most glorious petals opening up to the brightest sun.

When my main man Wili died, I received so many kind expressions of sympathy that I couldn't keep track of all of them. Scarlett and her brother, Harrison, attend both Christ Episcopal School and the Church. I remember they both wore red bandanas to church for "Welcome Home Wili" weekend after we returned from the Last Howlelujah Tour and someone snapped a photo of the two of them with Wili. It's one of my favorite photos: Cowgirl, Cowboy, and Cowdog. On what would be Wili's final visit to the church after he processed down the center aisle and out the back door, Harrison volunteered to take him for a walk. And I don't know how it happened, but Wili somehow convinced Harrison to lead him straight to the donut table. Harrison would be the last person from the church to have the pleasure of walking Wili.

The day after Wili died, Scarlett gave me a handmade sympathy card. On the outside she'd written: *To Father Bill, From Scarlett*, and below that she wrote, *Wili* with an arrow pointing toward a hand-drawn creature with five legs and a tail. I'd recognize Wili anywhere! Inside the card, below a drawing of an orange cross and a bright yellow sun crying big, blue tears surrounded by a rainbow, Scarlett wrote:

> *Dear Father Bill.*
> *I'm sorry Wili died. I'm so glad Harrison got*
> *to walk him. I'm also glad that Harrison and*
> *I got to know him. Did you know that when*
> *dogs die they cross a rainbow to get to heaven?*
> *He is in a good place now.*
>
> *Sincerely, Scarlett*

I need a moment.

In fact, I need a lifetime. I often remind people that if they want to draw closer to God, draw closer to children and dogs. They each have a particular gift for showing us the way to the heart of God and to the heart of what matters to God. My prayer for all of these special, small folks is that they grow up and not forget the truths they knew as children, that they always be true to themselves and to the unique calling their Creator has for their lives, and that they never forget to focus on the most important things.

In 2013, a young man who'd dreamed for many years of attending medical school and becoming a physician drove from New Orleans to Las Vegas to live with his aunt. He was broke and unemployed and would have to continue his college education online rather than attend classes in person at the University of New Orleans. One afternoon, as he was heading to his car to go to the grocery store, he saw some kids and a dog standing on the sidewalk. As he got into his car and was about to close the door, the dog ran to him, jumped into the car, and lodged herself between him and the steering wheel. She was a brown and white pit bull and looked a little like a dairy cow. He laughed and managed to shoo her out of his car and herd her in the direction of the kids. The kids told him they don't know where she came from. He looked around thinking *someone* needed to do *something* about *this*. The last thing he needed was a dog—especially a pit bull. As he was going back inside his house, Miss Pitiful rushed past him into the house, sat down, and made herself right at home.

That young man's name is Matthew. And while he thought the last thing he needed was a dog, the dog knew that Matthew was exactly what she needed. He named her Lily, as in the lilies of the field. In the Gospel of Saint Matthew, Jesus said that the lilies of the field demonstrated how we shouldn't worry about what we wear or about anything else for that matter, because lilies were clothed more beautifully than anyone wearing the latest fashions, and they worried about nothing. Lily had never been too worried about what to wear. But now she didn't have to worry about where she would live, or what she would eat, or who might love her as much as she loved them. And although Lily didn't smell like anything particularly floral, she did appear as bright and joyful as a field of flowers glowing in the sun. Lily was also a witness to the power of persistence. As Jesus often reminded his disciples, including Matthew and Luke, sometimes you just have to keep showing up and pleading your just case before things really begin to change.

Over the years, the young man sometimes experienced employment difficulties and financial challenges, but continued his studies in New Orleans hoping that someday he would be accepted to medical school. Whatever disappointment he may have felt, it always seemed to dissipate whenever Lily was around, which was all the time. He and Lily eventually had to move into a small van parked on top of a parking garage in New Orleans. They had occasional neighbors who lived in an assortment of campers and trailers, one of whom even tended a small rooftop garden. Matthew and Lily often went on long walks in the neighborhood, and everyone would greet the sweet pit bull with shouts of, "Here comes the happy dog!" As far as Lily was concerned, she'd hit the jackpot with her human. Economic status and living conditions really don't matter much as long as you're loved. And Lily was loved very much.

The day finally came when Matthew was accepted into medical school—a lifelong dream come true. But the school was located on a small island in the Caribbean where certain misunderstood breeds of dogs were not allowed. As heart-wrenching as it was to part with his best friend and perpetual ray of sunshine, he made the difficult decision to leave Lily behind, but only if he could find her the very best home. He put the word out on social media that he was looking for a special home for his sweet girl. Well, I always wanted a girl.

Mr. Rogers used to tell children during times of trouble that they should always look for the helpers. Such advice is still timely, even for adults, and especially in times when so many seem determined not to help, and even to hinder or to harm. I received a message from a friend with a link to Lily's information. The message was a simple question. "Bill, can you help?" I can't always help. But in this case, I knew that I could.

I admired Matthew so much for his thoughtful willingness to give up his most treasured relationship. He felt like Lily had saved him on more than one occasion. In a small way, it reminded me of another father who was willing to give up a child in the name of goodness and love. It's a sacrifice like no other, which is why the cross is such a powerful symbol, even now.

Matthew was serious about finding an exceptional home for his girl—I had to submit a resume with references. It helped that I'd written a book about my dog Sam, and that Wili and Sinbad were so welcoming, gracious, and accommodating. There was a formal interview which, apparently, I passed. Matthew asked if we could meet at City Park in New Orleans so that Lily and I could sniff each other to see if we were a match. I knew there was only one person I trusted enough to go with me to help me make such an important decision—one person who could see straight through any preconceived prejudice and right into the heart of a person, or a pup: Ashley Wennerstrom.

I first met Ashley at a wine bar on Oak Street in New Orleans. She's smart. She's compassionate. She's wise. She's beautiful inside and out. Ashley had only one flaw, as far as I could tell. She drinks Chardonnay. But that doesn't take away from how extraordinary she is. She teaches public health at the graduate level. She lives fearlessly in one of the grittiest neighborhoods in New Orleans. She's a crusader for the rights of the marginalized. She rescued a pit bull mix named Jughead. She's committed to doing the right thing every time.

Years ago, Ashley saw a documentary titled, *In the Land of the Free*. The film told the story of three Black men incarcerated in Angola State Penitentiary in Louisiana. In an attempt to bring attention to the horrific conditions of the prison and try to improve the lives of the inmates, they joined the Black Panther party. The Black Panthers, a political party not particularly in favor among anyone who might have racist tendencies, especially in the Deep South, immediately aroused suspicions among those who'd likely never met a Black Panther. Not unlike certain breeds of dogs such as pit bulls, there was a rush to judgement, believing them dangerous simply because of what people may have heard, not based on fact. Despite no physical evidence or credible witnesses, the three men in Angola were eventually convicted of the murder of a prison guard and spent decades in solitary confinement.

Many of us read books and watch movies that challenge our preconceived prejudices or that call into question our uninformed assumptions. Perhaps our exposure to such stories will ignite our compassion and our God-given desire for justice and equality. Moved, we may even demand that "someone" should do "something" about "that." Ashley actually *did* something—she began writing letters to Herman Wallace, one of the "Angola Three." When Herman realized she lived just a block from where he grew up in New Orleans, he wrote her back.

She began visiting Herman in prison, a kind gesture that may seem strange, but which Jesus says is one of the truly important things that he would like for his followers to be doing. Dear Reader, just as a reminder—Jesus' top priorities include: visiting those in prison, feeding the hungry, providing beverages for the thirsty, clothing the naked, comforting the sick, and welcoming the stranger. If those don't sound like your social, religious, or political priorities, you might either want to change parties, or change religions. Or, do what would make Jesus *really* happy—change yourself.

Herman had liver cancer, but he'd been misdiagnosed by a prison physician and without treatment, grew sicker and sicker. Ashley had told Herman many times that should he ever be released from prison that she had a nice guest room in her home where he could stay. Herman always responded that he wasn't about to stay in "no damn guest room," but that he would kick her out of the master bedroom and move in.

Thanks to the tireless efforts of many, a judge miraculously agreed that Herman would be allowed stay at her home for his final days on earth, so Herman was released into her care. Still lucid, but nearing the end of his life, he arrived at her house on a Wednesday. She asked him if he knew where he was. He opened his eyes, smiled, and whispered, "Yeah. Damn guest room." A whole host of concerned citizens and many Black Panthers called Ashley's house during those final forty-eight hours to check on Herman and offer, not just their "thoughts and prayers," but their real commitment to continue to work for positive change in our country, especially with regard to racial injustice and inequality.

As Herman drifted in and out of consciousness, Ashley would reassure him. "Herman, you're free now." And one of the last things he said was, "I'm free." The state of Louisiana attempted to re-arrest Herman and take him back to Angola. Perhaps cruelty has no limits, but neither does grace. On October 4, 2013 in Ashley's guest room—her damn beautiful, grace-filled, guest room—Herman Wallace died.

Ashley was the person I trusted most to judge every character with conviction and every canine with compassion. We met Lily and Matthew not far from George Rodrigue's giant sculpture of a blue, red, and yellow dog in the sculpture garden. Although I thought Ashley might fight me over her rights, we agreed that Lily was a true work of art—a big bundle of affection, all sweetness and light.

I continued to call her Lily, but I changed her name to the Hawaiian spelling—Lili. I gave her a full name that honored two women I deeply respected and reflected my most recent homes in Hawaii and New Orleans. My new pit bull would hereafter be known as Mahalia Jackson Queen Liluokalani. In a single name I was able to express my love for Hawaii, New Orleans, music, and dogs! Liluokalani was the Queen of Hawaii. Mahalia Jackson was the Queen of Gospel music, and Lili would quickly become the Queen of the Miller household. And even in her new neighborhood, she'd become known as "The Happy Dog!"

As it turns out, Mahalia Jackson was born not far from the parking garage where Lili and Matthew had been living. Mahalia grew up in a three-room house with twelve other people and one dog. She began her singing career nearby at the Mount Moriah Baptist Church, and she was baptized in the Mississippi River. She once said that when you sing gospel music, you have a feeling that there's a cure for what's wrong. The gospel message of God's unconditional love in Jesus Christ—good news for a world that's divided and enslaved—is *still* the cure for what's *still* wrong. If your gospel is not a cure for what's wrong, it's likely the wrong gospel. There's a lot of that going around these days.

As well-known as Mahalia Jackson was for her vocal abilities, the singular moment in which she changed the course of American history came *after* she'd finished singing at the Civil Rights March on Washington in 1963. After Mahalia sang "I've Been Buked and I've Been Scorned," a song about the pain and suffering endured by those who have been mistreated and misunderstood, but also a song about the hope that can still be found in times of turmoil and the hope that we can return home and be set free, she sat down to listen to her friend, the Rev. Dr.

Martin Luther King give the most important speech of his life. When he began his speech by equating the idea of oppression in America to having "insufficient funds," which sounded more like a bank statement than an impassioned plea for peace, Mahalia looked around at the faces in the crowd and saw that they were losing interest. That's when she shouted to Dr. King: "Tell them about the dream, Martin! Tell them about the dream!" Setting aside his prepared notes and grasping the lectern, King launched into a vivid and poignant description of his dream for America, a dream for all of our children that looks past prejudice and difference, and toward a nation characterized by equal opportunity and love for all our neighbors. His dream was of a country becoming a beloved community of justice, peace, reconciliation, equality, and understanding. Sometimes truth must not just convict us of a wrong, but move us toward the right—giving us an alternative vision, painting a beautiful multi-colored picture in which we can clearly see the symbols that can motivate us to become the change we want to see in the world. I wonder if there were any little girls in the audience that day, and if they drew Dr. King a picture, and if it contained a rainbow, a heart, or a cross?

Queen Liliuokalani's story and her legacy for our nation and for our world were equally compelling. She was the last sovereign monarch of the Hawaiian Kingdom who sought to preserve the joyful, creation-centered culture of Hawaii and the spirit of *aloha*. Liliuokalani lived aloha, recognizing that God is present in every person and in every created being—leopards and panthers, pit bulls and puppies, business leaders and indigenous peoples, sugar barons and hula dancers, little girls and even convicted felons.

In 1894, a group of American businessmen enlisted the local American ambassador and U.S. marines onboard the U.S.S. Boston, conveniently stationed in Honolulu Harbor, to overthrow the Hawaiian monarch and illegally occupy the sovereign nation of Hawaii. Whenever business interests solely determine American foreign policy, the moral compass is likely already skewed toward injustice. Having absolutely no shame, these embarrassing excuses for Americans imprisoned Queen Liliuokalani in her own palace. Her own Protestant minister sided with the businessmen and refused to provide her pastoral care. The Anglican bishop in Honolulu wasn't intimidated by the powers of this world, however, and visited her frequently. She was so moved by his kindness that she was later confirmed in the Episcopal Church. The *loving* thing is always the *right* thing, even if the powers of this world try to convince you otherwise.

But the most powerfully loving thing in this unfortunate episode of American history was offered by Liliuokalani herself. While she was imprisoned in her palace, many native Hawaiians wanted to fight for her and wage war against the occupiers. It would've been a just war, but she convinced them otherwise. With her musical talent, she could've composed an angry diatribe that would've been heard throughout the world. She could've been bitter and spoken harshly of those who unlawfully and unashamedly imprisoned her, and she would've been right. But it's better to be *loving* than to be *right*—and in *loving* we are always ultimately *right*. The Queen of Hawaii, instead, composed what has become known as "The Queen's Prayer." Still sung in many churches in Hawaii, it's a song about forgiveness and often follows the confession of sin and the pronouncement of God's forgiveness:

> *Your loving mercy*
> *Is as high as heaven*
> *And your truth*
> *So perfect*
>
> *I live in sorrow*
> *Imprisoned*
> *You are my light*
> *Your glory, my support*
>
> *Behold not with malevolence*
> *The sins of man*
> *But forgive*
> *And cleanse*
>
> *And so, O Lord*
> *Protect us beneath your wings*
> *And let peace be our portion*
> *Now and forever more*
> *Amen*

I'm so proud to call my dog Mahalia Jackson Queen Liliuokalani. My beautiful, loving, and happy Lili embodies the spirits of both of her namesakes. She's not perfect. She still fears thunderstorms, and even less threatening rain—perhaps the remnants of a life lived on the streets or perhaps a reminder of too many times caught in a storm without shelter. In these difficult moments, she seems to seek only my presence. If I'm simply there, that seems to be enough to comfort her. Well, that and a Xanax!

No matter what she's been through, her radiance speaks of a new day—her own discovery of the cure for what's wrong. All is forgiven. She's at home. Her enthusiasm in greeting, sniffing, and licking all people, regardless of race, color, creed, religious or political affiliation, background or species—calls to mind a certain dream for America. Though some still look at her and move to the other side of the street, assuming that her kind is dangerous and must be avoided, their prejudices don't change her positive way of embracing the world. She's still the happiest dog I know.

I always wanted a girl. Now I have a Queen.

THERE GOES THE NEIGHBORHOOD

I've always wanted to have a neighbor just like you.

Mr. Rogers

There's an old proverb: "good fences make good neighbors." As an avowed introvert, I value my anonymity as much as I value my masculinity. So I'm all in favor of fences. I'm for anything that puts the privy back in private, including peepholes, blackout shades, underground bunkers, drawbridges, and moats. However, it's not *good fences* that make good neighbors, it's *good neighbors* that make good neighbors. And good dogs don't hurt either.

I've moved around a lot in my lifetime, and I've lived in many different neighborhoods. Every time I think I've moved for the last time, God says, *Hold my beer*. That's how I ended up moving from "The Garden Island" of Kauai to the "Gator Swamp" of Louisiana. I had not anticipated exchanging pineapples for pelicans, slippers for seersuckers, leis for Mardi Gras beads, lava flows for Hand Grenades, "Surf's up!" for "Geaux Saints!" or blue water for a red state.

The first thing I did when I moved to Louisiana was turn my garage into the exact replica of the Tiki Bar I had in Hawaii. I'm the only guy on my block that's hosted a "Don Ho Hoe Down." My Cajun Luau featured Poi Boys and Crawfish sushi, and it has already become a Louisiana legend. We played Pin the Cornmeal Batter on the Thinly Sliced Catfish, Boudin Bingo, and held a contest to see who could strum a washboard and a ukulele while wearing overalls with a grass skirt. I knew I was in a different state when a man at my church brought me a "holster" for my hot sauce, giving a whole new meaning to "packing heat." At my first luncheon at a local retirement center, I realized I'd fully arrived when an 86-year-old woman allowed me to borrow her Tabasco. On the bottle she had affixed a large, printed label that included her name, address, telephone number, social security number, next of kin, power of attorney, and in all capital letters: "REWARD IF RETURNED." I'm pretty sure she'd also had it microchipped with a tracking device. I wasn't in Kansas anymore, and I was definitely not in Hawaii.

The best things about living in Louisiana—other than fried chicken, beignets, chargrilled oysters, and the sultry sounds emanating from Frenchman Street (or *any* street for that matter)—are my neighbors. I have the best neighbors. I enjoyed many blessings living on the island of Kauai, but good neighbors weren't among them. I'm pretty sure my next door neighbors on Kauai will never be mistaken for sheep *or* goats come Judgment Day—more likely sharks and snakes. They'll probably both be banished to an eternity living right next door to the Kardashians. For them A.L.O.H.A. had apparently gone A.W.O.L., and I doubt a mere fence would've improved relations between us. Perhaps a wall would have, but only if I could have gotten Micronesia to pay for it.

I did my best to engage my neighbors. I complimented their mud flaps and tattoos. I gave them the *shaka* sign at every turn. And I picked up the dog poop in the neighborhood, even though it wasn't my pups' poop. Take the neighbor to my left—we'll call him Leftie—the guy I bought my house from warned me about him saying, "That guy is an asshole." But I never make assumptions about anyone's character. I assume the best about all people until they prove otherwise. He proved otherwise.

One day, Leftie asked me to trim the "high biscuit" plants growing along the edge of my property. My hibiscus were apparently trespassing and randomly littering his lawn. I wasn't aware that dropping hibiscus blossoms was the gardening moral equivalent of launching dog turds from my front lanai. I'd noticed that he had no trees on his property, just a few bonsai-type bushes that looked like they visited the barber shop, if not the butcher shop, frequently. His lawn resembled a minefield in Afghanistan, but that didn't stop him from meticulously manicuring every blade of grass that managed to survive his plucking, pruning, nipping, ripping, and nitpicking.

I obliged by pruning my hibiscus bushes to look like they'd survived a square-down-the-middle chainsaw attack. He informed me that my efforts were grossly insufficient. What he seemed to desire was a large buffer zone, a sort of vegetation-free DMZ so that in gale-force winds, a hibiscus bud wouldn't be tempted to take flight and land on his ass-y, I mean grassy, paradise.

After the great hibiscus massacre, I'd hoped for a mutually-agreed-upon tree treaty before he could employ a chemical weapon assault to finish off my flora. Instead, he turned his attention to my nearby mango and avocado trees, in particular, any left-leaning limbs that might, at any moment, attack his property. I immediately regretted giving him permission to "trim my trees." My landscaping plan had to be updated to incorporate stumps into the design. For the rest of my years on Kauai, many of my mangos and avocados came from friends who I wished were my neighbors, but most came from the produce aisle at Foodland. I'm not saying that this guy was an asshole. It's just that I might need to consult an experienced proctologist for a more accurate identification.

The neighbor to my right—I'll call him Rightie—was even worse. I liked his elevated truck design—it was handy in floods. His girlfriend seemed sweet and his pit bull showed potential. When his daughter was born, I hoped he would assume a more gentle temperament. But, I knew we were in trouble when, one day, Wili wandered out of the gate to say "aloha" to the neighbor dog. Wili was no fool and sensed trouble. He immediately raced back to the safer confines of our backyard next to our hot tub, shielded by hibiscus, which I now guarded with perimeter cannons. Rightie was a serious MMA fighter, and I could imagine that he'd be pretty tough in a cage. Seeing that Wili stood by my side and wasn't afraid of me, he sought to explain to me what dogs *really* needed. He told me that the best way to "train" a dog was to lift them up by the scruff of their neck and then slam them against the ground. I told him that I was pretty sure that wasn't a good way to train or treat *any* animal or human. He laughed and told me to go back to the Mainland. I didn't laugh. But I did eventually return to the Mainland.

I later heard that not only had Rightie racked up several 9-1-1 calls for domestic violence, but also that several neighbors caught him in the act of "training" his dog and reported him to the humane society. I know that one day he slammed his dog so hard against the ground that the dog had to be euthanized. I don't relish telling you such painful stories. Perhaps it's important for us to be reminded that evil is real, and sometimes it lives very close to us—too close for comfort, and too close to let us become too comfortable. It's also important to recognize that anyone who is cruel to an animal will likely be cruel to a human. Harming any of God's precious creatures, including people, should be enough to get you kicked off the island, if not the planet.

When my dogs and I eventually moved back to the Mainland, I was a nervous wreck on the flights home. I'd asked the vet about a sedative, but she told me that I'd have to see my primary care physician. She knew that I'd be a lot more anxious than they would be. On both flights, before take-off, I sent the pilots a gift of chocolate-covered macadamia nuts with Wili and Sinbad's photo attached along with a note that read, "We're down below!" Everyone made it safely to Louisiana and as we started to sniff out our new digs, we began to realize just how lucky and blessed we were. There wasn't one plant or pet abuser in the entire neighborhood.

Our first Christmas morning, we heard someone shout, "Mele Kalikimaka!" It was our 90-year-old neighbor, Margaret, who lived two doors down. Her husband, who'd died thirty years earlier, had been stationed in Hawaii for several years. The two of them had traveled there often. Margaret would become a big fan of Wili's. The first time he nuzzled her, she said, "Wili, I haven't been that close to a man in thirty years. Good boy!" Margaret loved to flirt with Wili as she told us wild tales from when she was a young woman living in New Orleans. She had lots of health issues, but she always reminded me, and perhaps herself, that she'd been abundantly blessed in this life. Right next door to us lived Barbara, the Master Gardener. Her front yard was so vibrant and colorful it reminded me of my years in paradise, except her hibiscus plants had never known a chainsaw. Then there was Marianne, a young Filipina artist, and her husband, Rock, a local musician and mixologist. Marianne's parents had worked for the United Nations, so she'd lived all over the world. She was walking her dog the day that I picked up the posters for the Last Howlelujah Tour, the one with Wili's mugshot wearing a cowboy hat and flower lei. As she was walking by, a poster flew out of my hands and landed at her feet. "Is that your dog?" she asked. We've been good friends ever since. She even agreed to be a judge for the Howl-o-Ween costume contest the dogs and

I hosted to benefit the local humane society. Although my dogs were disqualified from winning, we all agreed that Lili in her coconut bra, lei, and grass skirt was the looker of the evening.

But if I had to pick favorite neighbors, it would be Helen and Cleo, their rescue dogs, Finders and Keepers, and their notorious cat, Bad Jack. He was originally named just Jack, but the adjective was added so often, it just stuck. They live in the house that I was thinking of buying right about the time that they purchased it. But, I managed to still find a perfectly fine house in the same neighborhood.

I now live in a very conservative part of the country, and that's fine by me. I don't really care much about labels because they rarely capture everything there is to know and appreciate about a person, and they often don't mean anything at all. Besides, I don't really care whether my neighbors are conservative or liberal. But I do care that they treat all people with dignity and respect, care for the earth, and show compassion to all. And if they can bake pies, that also goes a long way.

The first time I walked Wili and Sinbad past Helen and Cleo's house, I noticed some pretty unusual signs surrounding their abode—well, unusual for these parts. The signs indicated that some mindful, thoughtful, and kind folks lived there. There was one near their front door with a Dalai Lama quote: "Love and compassion are necessities, not luxuries. Without them humanity cannot survive." Mr. Lama nailed it again. On their front fence was a banner with a photograph of a large boat filled with refugees fleeing Syria. Above the boat it read:

"The only thing stronger than fear is hope." Sounded like something that guy in sandals might've said who was always talking about welcoming the stranger and how love casts out fear. Finally, there was a multi-colored yard sign that read: "In This House, We Believe: Black Lives Matter. Women's Rights are Human Rights. No Human is Illegal. Science is Real. Love is Love. No Matter Your Faith or Ability, Kindness is Everything." I had a feeling they might not be from around here. When I saw the sign that read: "Neuter your pets and not just your enemies," I knew they had a healthy sense of humor. Even if they didn't have a Tiki Bar, I had a feeling we wouldn't just be neighbors, but we would also be good friends.

Cleo and Helen met when they were in their 20s on Beaver Island in Michigan. They dated for a while, but eventually went their separate ways and lived separate lives—careers, marriages, children. Not too long ago they found each other again and the rest is history. Helen is a retired therapist with a knowing smile. Cleo is a retired contractor who's very tall. "Retired" is a relative term. Neither of them has slowed down at all. Cleo is black and Helen is white. Helen's mother, who came to adore Cleo, said to Helen, "You *would* fall in love with the only black man on the entire island." I heard that when Helen and Cleo moved in just a few months before I did, someone actually said, "There goes the neighborhood." Yep, there it went, all right. It improved exponentially.

Cleo has had to deal with racism his entire life, but, he approaches every incident of prejudice and hateful comment with his easygoing nature, disarming humor, and a perfectly timed "They must not like tall people!" For years, Cleo was a member of the NRA back when sanity prevailed, and he once tried to join the Ku Klux Klan just to "see what all the fuss was about." He made it all the way to the "download your photo" portion of the application, at which point he was rejected. Apparently, they don't like *tall* people.

Helen and Cleo aren't just good neighbors to those who live nearby, they're good neighbors to all neighborhoods, even those who may not align with their level of education or economic status. Cleo serves on the Board of Habitat for Humanity and Helen volunteers for an after-school program for low-income children. Wherever there's an opportunity to serve those in need or build bridges of support, Helen and Cleo will step up and be counted among the faithful. Their latest project has been to completely rebuild and renovate an old, run-down home in what used to be, and to an extent still is, the historically Black neighborhood in Covington called The West 30s.

We live in the Deep South, and reminders of our segregated past, and still-too-segregated present, are everywhere. You can still spot the sign for the "colored" entrance to the balcony of the now-shuttered downtown movie theatre. In my historic and beautiful chapel at Christ Church, built in 1846, the balcony was once the cramped galleries where people of color were made to sit. Even today, things aren't so different on your typical Sunday morning for most Americans—folks still often go their separate ways.

Decades ago, when the West 30s was a poor, but vibrant, neighborhood, there were neighbors of different occupations and a neighborhood school where the teachers not only knew the students' names, but they also knew their parents' names and where they lived. Segregation is a terrible thing, but the loss of neighborhoods where we knew our neighbors may be almost as bad. For many years, especially in the 1930s, 40s, and 50s, West 30th Street was an epicenter for what was called "The Chitlin' Circuit." There were more than a few hopping nightclubs that were safe places for Black performers and audiences to gather. It was the small version of Beale Street in Memphis, and people came to Covington from a hundred miles away to see shows. The Band Box, Dot's Ponderosa, and the Pheasant Club hosted greats like Fats Domino, Irma Thomas, Johnny Guitar Watson, Bobby Blue Bland, Ray Charles, Sam Cooke, James Brown, and B.B. King. The clubs are mostly gone, as is much of the quality housing, so Helen and Cleo decided to play a small part in the neighborhood's renewal by renovating and updating a home and selling it back to a neighbor at cost. There wouldn't be any profit in this endeavor. It's just the kind of thing good neighbors, and good people, do. Wili, Sinbad, and Lili would always pull me straight toward their house on our walks. Dogs know good character when they sniff it. Combine a great sense of humor with good character and you end up with excellent neighbors. Wili and I howled with laughter when we received the following letter from Helen and Cleo's dog, Keepers:

****

GOLDEN RULE RETRIEVER LEGAL SERVICES
"Justice Sniffed Out"

St. Wili a.k.a. Nawiliwili Nelson Miller
Father William Miller, said owner of St. Wili

███████████

Covington, Louisiana 70433

Dear St. Wili and Father William Miller,

Please be advised that my client, Ms. Keepers Curran-Seay, is seriously considering filing a sexual harassment suit due to your continuous attempts to hump her in social situations. She has clearly barked her total lack of interest in your sexual advances (bark translation: *get the hell off my back and keep your paws to yourself*). You apparently can't take "NO" for an answer. You appear to believe that your social fame and fortune grants you the right to hump whoever you want, whenever you want. You are greatly mistaken.

My client is insisting that you cease and desist this unwanted behavior and that you compensate her with unlimited dog treats, cost of past, present and future psychological treatment, as well as all present and future veterinarian bills including a tummy tuck to help restore her damaged self-image, and a supply of decent wine for her owners who are understandably distraught over what she has endured.

If these conditions are met in good faith, Ms. Keepers Curran-Seay will not disclose your sexual harassment to the press or to other dogs in the neighborhood (with the exception of yappy little dogs).

We await your response.

Sincerely,
Red Rover, Esquire

After Wili died, I made a vow to limit my dog family members to two—Lili and Sinbad. They were plenty. A few weeks later, Cleo was finishing up some electrical work in the main room of their renovation project when he suddenly felt a presence. It wasn't a malevolent presence, but it was an intruder, nonetheless. He looked up and saw peering at him from around the corner a gray, pit bull-mix puppy. He was so thin you could see his ribs. He appeared to be starving, not just for food, but also for affection—a kind scratch and maybe even a home. He'd likely been living on the streets since he was born, and judging by the pellet gun wounds all over his face and his big ears, he'd had a hard life for such a young pup.

Cleo had just been telling Helen she needed another animal intervention after she'd rescued a momma cat and her eight kittens that had made a home under the house they were renovating. In fact, Cleo would frequently ask both of us, given our soft spot for homeless critters, "What is *wrong* with y'all?!" But Cleo couldn't help himself. When confronted with a need or a needy one, it was hard for him to turn away and do nothing. He took a picture of the puppy, sent it to Helen, and texted: "What do I do?" Helen texted back: "I'll call Bill."

A new puppy wasn't in my plan. But that's when Wili got wind of it from on high and said to St. Peter, *Hold my beer.* I'm certain Wili orchestrated the whole thing. I'd just started writing this book and I'd asked for a muse to appear. Who knew the muse had such big ears? I said muse, not mouse! And certainly not a pit bull/mouse mix! I met Helen and the puppy at their house ten minutes later. I noticed immediately that he wasn't only shark gray, but he also had markings like that of a shark. Plus, he tried to bite my hand off, as well as anything and everything within biting distance. I named him Mano—Hawaiian for shark. I'd recently had a rare Saturday night off, so I ventured into New Orleans to the legendary music venue Tipitina's. Just inside the front door of the club is a bronze bust of Professor Longhair, the great blues and jazz pianist who was born in Bogalusa, just one town over. He wrote a slew of Louisiana-themed hits such as: "Tipitina" (hence, the name of the venue), "Big Chief," "Bald Head," "Mardi Gras in New Orleans," and "Ball the Wall." In keeping with tradition, I rubbed the head of the bronzed legend upon entering, a gesture that's supposed to bring good things into your life. I was hoping to win the lottery, so a pit bull puppy from a suspicious lineage wasn't exactly what I had in mind. But I continued my naming ways. "You will be Mano Professor Shorthair Miller," I declared. Not only because Miller is my last name, but also because I had a feeling I was going to need a beer of the same name very soon.

I agreed to foster Mano on a trial basis until we found him a more suitable home. But once you name a dog, he belongs to you, so you likely have no one to blame but yourself. His first night, I had the great and naïve idea that we could all sleep in my bedroom like one, big, happy family. The moments of bliss, which were few, were far outweighed by the moments of asking, "How did a terrorist get into my bed?" Mano kept me up all night. When he wasn't testing his teeth on my skin, he was farting in my face and straddling my head with his crotch. He'd only jump out of bed long enough to poop on the floor. In fact, he took care of his business (a song *not* by Professor Longhair), many times and in many ways—and all over my house. Plus, he nearly chewed the house down There's an old proverb that says: "good crates make good pets." I now know that to be true.

Despite his challenges, and my urgent pleas to every dog adoption agency from Louisiana to Hawaii, Mano is still with me and has taught me much. Many of the lessons I thought I'd already learned. Like most people, I seem to have to learn, then relearn, and then learn again, life's most important lessons.

Mano's big ears that stood straight up consistently reminded me of how important it is to listen, especially to those who may not vote the same, practice religion the same, or have athletic loyalties the same as mine. I believe it was Saint James who reminded us to be quick to listen, slow to speak, and even slower to anger. We could learn so much from not only our neighbors, but also from those who aren't locals and who are different from us—if only we would shut up and listen.

Mano has also reminded me of how important it is to take your time and teach your children well. The relationship between dog and human, teacher and student, parent and child, elders and youth, is the most important work of our age. There are too many strays wandering our streets without direction or guidance. It takes a neighborhood to raise a child and, sometimes, a dog.

We learn much more when we learn together. We learn what's right and what's wrong. We learn that you don't steal your neighbor's food, bones, or toys and that you bite without vicious intent, but only if you and your play partner are clear about the rules of the game. We learn to observe boundaries, listen to parents' instructions, and not pollute your home, whether that home is a crate or a planet. Mano is slowly learning how to correct the error of his ways with patient guidance from me, Lili, and Sinbad. He's actually getting better. And I already love him like a shark—I mean a son.

But he's definitely NOT staying here.

Ok, he can stay.

There goes the neighborhood.

MY PUPS RUNNETH OVER

Peter: *Brian, there's a message in my Alphabits! It says, Oooooooooo!*
Brian the Dog: *Peter, those are Cheerios.*

Family Guy

The state of being canine and the gift of being in a right relationship with a canine may be as close as we will come to experiencing God's original intention for all creation. Dogs, often better than the people who love them, live out the core values of the spiritual life: unconditional love for others, unqualified appreciation of all, authentic understanding of self, curiosity, loyalty, openness, affection, forgiveness, playfulness, and a keen sensual awareness of all that God is revealing in the world around them. Dogs are God's best work. I should know—dogs outnumber humans in my house four-to-one.

Don't get me wrong, I like people, too. Some of my best friends are people. I have nothing against human beings, even if in one of the creation stories in the Book of Genesis, it took God a day and a half to make the animals and only twelve hours to make humans. Draw your own conclusions. Still, if God says that it's good, then who am I to argue? The *Homo sapiens* are just fine, I suppose, if you've only got a half a day and a deadline. Plus, even though we have the *homo* (human) part down, we have a ways to go on the *sapiens* (wisdom) qualifier. For many humans, we know what the Master desires, but we're too stubborn or stupid to obey. Maybe somewhere along the way we began to believe that we were smarter than our Master and that Obedience School was only for dogs. But they may now be the wiser of the species.

So, my doctrine for a good life, or at least a better life, is not quite dogmatic, but more dog-centric. I believe that regardless of our religious backgrounds or political persuasions, we can't go wrong with a critter. It doesn't matter whether you are Catlick, Pawtostant, Barkhist, Hindog, Chewish, Muttlim, or even Agdogstic. It matters not whether you are a Demo*cat* or a Re*paw*blican—dogs can bring us together and help us overcome our differences. You can always find common ground with man's best friend. My mantras for better living are: *I Fawn Over Fauna, My Beastie is My Bestie, I'm Wild for Woofers, I Brake for Barkers, Floppy Ears Bring Me to Tears, Drool is Cool, Slobber is Da' Bomber, Puppies Over Yuppies, My Dog is Smarter Than Your Honor Student, I Like Big Mutts and I Cannot Lie, Get Your Tails to the Pound, Amazing Face— How Sweet the Dog,* and *Sniffing Makes the World Go Round.*

We live in a world and in a time when no news is good news, and most news is bad news. In the religious tradition, an evangelist is one who brings a positive message from God into the world. It's one who helps us make meaning out of the mayhem. The gospel is literally God's good news for a world that desperately needs to hear some. Experiences with our dogs and stories about our dogs give us hope and help us to carry on in a world that's increasingly "dog eat dog," or even worse "people destroy everything"—including themselves. These stories are really gospel stories told by evangelists, *not* in possession of television shows that make us feel guilty, but of tails that make us feel loved. They are truly from God.

Here is a true story—a gospel story. One Sunday morning right after my first book about my dog, Sam, was released, a pastor at a large church in a major southern city gathered all the children on the altar steps, as was his custom, to hear the children's sermon for the day. The pastor wanted to remind them about the four gospels of the New Testament—the uplifting stories told by true evangelists. The pastor asked the young children if they could name the four gospels, the four evangelists, of the New Testament. They quickly named the first three—Matthew, Mark, and Luke. But they were having trouble identifying that fourth gospel. The pastor said, "Come on children, you know this. The other gospel is The Gospel According to …" One little boy in the back stood up and shouted, "I know! It's the Gospel According to Sam!"

This little boy was obviously touched with the gift of prophecy. Perhaps our stories about dogs, God's best work, are not quite canonical and part of the traditionally accepted inspired sacred texts, but they are certainly *caninical*—which one could argue is just as sacred. Our dogs and their gospels, whether it's The Gospel According to Sam, Jack, Wili, Sinbad, Lili, Mano, or your own beloved beast, all share good news amid the bad. It's just what the Doctor, the Veterinarian, and the Great Physician ordered to help heal our wounded world. How can dogs lead us toward a more helpful and authentic spirituality centered in the good news of God's love for all creation? Let me sniff the ways!

First, we would be wise to adopt a spirituality that's more grounded, connected, and closer to the earth—a kind of spirituality on all fours, so to speak. Good theology doesn't rise above and dismiss the common stuff of life as too earthly or earthy, but appreciates and infuses the daily materials of our existence with a whiff of heaven—the markings of divinity. So much of what passes for spirituality is more pie in the sky than poop on the ground, operating at a plane of understanding that's stratospherically disconnected from real life. We think we may be washing our hands of the ways of the world when we are actually washing away the seeds of transformation, the remnants of the ground of our being in which true life might take root to grow and thrive.

There is a reason why we feel so alive when we dig in the dirt and plant something. When we get our hands dirty with the very materials from which God fashioned the world, including ourselves, it reminds us of the original connection God intended. We are called to tend the earth as caring stewards rather than destroy our planet as uncaring tenants. Remember that we are formed of dust, the scriptures tell us, and to dust we shall return. The more creation-conscious our theology, the more we recognize the good, seek the good, and do the good in the context of all the good that God has made. Remember this truth the next time your dog runs inside absolutely delighted to be completely covered in mud. Our mutts are simply reminding us of what we're actually made and what truly matters. *Matter* matters.

Second, my dogs' unconditional love empowers me to carry on, to walk on, regardless of who yanks my chain, tells me I'm a bad boy, or tries to tie me to a tree. Through thick and thin, whether I'm learning new tricks or failing miserably at the ones I thought I'd already mastered, regardless of my measuring up to anyone else's standards, for my dogs, I am enough. I am divine. I'm master of their universe. I can be myself, delight in myself, and celebrate myself. Whether or not I believe in Dog doesn't matter, because Dog believes in me.

When one of my canines looks me in the eye, I see love— unconditionally positive regard in its purest form. There is no judgment, fault-finding, limitation, restriction, or restitution. My dog seems to see something in me that I often fail to see in myself. They see God. What they see reminds me that I'm made in the image of God, and that God loves me even more than my dog does. Pay more attention to the critter than the critic. Remember, there's only one Judge, who is also your Creator, and it's not Simon Cowell! In the words of Willie Nelson: "If you really want to get along with somebody, let them be themselves." Start by letting yourself be yourself. Always remember—according to your dog—you are enough.

Third, dogs are comfortable in their own fur. They take

great delight in being just what God made them to be. Dogs aspire to be dogs. They don't aspire to be what they cannot be and what they weren't created or called to be. Dogs don't pretend to be cats, whales, or warthogs. Dogs don't desire to be nuclear physicists, meteorologists, bishops, or super-models. Dogs don't wish to trade places with anyone, unless there's bacon involved. Dogs are dogs. There are no apologies. There is no pretense or pretension. There are no regrets.

It's refreshing in a world obsessed with being someone or something else, or pretending to be what we aren't, to observe dogs simply being themselves and taking great delight in that state of honest-to-God grace. Dogs walk around naked and unashamed, regardless of their girth of belly or their length of tail. Not one of them is neurotic because they were neutered or languishing because they don't have a designer leash. Dogs are happy to be themselves. They're happy to be anywhere! They sniff indiscriminately and without regard to what some may consider off-limits or, at least, off-putting. They remind us that all ground is hallowed ground, and all the beasts that walk upon it are blessed by the one who made them just the way they are. From head to toe, from snout to tail, from paw to pelvis—it's all good.

Fourth, dogs are forthcoming about revealing their wants and needs. They often communicate more effectively than most humans. If my dogs have a need, whether they are hungry, itching for a belly scratch, or just want to be petted, they don't do what humans too often do. We, all too often, make people guess what we want, and then get mad when they cannot read

our minds. Or perhaps we project onto others our own inade-
quacies and inconsistencies rather than just acknowledge them.

Dogs tell it like it is. They aren't shy about making their
wants and needs known. If Wili wanted a belly scratch, he would
often flop over on top of me to reveal prime scratching real
estate. He had no shame in showing me the most intimate parts
of himself. His four paws would be directed to the four corners
of the earth. If I didn't catch on quickly enough, he'd do a head
bob toward his belly or take my hand in his mouth and redirect
it toward a more helpful location. If Wili wanted a bite of my
burger, he would simply come and gently sit right next to me
with the world's best "beauty queen" posture. I quickly got the
message that went like this: *Look. I'm sitting right next to you. I'm
a good boy. Please give me a bite-—extra beef or I'll cut the cheese.* If I
didn't move fast enough to comply with his clearly communicated
directive, he would start smacking his chops every time I took
a bite. Not once did I have to guess what Wili wanted from me.

Tell others, especially those you love, what you want or need.
Communicate in whatever way is most effective—wag, nuzzle,
or bark. Be assertive in expressing your desires and be active
in your listening. Many of our challenges could be resolved
by simple communication. Stop. Sit. Stay. Speak. Listen.
Your relationships will be more satisfying, and the world will
be a better place. You might even get a bite of cheeseburger.

Perhaps most importantly, pups teach us how to live more
balanced, grounded, whole, healthy, and complete lives. They
seem to understand that there's more than one way to skin

a cat, and certainly more than one way to save our own skin and our own souls. I call these The Four Spiritual Disciplines of Dog: Work Hard. Play Hard. Nap Hard. Sniff Hard.

Work Hard

There are some things in the world worth getting worked up over. There are some ways in which we are called to engage with the world that really do matter. There should be priorities in our lives that are worthy of our greatest focus and our undivided attention. And then there are some things that aren't worth getting worked up over at all. In higher learning terms, we might say we *major* in minors and we *minor* in majors. In even *higher* learning terms, as Jesus once told the Pharisees, we neglect the weightier matters of God's law—justice, mercy, and faithfulness—while focusing on the issues that really don't amount to much in the grand scheme of God's kingdom.

Occasionally, when my dogs come down with a digestive disorder and refuse to eat anything at all, my veterinarian will prescribe what she calls "canned crack." We joke that in Louisiana, a dog cannot refuse a can of that stuff anymore than a human can refuse what comes out of the take-out window at Popeye's. Put some spicy fried chicken in front of my face, or even within sniffing distance, and my concentration is unwavering until I've completely consumed every piece. I'm helpless in its presence. Nothing else matters. All my attention is on the tasty fried sacrament. Put some canned crack in front of Wili, and he couldn't think about anything else. For my dog Sam the one food that he couldn't refuse and that mattered above all others, was cheese. For Sam, there was nothing in this world more important than cheese, or even the possibility that there *might* be cheese.

Which of God's commands should be considered in the same way? Are there some truths that God desires for us to swallow and pursue with the same sense of passion and purpose? Another way to ask this question is: what is God's fried chicken? Or, for Sam, what is God's cheese? What is the one thing that really matters to God or that gets God worked up? Are they the same priorities that receive *our* undivided attention? Or do we spend too much time sniffing the side dishes or the plastic wrapper? Do we prioritize the peripheral and focus on the trivial, missing the tastiest, meatiest, and most satisfying of all God's blessings?

The more we listen, learn, taste, and see the goodness of God, the more we'll begin to understand what really matters in faith and in life and what deserves our undivided attention and most passionate efforts. While it's not chicken, canned crack, or cheese (sorry Sam and Wili), it is love without limits, peace for the whole world, compassion for everyone, and justice for all. It is to love God with all we've got, and to love our neighbor as we would ourselves. Without these truths fully pursued, the world cannot be fed, and we cannot be sustained as spiritual people. These are the qualities and values that matter to God, worth our hardest work, our deepest devotion, and our sustained persistence. Don't get up off the couch for anything less.

Play Hard

Life is too important to be taken too seriously. A sense of humor, the gift of joy and wonder, an attitude of fun and frivolity—these may be the only ways to save us from ourselves and from each other. When religion becomes the re-enforcer of bad news, the initiator of exclusionary judgment, the oppressor of joy, the leader of the pack of misery and woe, it ceases to be what it claims to be. What we need in religion is what we need in the world—more WAGGISHNESS!

We need more humor. More playfulness. More silliness. More light and lightheartedness. The one who gets the last laugh is always God, because God is the source of all that's comedic in this world. You want a good laugh? Look at the world around you. It's hilarious. Still not convinced? Take a look in the mirror. That's pretty damn funny (I know from experience)! When we laugh out loud, we breathe in the breath of God. We inhale the spirit of God. Serial solemnity and spiritual awareness have nothing in common. If you are easily offended or fail to see the humor in anything of God, you're likely sniffing the wrong behind.

When I lived on the island of Kauai, the moments I felt closest to God, other than in my dog's presence, were when I was kayaking the green sea cliffs of the Napali Coast surrounded by waterfalls and waves. Sometimes, after a long day of paddling, my energy would begin to fade. But just when I thought I couldn't continue, one of God's playful creatures would appear and inspire me to paddle faster, or at least inspire me to have a better attitude. Often it was spinner dolphins jumping out of the water just long enough to spin around in mid-air before belly-flopping back into the water. I'm sure that there's some reasonable biological explanation for this behavior, but the best explanation is likely that it's just fun! God gave dolphins a playful spirit just as God gives us the desire to engage in silliness for the sake of our souls. And it wasn't only spinner dolphins with their "slapsticks of the sea" routines; monk seals would race us to the beach and sea turtles would try to out-surf us. Everywhere we looked, nature would remind us of the playfulness of God.

My dogs are forever teaching me about the importance of simple joys and playful pleasures in life—chasing a ball, tossing around a squeaky Mardi Gras worm, running in circles for no apparent reason, smiling at humans, wagging their tails to let everyone know that they're in on the joke. As soon as little Mano arrived at our house, he began trying to get Lili to play. Although Lili is a little on the older side, she quickly rediscovered her inner puppy. Their pretend wrestling matches when they bare fangs that would put fear into the heart of a shark are as entertaining as anything Cirque du Soleil could create. Lately they've discovered that even though my back yard is mostly gravel and flower beds covered in pine-needles separated with a small strip of grass, there's one tiny patch of dirt that turns to mud after every rain. Lili and Mano have figured out that after it rains, they can dig really hard in that one small spot of dirt then bury their whole bodies in the hole and wallow in the muck to their heart's content—which is almost as much fun as seeing the expression on their dad's face when they show up at the back door completely covered in mud. Sometimes, when I see my dogs enjoying themselves with such abandon and enthusiasm, I'm reminded of the words of Rabbi Abraham Heschel when he said, "Everything is phenomenal. Everything is incredible. To be spiritual is to be amazed." I'm always amazed by my dogs and their ability to be amazed. May God give me that same desire—to play so hard that I forget every trouble, but remember every blessing—even mud! Play hard, my friends.

Nap Hard

Don't just do something, stand there. Or better yet, sit there or lie down. Take time to reflect, ponder, rest, and reconsider. Take time to pause your paws—to be renewed and clear your mind. Breathe deeply. Slow down. Sigh and snore like your dog. Take a nap. You might consider this canine tendency as *The Prone Position as Positive Force for Social Change.* Even though my youngest pup, Mano, has just arrived on the scene, he's still excited at the thought of, well, everything! He cannot sit still and he's excitable beyond description. But if I pick him up and place him on the bed right next to me, where he can be comfortable and secure, certain of my presence, he will often fall right to sleep. He will become an instant "good boy," and I become a better boy for having experienced these times with him. These moments have become the most renewing part of my day. When people ask me to describe my favorite memory with Wili, it's easy. It would be those moments when I'd be lying on the couch, maybe watching a game, maybe not, and Wili would approach the couch, climb directly on top of me, sprawl out, look at me intently for a millisecond, and then lie down his head and immediately start snoring. In those moments of simple stillness and closeness—of heavy breathing and an even heavier dog body—I'm pretty sure my blood pressure would finally drop to a more healthy level. I'd feel safe and secure in the presence of my dog, or better, the presence of my God.

I inherited workaholic tendencies from my father. Or, perhaps, I'm just not secure enough in my own skin and I'm still working to earn the favor of God, and of others. I once told my spiritual director that I felt like I was running ragged. I told her there was so much to do and not enough time to accomplish everything. She reminded me that God had gotten by without me for most of history and that the most productive thing, the most *needed* thing that I could do each day (other than meditative mindful prayer), was to take a cue from my dog. She said I needed to find a cool spot every afternoon, circle it a few times, and then lie down and go to sleep. Naps are apparently a highly underrated form of spiritual practice. They are that "needed time" spoken of in the old spiritual. And it's always needed—even right now. God rested on the Sabbath day. Given what we've done with what God created, and the work he still has cut out for himself, I'll bet God is glad he got in that nap.

Sniff Hard

While you shouldn't stick your nose into anybody's business, you should, however, insert your snout into God's ongoing revelation in the world. Curiosity may have killed the cat, but it saved the dog. The Jewish theologian, Martin Buber, once wrote, "An animal's eyes have the power to speak a great language." And Wili would add that an animal's nose has the power to reveal great truth.

On our Last Howlelujah Tour, Wili's nose went into overdrive at every turn. There were so many new revelations of things previously unknown. There were new tastes, new truths, new critters, new cultures, new plants, and new people. The world that God has made, and continues to remake, is inexhaustible. There will always be something new to discover with our eyes, ears, noses, mouths, minds, hearts, and souls—if they stay open. Albert Einstein, who was almost as smart as Wili, once said, "I have no special talent, I'm only passionately curious."

When we get to that place where we know enough to know that we know *nothing*, it's there where we can be taught enough to do *something*. It's there where we are aware of our *unknowing* that God reveals what we might become. It's there where we can discern our individual destiny and change the world for the better.

Sniff out truth wherever you go. Learn new tricks and you'll never grow old. Know that you weren't the first to mark a spot and that you will not be the last, but mark it, nonetheless. Remember from where you have come, but be open to where you might be called. My dogs have taught me much. As long as I'm not finished learning, their job is not done teaching me about the ways of the world our Creator has made. I never imagined I'd have so many critters. I also never imagined learning so much from them. My pups runneth over. *Thanks be to Dog.*

Second Paw:

ON THE ROAD (AGAIN)

Life ain't always beautiful, but it's a beautiful ride.

Tommy Lee Jones

BAD DOGNOSIS

Take a sad song and make it better.
The Beatles

As popes go, Leo the Great was a good one. Leo had skills—administrator, negotiator, theologian, and writer. Unlike his successor, Pope Hilarius, who sounds like a stand-up comedian, but wasn't all that funny, Leo left us several compelling nuggets of spiritual wisdom, such as: "There is no victory without strife" and "Those who aren't good to others are bad to themselves." Pope Leo may not be quite in the same quotability category as other Leos such as novelist, Leo Tolstoy, who said, "Everyone thinks of changing the world, but no one thinks of changing himself" or former Cubs manager, Leo Durocher's nugget of wisdom: "Baseball is like church—many attend, few understand." But he proved himself to be a superb negotiator without parallel. When all-around-bad-guy, Attila the Hun, threatened to ransack Rome unless the Emperor Valentinian sent over his half-sister to be his bride (and with her a small, meager dowry of half of the Western Roman Empire), Valentinian instead sent Pope Leo. Even in full papal regalia, Leo wouldn't likely have been mistaken for Valentinian's sister, so this unexpected response must have been a real Roman downer to Atilla. Somehow, by the grace of God and the Pope's promise of free pizza for life, not only did Attila not killa the pope, he retreated. The man who put the barb in Barbarian tucked his tail and ran back home to his wife Zsa Zsa, who forever thereafter referred to him as "Attila the Hunny Bunny." I can hear Mrs. Hun now, winning every argument with the words, *you got your ass whooped by the pope—the POPE for Pete's sake! Now take out the trash, altar boy!*

As pups go, Wili the Woofster was a great one. Greatness often involves the overcoming of great challenges in life. On the Feast Day of Saint Leo the Great, November 10, 2016, Wili and I found ourselves in the city of New Orleans, just across the lake from our charming small-town home. Unlike many who might find an unscrupulous excuse to visit this enticing city, we weren't there to engage in any sort of questionable behavior that might have elicited an edict of immorality from Pope Leo. There was no bull involved—papal or otherwise. I was there to attend a conference on Christian education. Thanks to the hospitality of our good friend and New Orleans Jazz Musician, Matt Lemmler, who always opens his home to both man and beast, Wili and Sinbad were able to tag along. Matt is the kind of New Orleans musician whose son is named Miles and whose dog is named Beignet—in other words, he's the real deal. When Wili, Sinbad, and I arrived in New Orleans, Matt was on tour, so all three of the Miller mutts had the entire place to ourselves. We were within sniffing distance of the streetcar, a bone's throw from a lovely park with majestic oaks that had been marked by many generations of the pups of NOLA, and next door to a dog-friendly neighborhood café that served excellent sausages. On that fateful feast day, the first twenty-three hours were nothing less than great.

After Wili and Sinbad had settled in and claimed their comfy spots, I headed out for lunch at a funky French Quarter spot with my good friend, Vince. A motivational speaker without equal, Vince is a Canadian now living in Dallas and decided late in life that he wanted to become an Olympic athlete. He did, and he's been inspiring all kinds of folks with his unlikely story of Olympic success ever since. Being around Vince always motivated me to be my best self, even if a delicious plate of shrimp creole isn't involved. Later that same day at the conference, I managed to make a new friend for life, Scott. He was from Milwaukee (a place where my favorite blue-ribbon beverages are brewed), and he'd decided several years earlier that religion and wellness should be inseparable. He was convinced that what is *healthy* is also what is *holy*. And in a world where there's so much that's unhealthy, unbalanced, and unhelpful about the way some practice a kind of life-denying faith, Scott wanted to be an agent of positive change and created a wellness ministry called Living Compass. He and I instantly bonded, and it didn't hurt that he played guitar, sang with the soul of Bob Dylan, and loved baseball. He even inspired me to cheer for the Brewers!

A great day was topped off with a delicious dinner at a storied Creole restaurant that serves crabmeat cheesecake, has a bar named after a duck, and is housed in a historic music store. Does it get any better than that? I was met there by my good friend Sean, the Engagement Director for a favorite charity, Episcopal Relief and Development. I've traveled with them twice on pilgrimage—once to Ghana and then again to Zambia. I've been proud to partner with them to support their disaster relief efforts, economic empowerment, food security, and early childhood development programs in Africa and around the world. Wili has raised more funds on their behalf than I have. In a previous life, Sean was a tour manager for a psychobilly band out of Dallas called The Reverend Horton Heat. That's cool as dog drool.

We were also joined by my friend, Danielle, a theology professor who looks like a model. A graduate from Yale, Danielle writes about Harry Potter and the theological significance of surrogacy, but not at the same time or in the same book. Our table was eventually filled with a whole host of wonderful people who all shared a common love for dogs, God, doing good, saints, and the city of New Orleans. It was a perfect end to a perfect day. My heart was fuller than my stomach, and I was giddy with gratitude as I headed back home to my most remarkable and beloved beasts. To quote another Leo, I felt like I was "king of the world."

I was also feeling just a tad guilty for not saving Wili any crab cheesecake, but I knew that Wili is the kind of dog who never met a morsel he was unwilling to munch. The beauty of going home to a dog is that regardless of how good or how bad your day has been—it's about to get better. If you are down, your dog will raise you up. If you are up, your dog will calm you down. There were always two certainties I could count on when returning home to Wili. One, he would jump up, wag his tail, and run to greet me—a response that consistently made me feel like I was the pope of pups and the king of his world. Two, I knew that whatever food or food approximation I'd set before him he would rejoice and devour it before I could say "those are my fingers." You could place a rice cake infused with essence of celery and encased in plain gelatin and topped with tasteless tofu and shredded cardboard, and Wili would salivate until the floor was transformed into a swamp. Wili loved food and Wili loved me—perhaps in that order.

When I walked in the front door, Wili didn't run to greet me. Instead, he was standing motionless on the other side of the room, rigid on all fours, head and tail down, eyes not registering my presence. My heart sank below sea level. I immediately felt like the levee of meaning in my life had burst open and I was about to drown in some unanticipated sorrow. I didn't know exactly what was wrong, but when he wouldn't eat anything I put before him, I knew something was terribly wrong. Wili wouldn't move and wouldn't eat. While that announcement may not be the end of the world as we know it, that realization felt like the end of my world as I knew it.

After texting everyone I knew asking where we could find a veterinarian that stayed open as late as the bars, I carried Wili down the stairs, gently placed him in the back seat of my car and raced to the 24-hour animal clinic. I felt frantic, hopeless, set adrift, and weighed down all at the same time. As Wili and I waited our turn, I did the only thing that I could do—I asked people to pray for Wili. I posted a simple prayer request on my social media around midnight. Within minutes, there were 368 emoji responses consisting solely and soulfully of hearts and tears, and 175 supportive comments from around the world. To put this kind of compassionate response in perspective, and to begin to understand the depth of empathy expressed by those responding to this special dog—when I was hospitalized with chest pains not long thereafter, I received ten likes, one frowny face, and two half-hearted comments. Everybody loved Wili. Some loved me only because of Wili, and that was okay, too. I, more than anyone, understood why.

I took comfort in their prayers and found strength in their concern. A new friend in Covington prayed for the veterinarians and their staff that "their hands be guided, their minds be sharp, and their hearts be kind." That would cover it. My Jewish chef friend on Kauai posted, "Praying for the world's best dog." Leave it to the Hebrews to get right to the heart of the matter. Someone I didn't even know posted, "Dear heavenly Father: Help *Wiki* in his moment of need and watch over your humble preacher teacher man." Spelling aside, I appreciated the sentiment for Wili, and his description of the priest had a nice ring to it. Wili and I could be the dynamic duo of preacher-teacher man and his sparky, barky dog.

After examining Wili, the vet told me she would be admitting him immediately so that they could conduct further tests to determine what was going on. She'd already diagnosed Wili as having high fever, swollen lymph nodes, excessive licking of veterinary staff, tail too large and waggy, and indiscriminate sniffing of medical waste. Although it was difficult to leave, I knew that Wili was in good hands. For the first time in my life, I was grateful for late hours in New Orleans, and for a reason that had nothing to do with food, drink, music, or dog-like behavior exhibited by a human.

The nights of unknowing can be the hardest. It's during those darkest hours when we hope against hope and pray against probabilities that we fret, fidget, and fumble. We assume the worst and worry without warrant. We toss and turn and weep and wail. At least for that night, I did all of those things, and more. I prayed and I pleaded. But I didn't sleep. I felt like howling but not at anything in particular. I wanted to chase something that I could catch, but I couldn't identify what I was even chasing. I wanted to dig something up that would make everything better and right and good again. All I really wanted was Wili back—back to his eating, dancing, prancing, tail-wagging self.

The next morning, I kept watch over my phone—never setting it down, even for a second. I stared at it in the hopes that such intensive attention might cause it to ring sooner with tidings of good news. Sinbad did his best to provide comfort, offering his sweet and gentle presence as I alternated between stroking my chin and scratching his. When the clinic finally called, I clutched the phone as if I could squeeze out of it the news I desperately needed to hear—that my boy was okay, that he'd be fine, that he'd be coming home with me, and that he'd be better than ever. As a priest, I know all about dire diagnoses. My people have allowed me to provide a pastoral presence amid all possibilities and every conceivable prognosis. When the veterinarian began by affirming what a good dad I was and how obvious it had been to the staff how much I loved and cared for Wili, I wondered if this was how Wili felt when I'd tell him that he's a very good boy. As the good veterinarian continued, his impassioned praise of my parenting skills turned to an unimpassioned discourse on Wili's condition. I don't remember everything he said, but the three things that I definitely heard were *cancer, serious,* and *three months.* I held the phone as far away from my head and heart as I could. I felt a crushing weight of disbelief, depression, and denial. There are rare moments in this life when one's pain is so deep, it's inexpressible. In that moment I couldn't breathe, speak, or even cry. It was only after I hung up that I heaved and wailed and crumpled into a pile. I loved Wili with every part of myself, and now every part of me was in agony. I knew only one thing—I'd do *anything* to save Wili.

Wili's official diagnosis was that he had a malignant anal sac tumor. That was bad enough, not to mention embarrassing. But even worse (or as Wili would say, *Butt* even worse*),* it wasn't a laughing matter that the cancer had spread to his lymph nodes. After exhaustive consultation with the great veterinarians who wanted to give Wili his best shot at a good life, we decided he would have surgery to remove not only the tumor, but also the affected lymph nodes. The surgeon admitted it would be a complicated surgery, but he also assured us that he was a competent surgeon. And his wife, the co-owner of the clinic, was also an oncologist. We agreed that the best course of treatment for Wili would be the surgery followed by chemotherapy. After speaking to a good friend who is a natural vet, we also decided to put him on a healthier diet—ground turkey and vegetables—and to start him on some Chinese herbs. Wili immediately protested, asking to exchange the Chinese herbs for Chinese food. He also received acupuncture, which helped him tremendously, although he tried to trade it in for a massage. *Nice try, buster.*

Even with the course of treatment we'd all agreed on, the vet wouldn't guarantee that Wili would live much beyond three months. But, she told us, he might, and our plan was the best option for extending his life. I could've purchased a Porsche for what I'd eventually spend on my pup. But it was worth every penny. How do you place a value on your most faithful friend? What is the price of another day with the most loving creature you've ever known? I'd pay top dollar for my top dog—whatever that amount might be. And Wili and I counted each day as pure gift—giving thanks for every precious moment that we had together. When you are keenly aware that you're living on borrowed time (gifted time, actually), it changes everything. The quality of your life increases exponentially, if not eternally.

You can tell that you are in a good place and that your perspective has shifted from gloom and doom toward health and wholeness when your sense of humor returns. Our anxiety over Wili's condition never completely dissipated, but Wili and

I got to the point where we could find humor in the situation. Perhaps that was our ultimate salvation. Laughter is always the best medicine for whatever ails us and our dogs. Thanks to his anal sac tumor, not to mention his human's *caninical* approach to comedy, we came up with some doozies: *What do you call a dog proctologist? A pooper scooper. What's another term for prognosis of the posterior? An oracle of the orifice. What did Wili say to the surgeon? Let's get to the bottom of this, doc.* Wili also came up with an entire series of slogans worthy of bumper stickers, or what Wili called "back-end band-aids": *Cancer is a pain in my ass! What's the rumpus about my rump? Don't wreck my rectum! I bark for buns! Do you know jack about my sac?* We thought about taping a sign to his backside just before they wheeled him into surgery that would read, *Exit Only.* Wili even tried to insist that whenever I wrote about this experience, that I title the chapter *The Tale of My Tail* or *There Butt for the Grace of God Go I.* Perhaps none of these have quite the theological poignancy of *There is No Victory without Strife.* But Wili and I agreed—there's no sanity without humor. Or sanctity, either, for that matter.

On November 28th, we celebrated the Feast Day of the Saints of Hawaii, King Kamehameha IV and Queen Emma. In our house, this day is observed with great fanfare. The dogs all get to wear leis, eat spam, and call each other Duke Kahanamoku. Other than Francis, these compassionate rulers of Hawaii are my favorite saints. They knew great sorrow, having lost their only son, Prince Albert, when he was just four years old. Albert was Queen Victoria's godson. The King died only a year later, and while some suggest that he died from asthma, it's more likely that he passed away from a broken heart. Emma eventually emerged from these dual tragedies of losing both her little boy and her precious husband, more determined to make a difference. One never gets over such loss, but one can turn sadness into devotion and the pain of heartache into the passion of heartfelt deeds, and Emma devoted the rest of her life to doing just that. She built a hospital, created a school for girls who'd previously been denied an education, and celebrated the beauty of art and nature as pathways to a deeper relationship with the Creator. She's still known throughout Hawaii as "our beloved queen." The next day, on November 29th, Wili had surgery. The tumor was removed as were three lymph nodes, one of which the doctor described as being "the size of a lemon." Wili later corrected him, suggesting that it was the size of a meatball. For the rest of his days on earth, Wili would devote himself to doing good and lifting the spirits of all he met. He created a foundation to help his animal friends, and he's still known throughout the southwest, and even the world as "our beloved dog."

I wouldn't wish cancer, or any disease or disaster, on anyone. And I don't believe that God causes anyone to suffer to make a point, teach a lesson, or as a punishment for misdeeds. Whenever disaster strikes any place of which we're not too fond filled with people who may represent a viewpoint different from our own, the dumbest, most dishonest and ungodly thing we can think or say is, "these folks had it coming." Don't presume that God happens to hate the same people you hate. If your God shares your intolerance, you have created such a god in the image of your own prejudices and ignorance. Traditionally, such a viewpoint is called *idolatry*. It's not to be celebrated, nor praised. However, I do believe as scripture tells us that in all things, God is working for good with those who love God, and are called according to God's purpose. Some might argue that there's just a dog hair's difference between believing that God causes bad things to happen and believing that God works within each of us to bring blessing amidst what feels like a curse. But if you're a dog and it's your hair, that might be all the difference you need.

The most powerful verse in the Bible is not necessarily the longest one that speaks of the most dazzling power. It's likely the shortest one and most succinct in all of scripture: "Jesus wept." When Jesus' good friend Lazarus got sick and died unexpectedly, Jesus' response wasn't that Lazarus had screwed up and therefore God zapped the life out of him. Jesus didn't yell and scream and demand to know how God could cause such a thing to happen. Jesus didn't blame his sisters, Martha or Mary, or blame Lazarus, or even blame himself. Instead, he felt the same kind of anguish that we feel when someone we love is diagnosed with a terminal illness or succumbs to disease. Jesus wept. In this story, the power of Jesus' love for his friend changes everything, and not only redeems, but resurrects. The miracle was motivated not by a need to show off or to prove a point, but by love. There is power in that kind of love—even now. I don't believe that God gave Wili cancer. But I do believe that Jesus wept with me that night in New Orleans. I also believe that God led us to the most caring and competent people who helped heal him. And I'm certain that God was onboard and accompanied us every mile on the Howlelujah Tour. God led us to the people who needed to hear Wili's story, and God led people to us whose stories we needed to hear. God was with both of us, working for good along our way, empowering us to tell all who would hear that life is a gift, love is the way, and that miracles can still happen when we share the unconditional compassion of Christ.

Once upon a time, Jesus and his disciples came upon a man who'd been blind from birth. The disciples asked a question that suggested his blindness was a result of someone pissing off God, because otherwise how could such a thing have happened? They wondered aloud, "Who sinned? Was it this man or his parents?" In other words, surely someone is to blame when bad things happen to good people. Jesus tells them that the answer is neither—sinning didn't cause this man's blindness. But Jesus did remind them that when bad things happen, God is there to create something good and that we can be a part of the miracle of healing—if we are willing. As another rabbi once reminded me, "pain is the price we pay for being alive." The good news is not that we never get sick, we never suffer pain, or we never experience loss. The good news is that there's always more to the story, and even in life's most horrible situations, a kind of holiness can emerge—a loving presence that will never forsake, abandon, blame, or condemn. There's always a way out, a way forward, a way onward and upward—and that's the way the true God leads anyone who's willing to follow.

I'd lived in Louisiana long enough to have heard many tragic stories about Hurricane Katrina. It was a devastating and destructive hurricane. Everyone had a story related to the storm—even from those who got out before the levees failed. Our gracious host in New Orleans the night of Wili's diagnosis, Matt Lemmler, had one of the most compelling stories. And it reveals how sometimes the most terrible thing can eventually be transformed into something beautiful. I wish Katrina had never happened, but if it hadn't, I would've likely never met Matt nor come to call him my friend—and for that part of the story I'm truly grateful.

New Orleans was literally in his blood. His ancestors were some of the very first to call the Crescent City home. In the mid-eighteenth century, the Spanish sent about 2,000 folks from the Canary Islands to New Orleans to keep an eye on the British—which wasn't unlike a hound keeping an eye on a terrier. Interestingly, the Canary Islands were so named from the Latin *Canariae Insulae* which means "Island of Dogs." Apparently, dogs were held in very high esteem on the island, even mummified and worshiped. Perhaps there was some connection to the Egyptian god with the black dog head who greatly resembled Wili—Anubis. Apparently, Anubis had one job that dogs do well—the weighing of the human heart. There are depictions of Anubis determining whether the hearts of the deceased were heavy, in which case they would be devoured, or light, in which case they'd ascend into heaven. Dogs continue to be the best judges of human hearts, so maybe the *Canarios* understood that. Or maybe the islanders simply knew a holy animal when they saw one. In any event, there were lots of dogs on the island, so anyone from the Canary Islands already had a head start on understanding what really mattered. Matt's ancestors were members of that original 2,000, and would settle in what would eventually be called the Lower Ninth Ward. Thanks to Andrew Jackson, the British eventually got kicked off the island *and* out of the swamp.

Over the decades, the neighborhood where the family raised generation after generation drastically changed. On May 17, 1954, the Supreme Court ruled in *Brown vs. Board of Education* that segregation of schools was unconstitutional. Then, almost six years later, on November 14, 1960, New Orleans was ground zero for desegregation, and the first two public schools to be integrated were both located in the Lower Ninth Ward. This ugly chapter in New Orleans' (and human) history saw lots of white folks behaving appallingly—below that of even animals. I dare say Wili would've never engaged in such hateful behavior. Then again, he was more evolved than most humans.

Six-year-old Ruby Bridges was the very first African American student to enroll in first grade at William Frantz Elementary School in the Lower Ninth Ward. When little Ruby arrived at the school, accompanied by U.S. Marshalls, she saw a big crowd of white folks shouting and throwing things. Being raised in New Orleans, she assumed it was a Mardi Gras parade. It wasn't. The anger of the assembled was palpable and vile. Every white student boycotted that day and walked out of school. However, the next day, one white parent, a Methodist minister named Lloyd Forman walked his daughter, Pam, through the angry mob and into the school. A few other conscientious parents followed his example. It's important to mention this moment in American and New Orleans history. There will be other moments in our history when white people will be given the opportunity to do the right and conscionable thing. They should understand that it won't be easy or comfortable. But God, and Wili, will be with them and with you. Keep your heart light, and do what is right for every living thing on earth—critter and human—and you will eventually be welcomed into heaven.

After integration, when 80% of the whites in the Lower Ninth Ward fled, Matt's family stayed. By the time he was born, the demographic shift was in full effect. Matt remembers growing up in a house filled with music, in a neighborhood that was quiet and peaceful. His house was just a few blocks from where Fats Domino lived. He said the neighborhood kids always knew when Fats was home because his long pink Cadillac would be parked in the driveway. Matt was too shy to go by and visit with Fats, and locals knew not to bother the celebrities who lived in town. Still, he says, he wishes that he'd summoned up his courage and knocked on Fats Domino's door. He guesses that he would've been welcomed with open arms. Most people will welcome us if we seek to connect with them—if we come with no personal or prejudiced agenda, just a heart full of love, an attitude of grace, and a spirit of humility. And if not, well, in the words of Fats: "Ain't that a shame?"

The turning point in Matt's career came one night at Snug Harbor, the legendary New Orleans jazz club. As a teenager and music student in college, Matt had studied with the larger-than-life patriarch of one of the best-known musical families in the world—Ellis Marsalis. On this particular night, a host of all-star pianists had been enlisted to perform with Ellis as part of a dueling piano concert. There were two pianos onstage, and the performers were nervous because Ellis didn't believe in rehearsing, or in revealing what songs they might be playing together. As Matt approached him, his heart sunk a little when it became clear that Ellis didn't remember him. When they finally sat down opposite each other on stage and Ellis launched into the 1920s Fats Waller standard: "Squeeze Me," Matt didn't miss a beat. He matched Ellis note-for-note—feeling all his improvisational capabilities squeezed right out of him and onto the keys. At one point, Matt looked across the stage and saw Ellis smiling right at him. Their planned 45-minute performance went for longer than an hour, and when it ended, Matt realized he was no longer Ellis' student, but was now a colleague.

Matt would take that collegiality to the next level when he was hired as a full-time piano professor at the University of New Orleans, replacing—guess who—the legendary Ellis Marsalis. Matt had just started teaching music at the University of New Orleans when the local weather forecast started reporting that a tropical storm was forming in the Gulf of Mexico. Five days later, Hurricane Katrina would make landfall as a category five hurricane. But New Orleanians had been through more than a few hurricanes and they knew how to hunker down and wait them out. Still, Matt tried to book airfare for his wife and infant son, but by the time they decided to bug out, the airline tickets had sold out. But that turned out to be a blessing. Had they gone to the airport, they would've ended up stranded and eventually bussed to the Superdome. So, they drove to The Woodlands, just north of Houston to stay with friends. What would normally have been a five-hour drive became a twelve-hour journey. They eventually arrived safe and sound.

In the wake of Hurricane Katrina, New Orleanians were displaced and scattered from the east coast to the west coast and everywhere in between. Thousands wound up in Houston and faced with the daunting task of rebuilding their lives decided to stay—Matt was one of them. Matt was eventually hired as the music director for a popular restaurant and club that was considered THE place to go if you wanted to hear live jazz. This unexpected opportunity allowed him to hire a lot of displaced New Orleans musicians who had no place to play, and in many cases, no place to stay. Such amazing musicians as Don Vappie, Leah Chase-Kamata, and George French all played in Houston. Matt never imagined when he evacuated New Orleans that he'd be giving up his plum position at UNO, his home, and his marriage, but, for better or worse, all of those happened when he sought a new life in a new city. But, one Sunday morning, things went from bad to worse. He received a call from the restaurant owner releasing him from his position as music director. He felt his entire world collapse. But God is faithful if we seek to do what's right, even when we cannot see the way forward. Within twenty minutes of his termination, the priest at the historic Trinity Church called him to take over the 12:30 jazz service that I'd founded a few years prior. It was because of that jazz service that Matt and I eventually met and became fast friends. In the years since, our collaborative efforts have resulted in hundreds of services and concerts that we would've never imagined before Katrina. It was a terrible hurricane and a tragedy of epic proportions, but sometimes, from such scenarios grace happens. Twists and turns of fate (or faith) lead us to connect and create in ways that we never could've conceived.

After spending three years in H-Town, Matt had a vivid dream: Louis Armstrong appeared. He was wearing a tuxedo and was performing in a showroom. Matt was there. But after the show, Louis invited Matt backstage to his dressing room. He led him to his trumpet case. He opened it to reveal a whole set of skeleton keys. Matt could smell the sweat on Louis that only happens after a performer has given everything he's got—the body, the heart, the soul, the tears, and the energy. Louis picked up the keys, handed them to Matt and said, "These are for you, daddy." Not long after that dream, Matt found his way back to New Orleans where, for the first time in his life, he started singing. The first album he recorded with some of the best musicians from New Orleans was prophetic and profound. He titled the album *Ubuntu*, a Zulu expression from South Africa that means "we are all connected." Literally translated it means "I am because we are." When asked if anything good came out of Hurricane Katrina, Matt would say, "I found my voice. My voice came out of it."

Good things can come out of bad situations. That's the way

life is if we're willing to embrace all of it—the tragic, the terrible, and the unfortunate. Whatever situation we find ourselves in, if we are willing to reach out and connect with God and our fellow human beings, our story becomes enriched and empowered. We may find our voice, our bark, or even our purpose. Katrina sucked. So does cancer. But sometimes, we find our way back home after a storm in a way that reveals new life. If it weren't for the bad news, the good news would've remained no news at all.

Wili got a bad diagnosis that night, but Wili's a good dog. And Matt is a good friend. And God is a good God. And good things eventually emerge out of bad news—things we had not planned and couldn't see. Here is the good news: the worst news is not the *last* news. God can turn our wailing into dancing, our mourning into rejoicing, even our howling into *Howlelujahs*!

MIXED BREEDS, KIND DEEDS

Not all of us can do great things.
But we can do small things with great love.

Mother Theresa

We are all mixed breeds and mixed bags. Within each of us is the capacity to do right and good, and the audacity to do wrong and bad. But the more we practice kindness, the kinder we become. And the kinder we become, the kinder the world becomes. Kindness happens and the world is changed—one small deed at a time.

Before Wili and I had even pulled out of the driveway of our home, we had been blessed by the kindness of others. Our friend, Cindi, and her husband, Perry, just had to put down their daughter's small, sweet poodle, McGee. In honor of McGee, and to keep us nourished all the way to Las Vegas, Cindi put together a care package for us with some treats of both the human and the canine variety. Even more thoughtful, in case she'd selected items that weren't on Wili's Top Ten Treat list, she enclosed a twenty dollar bill to help in purchasing additional provisions. I talked it over with Wili, and he agreed that we'd spend the twenty dollars on a Butterfinger, some Peanut M & M's, a Mr. Good Bar, a large bag of Cool Ranch Doritos, and a 40-ounce bottle of Miller High Life. I was continually amazed at how Wili's "tastes" so closely resembled my own. Perhaps Wili's "kindness" was the result of my consuming "his" treats somewhere around Gallup, New Mexico. After so many miles, I was having a hard time telling the difference between a ginger snap and a liver snap. Wili made up for it by stealing bites of my Whataburger when I wasn't looking.

While deciding on what to pack for our road trip, we were also able to pay the kindness forward to someone else in need. Our friend, Charlotte, had recently lost her adorable Dachshund, Delta Dawn, who would've turned two on the Fourth of July. On June 4th, Charlotte snapped some photos of Delta wearing her favorite patriotic attire. She planned to send these "Delta Doodle Dandy" shots to all their grandkids, nieces, and nephews. But on June 5th, tragedy struck. Delta Dawn somehow managed to get out of a locked doggy door, ran into the street, and was struck and killed by a car. Charlotte asked if Wili and I would mind carrying Delta Dawn's photo with us on the tour as a way to remember her, to celebrate her life, and honor her memory. It would also give Delta a chance to "see" the Southwest. A photo of a dachshund doesn't take up much space in a car, but knowing that her precious pup will be riding shotgun with Wili on his Howlelujah Tour would maybe begin healing the Delta-shaped hole in

Charlotte's heart. Delta Dawn was a wonderful third wheel.

On the tour, Wili and I were the recipients of so many small (and large) acts of loving kindness that sometimes we felt our hearts would burst with gratitude. The simple awareness that people cared enough to come from far and wide, sometimes driving hours to lend their support to our mutual cause, would've been enough to fill our hearts to capacity, but their offerings of toys and treats, food and beverages, cards and mementos, meant that our gift bags were also overflowing, too. Beyond the doggie bags, there were also generous financial contributions given to support Wili and his animal friends who were sick, hungry, troubled, or homeless. Often the gifts reflected choices that testified that his new friends had gone to a lot of trouble on his behalf. Love does that. It goes to a lot of trouble. It travels great distances. It thoughtfully selects just the right gift, at just the right time, in just the right place.

Sometimes the gifts were completely spontaneous. Just outside of Austin, Wili and I caught up with Sarah and Chris, a couple I'd married years before. As their officiating priest, I'd been invited to their wedding reception, and it was a memorable one. It was held in a character-laden, old, country and western honky-tonk that featured toe-tapping music and delectable Cajun cuisine. Sarah and Chris knew how to throw an awesome party. My fondest memory of the evening was smoking cigars with an entire table of bridesmaids. What can I say—sometimes there are perks to the priesthood. In 2016, Sarah and Chris purchased an old church that had been built in 1910 and lovingly restored the sacred space to reflect its original simplicity. They called it Pearl Snap Hall (named for the kind of Western shirt I often wore on the trail) and turned it into a popular wedding and event venue. While even a celebrity like Wili sometimes had to rent his tour stop venues, we were surprised to learn that Sarah and Chris offered us way more than a clerical or canine discount—they comped our use of Pearl Snap Hall for our event and even promoted it on their own time with their own dime. And when you add a dog with charm to a space with character owned by people with compassion, the whole world will come. The Austin Dog Rescue showed up with many fine critters like Nala, TommyBoy, Jayla, and Pringles (the last of whom gave me the munchies). My good and giving friends, Everett and Sheree, offered craft beverages and freshly baked delights. I'd lived in Austin for more than eight years, so this stop on the tour gave me a chance to reconnect with many old friends, some of whom I'd not seen in ages. Lots of folks showed up, as they did at every stop along the tour. Many who came had never heard of me, but they wanted to meet Wili. One of those people was a young man best described as an Austin alterna-dude. Donnie lived just down the street, and he was hipper than I could ever hope to be. He had tattoos about subjects that would require a PhD in Mythology to understand, and he was adorned with all manner of metal-studded bracelets that would've made a poodle look as tough as a pit bull.

During my presentation, I told the story of how I met Wili and happened to mention my world-class Pez collection that had made its way with me from Texas to Hawaii to Louisiana.

I take some pride in my Pez Collection, which probably reveals just how sad my life might be. When my presentation ended, the Tattooed Young Turk high-tailed it out of there faster than a cat who had stumbled into a confessional booth. I thought perhaps my presentation hadn't been edgy enough for him. But I understood the reason for his quick departure when he returned moments later and handed me a box containing the limited edition *Lord of the Rings* Pez collection.

So moved by Wili's story and by my love of refillable, regurgitating plastic receptacles with the heads of various animal and comic book heroes attached, Donnie ran home, retrieved prized Pez from his own collection, and gave them to me. I held the gift aloft toward Valinor, the land of Tolkien's immortal beings, or it may have been toward Dog Heaven (I'm directionally-challenged, and both are worthy of oblations). I couldn't wait to get Bilbo, Frodo, Sam, Gandalf, Gollum, and the entire gang back home to display on the Pez shelf of honor in my home between my El Diablo Bubbletown Soap-on-a Rope and my "For Fun and Prophet" Answer-Me Jesus.

Wili and I headed out from Austin accompanied by most of the Pez citizenry of Middle Earth. I was somewhat alarmed that Wili had taken to grinning like Gollum and calling me "my precious" for the next ninety miles. Fortunately, Wili still had the good sense to follow the lead of one of J.R.R. Tolkien's profound truths of *Lord of the Rings* when Galadriel says, "Even the smallest person [or dog] can change the course of history." All it takes is the heart of a servant, the soul of a lover, and the deep desire to change things for the better—one good deed at a time. Wili had all those qualities, as did most of the humans who sniffed us out on the trail.

In my Tiki Bar, it's not Answer-Me Jesus, but Aloha Elvis who keeps watch over my prized possessions. Among them are three beer bottles lovingly crafted by a homebrewer in Albuquerque to commemorate Wili's arrival in New Mexico. Albuquerque is not unlike Austin in that it attracts an interesting assortment of humanity. Fortunately, the folks we met were as kind as they were interesting. Kirk, an engineer originally from South Carolina, is a standing member of the *Dukes of Ale*. He's the kind of guy who shaves his head to raise money to fight children's cancer. He's also the kind of guy who brews special beers for causes such as the Howlelujah Tour. While in Albuquerque, we discovered that Wili somewhat resembled the University of New Mexico mascot, Lobo Louie. Lobo is the Spanish word for wolf, and given Wili's fondness for wolfing down tamales, I wondered if he might be related.

If you know anything about brewing beer, you know that it's a painstaking process; one must pay attention, keep everything clean and pure, and select and blend just the right ingredients. It's a labor of love. Kirk had gone to the trouble of brewing three different kinds of beer in Wili's honor—A British Brown Ale, a Scottish Wee Heavy (which made me feel a wee heavy after consuming one or three), and a Saffron Tripel. Not only did Kirk brew the beer, but he bottled it with great care, attaching special Howlelujah Tour labels that featured Wili's mug shot wearing his Texas cowboy hat and Hawaiian lei. If beer is proof that God loves us and wants us to be happy (as Benjamin Franklin likely didn't actually say, but surely believed) then homebrewed beer with Nawiliwili Nelson featured on the label must mean that God *really* loves us and *really* wants us to be *really* happy. Kirk even inscribed one of the bottle caps: "Safe trip!" Attending to such minute details reflects some major love. Wili felt it in Albuquerque. I drank it in Albuquerque (and I felt it the next day).

Our Howlelujah helpers seemed to think of everything at every place we visited. They somehow covered all three major food groups on our behalf: Pez, beer, and tacos! During our appearance in Lubbock, a nice lady named Charlotte heard that we were on our way to Cloudcroft, New Mexico for our next event. She and her husband had a cabin there, so they knew the drive intimately. She approached the table where Wili was busy *paw*tographing his chapter titled, "My Wili" in my book *The Beer Drinker's Guide to God*, and informed us that we would be passing through Artesia, New Mexico about lunch time. She also told us about a favorite Mexican restaurant there that served the most tempting pork tacos in town. Tacobout love! When someone shares their secret taco haunts, you know you've become a treasured friend. She said that a place called La Fonda prepared tacos that are the stuff of dreams. How did she know that I dreamed about tacos? This restaurant's motto is: *When you find true love, hold onto it with both hands.* It's also apparently where the Taco-Cleanse Diet originated, where motivational words of wisdom by the wait staff include such nuggets as: *One* *word can change a person's day from bad to amazing: tacos*, and *Plot twist—maybe eating tacos isn't cheating on my diet—maybe going on a diet is cheating on my tacos.* Even the local elementary school had hopped onboard the taco train with lesson plans catered accordingly. Featured on the wall of the restaurant was a page neatly torn from the coloring book of a second-grader with a picture of a magic genie's lamp. Scrawled on the blank line next to the words: "My One Wish Is," in shiny black crayon were the words: "for it to rain tacos!" That young man is a true believer. I'm all for changing the world—one taco at a time.

But the million-pepper question for someone traveling with a taco-devouring dog is always: "Do they allow animals?" Charlotte's response took the corn out of my tortilla and removed the picante from my sauce. "No," she said, sadly. "No dogs are allowed." I resigned myself to the cold, non-spicy reality that there would be no carnitas for this canine. But why should I have doubted? Charlotte already had a plan. She told me that just across the street from La Fonda was an antique store called Sagebrush Annie's and that the lady who runs the store would watch Wili for me while I enjoyed my tacos. Who knew that Artesia would be the place where I'd find the Living Water that Jesus spoke of at Jacob's well—the kind of kindness that wells up and never runs dry? Was Artesia actually heaven? Tacos: check. Nice lady to watch my dog: check. Tell me there's free beer, and I'll move there!

Charlotte spoke the truth. When I got to Artesia, I walked Wili right into Sagebrush Annie's. Right behind the counter was a lady named Lou Ann (of course). She had the most radiant smile and looked so happy to see us. Let me rephrase that. She looked so happy to see *Wili*. I quickly told her our tale of potential taco woe, expecting her to turn us away and send us on to the next town. "Of course I'll keep him!" she said. "There are lots of things for Wili to sniff in here." Sure enough, Wili had already set off to sniff the stories of every item in the store. He wandered past the antique wagon covered in cowhide, past the giant illuminated ice cream cone, the vintage Pearl Beer sign, the old church doors, the sombreros and cowboy boots and metal cacti sculpture. He did, however, pause at the framed Jefferson Starship and Jerry Garcia gold albums (wait, what?). Wili was in dog-sniffing heaven.

After setting a world record for the number of tacos consumed by a priest in an hour without the support of tequila, I returned to the antique store to retrieve my road hound. As soon as I walked in, there he was, grinning ear to ear and sporting a brand-new red bandana. Wili looked like he'd had more fun sniffing than I had eating. Lou Ann said, "Well, with a name like Wili Nelson, he *had* to wear a bandana." True. With a name like Wili Nelson, he should also be smoking dope. But I didn't want to press our luck after hitting the jackpot. Lou Ann didn't know us from Pancho and Lefty, but she welcomed us with open arms. Perhaps Artesia *is* heaven, or at least a slice of it on earth. Artesia was a place where no one is turned away, even if they have paws and a tail. Artesia was a place where God must dwell.

Our good fortune was the result of Charlotte's willingness to share good news with us. She knew something important and realized that it was worth sharing with her fellow travelers, knowing that it would make a big difference in our lives. There's a spiritual tradition of sharing the good news. It's not that the faithful force-feed folks a steady diet of formulaic recipes or insist that they memorize old menus that never change and leave no room for personal preference or substitutions; it's simply that we know a place where folks can be fed, welcomed, nurtured, and nourished for their journey. People are tired and hungry for such authenticity. Why wouldn't we share such good news with those in need of such a place of refuge and renewal?

When I was a young man growing up in an evangelical religious tradition, I remember a teenage girl once telling me that part of our calling as Christians was to "share the gospel" with those who haven't heard. And her description of what that looks like has stayed with me all these years. She said, "It's really simple. It's just one beggar telling another beggar where to find bread." In Texas, one might say it's like one Texan telling another Texas where to find tacos. Maybe it's even like one dog telling another dog where to find a treat or where to find a safe place to sleep. Here's the good news about sharing the good news—it's really simple: we know a place that will accept you, love you, and allow you to sniff around until you feel comfortable. That's what it means to share the gospel with the world. The world needs to hear that. What's more, the world needs to *feel* that. In English, La Fonda means The Inn. In the inn of God's grace, the only status you need to stay there has already been secured for you. At such a place there's always room for you—*and* your dog. Regardless of your breed ranking, your bark pitch, or the color of your coat—even if you don't like jalapenos, you're in! But come hungry. In such a place, a feast has been prepared and a place has been set for you at the table.

One afternoon, after Wili and I had traveled a great distance across the desert from New Mexico, we arrived in Winslow, Arizona just in time for a late lunch. We were so hot, tired, hungry, and thirsty that we forgot to "take it easy" long enough to get a photo together "standing on a corner in Winslow, Arizona." But surely the Eagles will forgive us for heading straight to La Posada, a restored railroad hotel built in 1927 by the Santa Fe Railway. We'd heard that the hotel restaurant, The Turquoise Room, was excellent. Given its location, Wili and I could only hope that they might have some Piki Bread tacos—the Hopi's version of the tortilla made from blue corn. We pulled up to La Posada which *also* means "The Inn" in Spanish—another sign that Wili and I were on a true religious quest and might give birth to something far holier than we were aware of.

No one had given us the name of a nice woman in Winslow who might be willing to watch a dog, and the blazing sun meant that Wili and I would have to take our chances that the hotel might welcome a disheveled dog and his bedraggled human. We marched in the front door like we belonged there and immediately found The Turquoise Room. We approached the maître d. "Two for lunch," I told him. Hoping it might help secure us a table I added, "My pup is a Piki Bread pundit." His reply was courteous but curt. "I'm afraid the restaurant doesn't allow dogs." My hopes for Hopi cuisine were immediately dashed. "However," the man continued, looking at Wili like he was on to us, "your dog would be welcome to dine in our bar." Wili's ears perked up. The man had said the magic words. "My dog would actually *prefer* to dine in the bar," I assured my new best friend. Wili and I made our way to the bar. It wasn't our first rodeo. Nor was it our first visit to a bar.

As we took a load off, got comfortable, and celebrated our good fortune, I noticed the bartender—a young woman with dark hair and Native American features. She was working by herself and seemed to be flustered and overwhelmed. After giving her some time to catch her breath, I tried to catch her eye. She seemed to look right past me, an exchange I've experienced more than once in a bar. But I think she was looking right *beneath* me to the sprawled-out clump of panting fur—his tongue already lounging on the lounge floor. I was used to women in bars fixing their gaze on my better-looking wing dog, so I wasn't surprised. But I was thirsty. I was starting to have a margarita mirage, imagining swimming in a turquoise pool infused with spirits right there in the desert bar, when I heard a clunk on the floor. "Here ya go, buddy." She'd placed a water bowl just in front of Wili's nose. Wili stood up, perhaps more for her than for the beverage. After casting his usual coquettish glance, he began to lap up the refreshing liquid like the thirsty lad he was. "It's hot outside, so I put some ice in his bowl. I wanted to make sure he had *cold* water to drink."

I was so touched by her thoughtful gesture that I wanted to buy *her* a drink. She asked where we were from and where we were headed. She told us that New Orleans and Las Vegas were her two favorite cities and that she loved dogs—more than people, in fact. I'll drink to that. She laughed when I told her Nawiliwili Nelson's name, and started quoting the lyrics to "On the Road Again." Then she shared some of her story with us. Her life had obviously been more "melancholy Willie" and less "sentimental Eagles." She'd not had much opportunity to take it easy, although there'd been plenty of running down a road that never loosened her load, followed by an endless chorus of single parenthood, overdue bills, and unfaithful lovers. She'd lost more than she'd won and could never afford a flatbed Ford. Such a hard life can lead a person to become bitter and hardened. But her heart was open and honest, and her smile warm and welcoming. She welcomed Wili with not just a bowl of water, but a bowl of *cold* water on a hot day. She showed great kindness to a critter she'd never met, and that gesture was more satisfying than all the Piki bread in the world. I remembered immediately the words of Jesus about such actions. He said that if one offers even a cup of cold water to one of the "least of these" little ones, that person will surely be rewarded. And surely, she was that kind of person. We left her a big tip. But she left us with something far bigger—the knowledge that good people, even those who haven't had a particularly good life, will go out of their way to do good for others. Giving the smallest gift to the shortest one in the room can slake more spiritual thirst than all the margaritas in all the bars I've ever known.

As we were nearing the end of our tour and beginning to

make our way back home, Wili and I decided to practice what we were preaching. We'd told people in our many presentations how important it was to take time for those you love, to value your friendships, and prioritize your relationships. And while we'd hugged and waved at many good friends at various events along the way, we'd also blazed right past many others to get to the neon lights and greater glory of Las Vegas. Now, on the return trip home, it was time to take our time—and to take time for our friends. Our mission, in many ways, was accomplished. Now, the greater mission of honoring friendship would be our primary focus. So, in one day, we drove the entire 649.7 miles from Albuquerque to Dallas so that we could have dinner and hang out with our old friend, Kevin, and his girlfriend Tarri. Slowed by pit stops, sniff stops, and major traffic, it took us thirteen hours before finally arriving at our hotel in Dallas. I had just enough time to let Wili pee and check into the hotel before I had to head out to meet my friends.

Wili and I walked into the hotel and approached the front desk. I'd managed to book the only dog-friendly hotel room available within 100 miles. Since this stop wasn't part of our original itinerary, I'd booked it only a few hours earlier, so I was feeling very grateful to have snagged this room. I was only a few blocks from the Mexican restaurant where I'd be meeting my friends and where I'd finally enjoy that margarita I'd been craving for the last 4,000 miles. The front desk clerk looked at Wili, but not in the way that our bartender friend had looked at him back in Winslow. He looked at Wili, looked at me, and then looked at Wili again. He spoke in a rather stern-sounding voice. "That's a service dog, right?" the man asked. Silly truth-teller that I am, I replied, "No. He's a special guy for sure. But technically he's not a service dog." "I'm sorry sir," the desk clerk announced to two very tired beasts just about out of gas, "but we don't allow dogs on our property that aren't service dogs." My heart sank. I wasn't sure whether to bark, bite, or bawl. I told the desk clerk about Wili and the purpose of our tour. I shared with him that we'd driven thirteen hours that day to see an old friend. I may have even mentioned Wili's cancer and that I was a priest. I can't exactly recall, because for the first time on the tour, I thought I might roll over and play dead.

The clerk's matter-of-fact facial expression didn't suggest that he was going to waver from enforcing the rules, but he leaned over the counter and locked eyes with me. Nodding toward Wili, he very slowly raised his eyebrows in a way that suggested he might be in on something good and said, "Sir, let me ask you again about this dog, Mr. Nelson, who is providing such a good and significant *service* to our world. Emphasizing every charitable word he said, "He…IS….A…SERVICE… DOG…isn't…he?" Now, I'm a person who can sometimes be slow to recognize the scent of sympathy or the gesture of generosity, even when it's staring me in the eye, so it took me a second before I realized the kindness that was being offered. I responded, "Oooooh. Yes. Yes, he *does* provide a significant service. Yes, he is a dog of service, Sir. Yessiree, he is a *service* dog! Thank you, Sir." The clerk smiled and said, "Very good.

I thought that was what you said, but sometimes my hearing is not what it used to be." As he handed us our key, he said, "You and Wili Nelson have a good stay. And let me know if I can be of any *service* to you or to your very fine *service* dog." That may have been the best service I'd ever received anywhere.

It was a great night. And the best part had nothing to do with tacos or margaritas. The best part was the way it started—by someone providing a place for us to lay our stray heads. Even though there was no room for us in the inn, the innkeeper made room for us. Love does that. Love finds a way. Love makes a way. Love seeks to fix what's broken, to open what's closed, to soften what's hardened, to heal what's hurting. Love will even break the rules on behalf of the object of its affection. Religion can do great harm if it seeks to regulate rather than liberate. Creating, dictating, interpreting, and enforcing rules may keep your dog in the crate, but it won't create a relationship of companionship. We miss the mark whenever we put labels on people or pets, or when we use the rules to keep out those who are simply seeking shelter. Whenever we quote laws to keep people away—to exclude, separate or judge—you can be certain that God has left the building.

Jesus told those who sought to use the commandments to harm people that the commandments existed only to *help* people. When Jesus healed someone on the Sabbath day, the religious leaders of his day criticized him because, technically, one wasn't supposed to "work" on the Sabbath. But Jesus pointed out to them that they were missing the point. He reminded them: "The Sabbath was made for man, not man for the Sabbath." Jesus told us clearly that there are only two rules that really matter and that if you keep those two, you have kept them all: Love God and love your neighbor. That hotel clerk in Dallas gave us one of the greatest gifts of our entire trip. By not enforcing the law, he observed the law of love—the law that takes precedence over every other law. Love does that. It even reinterprets facts so that they might help our cause, so that they might support us along the way.

Kindness made a way for us that night in Dallas. Kindness made a way for us everywhere we went. Wili wants you to know that kindness matters more than anything else—except tacos.

ARE YOU GONNA EAT THAT?

Barbecue may not be the road to world peace, but it's a start.

Anthony Bourdain

When Wili was diagnosed with terminal cancer, in addition to high blood pressure, he was placed on some high-powered medication to get him ready not only for surgery, but to also move him along his path toward healing. I discovered that it wasn't a "spoonful of sugar" that made the medicine go down, but a chunk of rotisserie chicken to hide the wonder drugs.

Buying a rotisserie chicken in Louisiana is not as simple as buying a rotisserie chicken in most other places, but it's a hell of a lot more fun, not to mention exponentially more delicious. Elsewhere, one would typically go to the store, find the rotisserie chicken section, then simply select and purchase a rotisserie chicken. But, in New Orleans, there's no such thing as typical. One has many culinary options and they are *all* delicious. Though our bellies may resemble more keg than six-pack, our taste buds are well-developed and tightly-toned. The average taste buds of any New Orleanian could compete in most body-building competitions. Our taste buds don't just favor a particular flavor, they pull, push, press, squat, and even downward dog toward their full tasting potential. Every *caliculus gustatererius* within 300 miles is on steroids. We put the gusto back in gustatory. Just call us the triathletes of taste. We will go the extra mile to make our tongues happy. You've heard of the seven basic tastes? We have 107! And that's just for breakfast.

So, when we go the grocery store to pick up a rotisserie chicken, we are rarely faced with just one option. We frequently come face-to-face and nose-to-nose with dozens of revelatory roasting options. One can choose among the following poultry possibilities: Cajun, Creole, Cajun-Creole, Creole-Cajun, Italian, Cajun-Italian, Creole-Italian, Italian-Cajun-Creole, barbecue, lemon-pepper, oyster-stuffed, crawfish-coated, fried, southern fried, Caribbean fried, pan fried, fried-fried, bananas foster-style, and daiquiri-flavored. New Orleans is the only place I know where the primary topic of conversation during breakfast is about what you're going to have for lunch, and during lunch, where you're gonna eat dinner. This is a place where food and the partaking thereof is a religious experience. Every meal is as sacramental as the Lord's Supper, and every table is someone's altar on which loving sacrifices are made. We have museums that celebrate our cuisine and every variation thereof. Our chefs are elevated to sainthood and are quoted in sermons more reverentially than the church's greatest theologians (guilty!).

Around here, fast food is not given a passing glance or a single chance—unless it's Popeye's, which is a category unto itself.

And don't get me started on beverages. If the cocktail wasn't invented in New Orleans (it was), it was certainly perfected here. My first lesson on the significance of savoring every last drop of a libation occurred during my first bar-hopping excursion through the French Quarter before my very first New Orleans Saints game. While other fan bases set up barbecues in stadium parking lots, Saints fans scour the restaurants and bars of New Orleans seeking pre-game sustenance. Such palatable pilgrimages take our local tailgating to the level of the Michelin stars. Toward the end of my first such appetizing experience, my friends and I found ourselves in one of those brand new taverns in New Orleans that's only been around for about 200 years. It could've been the bar where the Sazerac was invented, or the Grasshopper, the French 75, the Gin Fizz, or the Hand Grenade—it matters not.

While enjoying one of the above mentioned beverages during my maiden, pre-game bar hop, my friends announced: "On to the next watering hole!" Not wanting to waste a drop I said, "I haven't finished my drink yet!" They all looked at me like I'd just ordered a Perrier, or I'd told the waiter to hold the Pontchartrain sauce on my redfish, or I'd questioned whether crawfish were edible, or I'd said I found Crystal Hot Sauce displeasing to the palate—all potentially blasphemous blemishes on my gastronomic character. But without uttering a word, they collectively pointed toward the omnipresent "Go Cup" section near the door. A mere exit from an establishment in this town certainly didn't preclude one from continuing to enjoy his or her adult beverage; one simply had to dump it into a plastic cup! While perhaps not quite as history-altering as the U.S. Constitution, I now rank this beverage consumption enlightenment right up there with, well, THE enlightenment, as well as my own conversion experience. When I eventually learned of the "drive-thru" daiquiri shops, I had a little talk with Jesus in which I demanded to know why I wasn't sent here sooner. Don't be alarmed at the concept—the plastic lid placed firmly on top of each cup, as well as the paper covering the top of the straw act as deterrents until one safely arrives at home.

After Wili and I arrived home from the emergency vet hospital and I'd laid out his truckload of medication, I headed out to pick up a rotisserie chicken at our local grocery store that's owned and run by a nice Creole-Italian family. This small IGA, by the way, though stocking a limited assortment of canned goods, contains a warehouse-sized wine selection and enough cheese to replenish every store in Switzerland. Not to mention they make a po-boy that would make any poor boy feel like a rich man. Although I knew I'd be confronted with the usual amazing assortment of rotisserie chicken, I recognized that the right choice for Wili, given his high blood pressure, was the low-salt variety. I don't know how they do it, but in Louisiana, even the low-salt cuisine is seasoned to perfection.

As I approached the rotisserie chickens, I noticed an older gentleman standing off to the side, gazing longingly, yet looking confused at the choices available. Too many chicken choices, like too many life choices, leave some people paralyzed. I also noticed there was only one low-salt option, so I stepped in, scooped it up, and headed toward the check-out counter. The man quickly held up a hand in my direction, looking intently at my singular possession. "Say, whatcha got there?" he wondered. "I have a low-salt rotisserie chicken," I responded matter-of-factly, hoping to dispatch him faster than a Jehovah's Witness at your front door on Super Bowl Sunday. "Oh," he said, his shoulders slumping. "That's what I wanted. Looks like you got the only one. Did you pick that on purpose, or just by chance?" *Dammit*, I thought to myself. *A priest can't go to the friggin' grocery store without encountering a major moral dilemma.* Paging Saint Thomas Aquinas for a major moral theology clean-up on aisle seven!

The kind part of myself, the part I sometimes have difficulty locating, wanted simply to give the nice man my chicken. But then I thought of Wili, the love of my life. Relational ethics, I recalled from my seminary days in Chicago, always supersedes the relative or objective approach. At least I *thought* that's what I remembered. I definitely remembered that telling the truth is almost always the right option. So, I told the man the truth. "Yes. I picked this one on purpose. My dog was just diagnosed with a serious cancer and he has high blood pressure. This chicken is the only thing he'll eat right now. Plus, it's the only way he'll take his medication. But look," I continued, "I live just up the street only a few blocks away. I can come here any time. I know they'll have more soon. You take this one and I can come back later. I want you to have this one." I attempted to hand him the chicken.

The old man's eyes seemed to grow misty, his lips pursing a bit. He slowly lifted his finger up into the air and shaking his head said, with the conviction of, well, Saint Thomas Aquinas, "I will NOT take that chicken! I love dogs. Dogs mean the world to me. I want your dog to have it. Say, what's his name anyway?" I told him Wili's name, and he put his hand on my shoulder and looked deeply into my eyes and said, "Well, you tell Wili I'm pulling for him. And I'm gonna say a prayer for him, too. God bless Wili."

And God bless that man. I took the chicken home and Wili loved it. He took his medicine wrapped in that chicken. Later he'd take his Chinese herbs wrapped in that chicken. And sometimes he ate the chicken all by itself. Wili lived not just the three months he'd been given, but eighteen months. Over the next year and a half, Wili and I shared a lot of chicken together. Don't tell his vet, but sometimes we had the Cajun kind. Wili way outlived the odds. There was likely more than one reason why he survived for so long. But certainly one of the primary factors was the great love that Wili was shown by so many people along the way. From that man at the grocery store to the thousands of people who showed us kindness on the Howlelujah Tour, people demonstrated unconditional and even sacrificial love. Some of those folks gave Wili the food off their own plates—food they'd planned to eat themselves. There were countless strangers who fed us and showed us extravagant good will, often manifested in good taste (or at least in what tasted good). Through their concern for Wili (and by association, for me), these people became friends and even family. I will never forget them. I can still see their faces. Just as I can see the old man's face at the grocery store and feel his supportive hand on my shoulder, sensing the tenderness in his words, the reassurance in his voice, and the support in his prayers. It was like that every day for Wili and me—for all 5,000 miles of our journey.

Wili and I covered a lot of territory on our trip, not to mention types of cuisine. From New Orleans we traveled to Houston, Tomball, College Station, Bryan, Austin, Salado, Corsicana, Dallas, Lubbock, Tulsa, Oklahoma City, Cloudcroft, Alamogordo, Albuquerque, Sedona, Flagstaff, and Las Vegas. While we sampled some delicious dishes, it was the barbecue that Wili seemed to find most satisfying. And hopefully, as we were fed and sustained, our stories of spiritual sustenance found their way into the hearts and souls of those who fed us. Although food ended up being a highlight for all of us, we set out on the Howlelujah Tour for three primary reasons—all of them seemingly unrelated to food.

First, because I loved Wili and he was my best friend, I simply wanted to spend time with him, just the two of us, on the road again. When your best friend is dying of cancer, you take time to enjoy each other's company and to treasure each moment together, counting every day as a blessing. Some of my most treasured memories were the times when it was just the two of us headed down the highway and howling to Willie Nelson tunes. Sometimes I could hear him snoring in the backseat, where he had a very comfortable bed, an assortment of toys, and a portable "no-spill" water bowl. Sometimes Wili would sit up front right next to me and look out on the road that stretched out before us. Sometimes he would put a paw on my arm or nuzzle my shoulder. On occasion, he'd try to crawl all the way into my lap and lodge himself between me and the steering wheel. I cherished those quiet moments of solitude we had on our early morning walks, sometimes even before the sun rose. It's amazing how beautiful the grounds of cheap hotels appear when you walk them with someone you love. Apparently, according to Wili, the smells were quite enchanting, as well. There were nights when we were both so tired we'd fall asleep in each other's arms. Sometimes we'd fall asleep on the floor, not even making it all the way to the bed. When you're with a good friend, the carpeted floors of La Quinta might be the most comfortable place on earth, even downright luxurious. True friendships aren't based solely on tossing the stuffed alligator around so your friend can wrestle him to the ground (although alligator wrestling was important to Wili so it was important to me), but most of the time just being in each other's presence was enough. To be with my favorite being was all I needed. And if there happened to be a "go plate" of barbecue in the fridge that we could share as a midnight snack, then all the better.

Secondly, we wanted to remind those we encountered at our twenty-three stops that the most important thing in this life is not necessarily among those things to which we devote most of our time, energy, and attention. What is most important is not our careers. Although I've been guilty of thinking that God cannot accomplish God's purposes without my help, so I work long hours to make sure my Boss' lofty goals get implemented. Interestingly, God has been getting along just fine without me all these years, and the coming of God's kingdom is not entirely dependent on my efforts. The church will survive without me. Chances are good that your place of employment won't crater should you take a few days off as well, especially if it's for something more important than your work. Our careers aren't the most important thing, and neither are our educations, our hobbies, our accomplishments, our possessions, our savings, our awards, or even our volunteer hours. Only one thing is of supreme importance in our lives and that's our relationships with our partners, spouses, parents, children, grandchildren, neighbors, friends, and yes, our pets. These relationships matter above all else. I know because God revealed it, and God's best messenger, a dog named Wili, confirmed it. Love the ones you're with. Value them. Make time for them. Prioritize them. Put your energies into the objects of your affection. Cherish and honor each of them, because they are the most precious parts of our human existence. When I shared these reminders on the Howlelujah Tour, I would motion toward the lump of fur lying next to me as living, breathing evidence of this truth. I believe people recognized how valuable our relationships are with those we love, those who love us back, and even those who don't.

Thirdly, Wili and I wanted to raise both awareness and funds on behalf of our animal friends and the special humans who support them. There's plenty of bad news in this world. There are even more than enough bad people in this world. But what we discovered on the tour is that there are also a lot of good people out there doing good work and making a positive difference in the lives of animals in need. Wili and I wanted to identify them, celebrate them, and support them. We wanted to share their stories. We held the Howlelujah Tour kickoff event at Abita Brewery in Abita Springs, Louisiana, with all proceeds going to our local animal shelter, the Northshore Humane Society. Since that very first event, our collaborative efforts with the Northshore Humane Society have continued with Wili, Lili, Sinbad, Mano, and I hosting their annual Howl-O-Ween benefit. I also dedicated their new pet cemetery and officiated the burial service of a favorite dog named Klunk. The very last organization we supported on the tour was the Las Vegas Animal Foundation, a packed event hosted by Mountain View Presbyterian Church that later founded a pastoral care team for those who grieve the loss of a pet. When Wili eventually passed on, we received the kindest note from those good people. In between these two organizations were countless others—good people doing their part in small towns and big cities to acknowledge that when the Creator created the world and everything in it and said it was good, that was our cue to do everything in our power to care for the critters that inhabit it. When we are good stewards of creation, we honor the Creator. If God says it's all good, that's good enough for me.

But perhaps even these three reasons for going on tour are still connected to the common table we share with our fellow human beings and fellow critters in God's world. In my spiritual tradition, there *is no* spiritual tradition without a table. The most powerful moment in our liturgy is when we gather at the Lord's Table to "take and eat." The Holy Communion sustains our souls, but the parish potlucks that often follow are sustaining in an equally powerful way. It's around those tables that we share our stories and become a community. Around the table, we open not only our mouths, but also our minds and our hearts. We let others in, and in so doing, we are changed. Being fed as part of a community while gathered around a common table with folks we may have not previously known became a central part of virtually every gathering on the Howlelujah Tour. When word got out that Wili's favorite food was barbecue (I'm not sure who leaked that, but I have a pretty good idea), the grillers of the world began to rise up and render unto Wili their unique and savory gifts. The process of barbecuing, particularly in my home state of Texas and the home of Nawiliwili's namesake, is truly a hallowed process—a "holy smokes" undertaking. It cannot be rushed. It cannot be store-bought. It cannot be thoughtlessly prepared. Like a deeper spirituality, you can't just "slap on some sauce" at the last minute; true transformation takes more than a glaze. This marinade goes all the way to the bone. Such a flavorsome feast begins when an animal makes the ultimate sacrifice (note to vegetarians: I'm with you philosophically, I'm just slow to get onboard practically). The pit master is truly masterful—taking his or her time to thoughtfully prepare a fire with just the right kind and amount of coal, wood, heat, or flame. Even the container in which the meat is prepared is carefully considered—the smoker or grill is their version of the Ark of the Covenant. Its contents are worthy of the very best. The right seasonings have been blended, tested, and sampled. Only when they have stood the test of time and taste bud are they applied liberally and graciously. On behalf of a dying dog, there were countless good grillers and proficient pit masters of the amateur and professional variety who stepped up to feed the multitudes. Some of them drove great distances. Some came out of retirement. Some spent days to prepare the very best that they could offer. Some of them hadn't set foot in a church in years, but they did so for Wili. The great Texas fire god, Bubba Barbecue, must have been pleased. I can tell you for certain that Wili and I were!

From College Station to Corsicana, from Dallas to Lubbock, from Albuquerque to Las Vegas—the most moving moments were watching the masters watch Master Wili taste their masterful creations. While he often woofed their offerings down, I can confirm that he savored every bite. By the time of the tour, Wili's appetite was back to its original Louisiana proportions. If given the opportunity, I do believe Nawiliwili Nelson could have consumed an entire side of Bevo the Longhorn. There were some Aggies along the way who likely wished he would've.

If Wili were to write his spiritual autobiography, it wouldn't have been titled *Eat. Pray. Love.* It likely would've been titled *Eat. Pray. Eat.* Or perhaps *Eat. Nap. Eat.* Or even *Eat. Love. Eat.* But most likely *EAT. EAT. EAT.* For Wili, the most spiritually significant question is: "Are you gonna eat that?" And Wili, being a messenger of the gospel, might also add: "Are you gonna *savor* that?" Because if you truly savor something, if you enjoy, appreciate, and give thanks for it, you are much more likely to share it. It's usually those who refuse to "taste and see that the Lord is good" who are most likely to misunderstand God's goodness and the ultimate point of the spiritual life—to share with others. Savoring and sharing are the flip sides of the same biblical brisket—you can't taste one without experiencing the other. Besides, everything tastes better when shared.

Jesus knew this truth. He taught it and he lived it. He was a religious leader who appreciated good food and drink. He was the one who grilled fish (a Galilean barbecue) for his disciples after his resurrection. During the Last Supper, Jesus took bread not to save it, but to share it. He took, broke, blessed, and gave. When he did that, the food was transformed into something life-changing. He did the same with a single cup of wine. Take a drink he said, and you will be satisfied. When food and drink are lovingly shared, they become sacramental, holy—something so powerful you will begin to hunger and thirst for things that change the world. Jesus was constantly reminding folks of the power of what we ingest. His first miracle was at a wedding reception where he turned 180 gallons of water into wine. Those are Texas-sized proportions! Another miracle occurred when, after a long day of teaching, he told his disciples to feed the hungry hillside crowd. The disciples wondered how they were going to be able to feed everyone. Jesus told them that by taking what you have available, blessing it, and sharing it—that's when the miracle happens. They found a little boy who had a few loaves of bread and some fish. Jesus blessed them and passed them around. Before anyone could even ask for mayo, Jesus fed 5,000 people. Hoo wee! That's alotta po'boys! Add some love and prayer to plain bread and meat, and it's amazing what can happen.

Wili and I did our best to validate the Creator's savory gifts as one way to access God's tasty truth. One of our most memorable, if not mouth-watering, moments was in Tomball, Texas when we made an appearance, not at a church or bookstore, but at Tejas Chocolate and Barbecue Restaurant. If there are two foods that reveal God's love more than these, I'd sure like to taste them. Located just up the road from where my brother and his family live, this sacred space occupies the oldest building in Old Town Tomball. Their motto: *Come Early. Eat Well.* That also sounds like a good church motto to me. Like good theology, their methods for making chocolate and for grilling meat are simple and sound. They use only premium cacao beans sourced from quality farms around the world. Before the beans ever get to Tomball, someone has already gone to a lot of trouble to grow, harvest, process, ferment, and dry them. Once these beautiful baby beans arrive in Texas, they are cleaned, sorted, fire-roasted, ground, aged, melted, tempered, and molded. Hmm, sounds suspiciously like the work of the Holy Spirit. For their barbecue, they start with the choicest cuts of meat and use a simple Texas "black and white" rub (that's salt and pepper to the novice). They let the fire, smoke, and meat meld together to create a dance of deliciousness. Wait, that also sounds like the Holy Spirit! Are we sure this is not a church that serves chocolate and barbecue?!

When I spoke to the proprietor, Scott Moore, and told him

Wili's story, he simply said, "I feel for you, man. I've been there." I knew anyone who could create such a special place must also love dogs. When Wili and I arrived at Tejas, almost two hours before they officially opened, there was already a line. Those who want to taste the good stuff always know to show up early because when they run out, they're out, and if you get there too late, you miss out. That hot July morning deterred no one from showing up. As the patrons waited in line, I shared dog stories and Wili rated the barbeque (he gave everything four paws). It was hard for us to believe, but the first two men in line that day got there early, not to buy barbecue, but to meet Wili. And some folks, including my cousins, drove for hours because good dogs, good food, and good people are all worth driving a great distance for.

In the Bible, the gathering of God's family, both on earth and in heaven, is frequently described as a feast. It sure felt that way that morning in Tomball, as it did every place we went on the tour. People got fed physically and spiritually. We celebrated. We blessed. We connected. We shared. Animals (and people) got cared for. I can't imagine anything better on earth or in heaven.

One of New Orleans' most celebrated chefs, Leah Chase, who found her way into my sermons on more than one occasion, recently passed on to the great banquet beyond. Leah has surely been cookin' up a storm in heaven, and has likely been working on a new food program called *Gumbo with God*. Leah was world-renowned for her gumbo recipe. She knew just the right ingredients. But she always insisted that even if your proportions were just right, if you didn't add love, the result would be bland, tasteless, and unsatisfying. Spices are no substitute for the most important ingredient of all. Leah understood and often talked about how food builds bridges and connects us to each other, even if we come from different places. Gathered around a table to share a meal, we learn from each other, and we learn how to change the world together. She said she always tried to live by her father's motto: "Pray, work, and do for others." She also said her last prayer each night was simply: "Thank you God."

At the end of each night of the Howlelujah Tour, Wili and I would give thanks for all those who are so filled with love that they lovingly feed others—those who know how to savor as well as share. Each night our stomachs were full.

But not as full as our hearts.

DOG BLESS AMERICA

Careful, man, there's a beverage here.
The Dude, *The Big Lebowski*

I love my country, but I rarely get to celebrate my nation or declare my independence on the Fourth of July. Traditionally, I stay home to boil wieners for my dogs' hotdog eating contest and cover their ears so they don't destroy my home, themselves, or each other when the fireworks start. In a patriotic attempt to lower our levels of anxiety, the dogs and I drink at least one American beer, preferably a micro-brew, hoping to stimulate the economy and sedate ourselves. On this national holiday, while it may seem un-American, the dogs and I always listen to reggae music which is scientifically proven to be the one musical genre most likely to help dogs chill. In our household, the red, white, and blue commemorating our founding fathers are briefly set aside in favor of the red, yellow, and green celebrating our Rastafarian friends. While Mano insists on *Noah's Ark* by Eek-A-Mouse, we also crank up anything by Bark Marley or Dog Marley and the Woofers. Our set list typically includes such Caribbean canine preferences as *Stars and Red Stripes Forever*; *No Fireworks, Woman, No Cry*; *Buffalo Wings Soldier*; *Don't Shoot the Fireworks*; *One Love—One Lick*; *Sit Down, Scratch Me, Before You Get Up, Stand Up*; *Bed, Bed, Dine* (by EweBeeFarty), and *Puppy I Love Your Way* (by Big Muttain). Hanging back and throwing back with my pack while trying to tune out the explosive tendencies of my neighbors is not a bad way to celebrate this big, booming, loud land we call America, *Mon*.

But there have been two flag-waving festivities on the Fourth for which I bravely ventured forth that will remain in my heart forever—one involved a Willie, and the other involved a Wili. I think the whole world would agree that two Willies always make it right. On July 4, 1996, I made my one and only pilgrimage to Willie Nelson's Fourth of July picnic. If there's anything more American than sweating your balls off while surrounded by a shining sea of boobs, beer, and dope-smoking cow-hippies listening to Willie Nelson, I can't imagine what that would be. While Willie's all-American, throw-down hoedown has moved around a bit—Tulsa, New Jersey, Kansas City, and Montana—it belongs in Texas. And in Texas, it belongs in Luckenbach. *I GOT LUCKY IN LUCKENBACH IN 1996* sounds like a great t-shirt slogan. It also sounds like a Willie Nelson song. Not only did I time it just right to catch Willie in this tiny town where time may not stand still, but it sure slows down, but I heard the one and only Waylon Jennings join him on stage to sing America's greatest anthem: "Luckenbach, Texas." If there's a more profoundly patriotic sentiment than "maybe it's time we got back to the basics of love," I haven't heard it. While those words aren't explicitly in the constitution, they are implicitly in the Bible. It was so hot that day that the water ran out by five o'clock, and all 55,000 beers were bought, drank, and peed out before the sun set. But that didn't stop Waylon and Willie from singing, and it didn't stop me from staying all the way to the end. Who needs fireworks when your heart is on fire after hearing Waylon and Willie?

My other most memorable Fourth of July didn't involve an infamous Texas troubadour, but a famous Texas trooper dog. It also took place in a small Texas town, the smallest we visited on our tour, Salado, Texas—which in Latin means *Taco Salad*, and in Spanish means simply *Salty Texan*. Salado has produced more than its share of salty characters including Ma and Pa Ferguson, both of whom served as Texas governors during a short-lived spell of sanity in state politics. The Chisholm Trail Cattle Drive passed right through Salado from 1867 to 1884, often stopping at the Stagecoach Inn (back then called the Shady Inn), the oldest continuously operating hotel in the state. There was a kind of first lady of Salado much later who wasn't only worth her salt and pulled no bull, but she also seasoned the lives of most Americans in ways most Americans are unaware. Liz Carpenter was the author of such literary gems as *Unplanned Parenthood, Getting Better All the Time, Start with a Laugh,* and *Presidential Humor.* Liz not only served as speechwriter for President Lyndon Johnson and press secretary for Lady Bird, but she also worked beyond the aisle of partisanship, serving on a White House Commission for President Gerald Ford, and often eluding to the Bush family's extraordinary sense of humor—intentional or otherwise. One of her favorite stories revolved around the time George, Sr. attended a 1992 banquet given by the Prime Minister of Japan, Kiichi Miyazawa. During dinner, President Bush vomited in the Prime Minister's lap and then passed out. While I've had dates that ended in a similar fashion (about which I'm still embarrassed), Bush seemed to take it all in stride. When Miyazawa showed up at the dedication of his Presidential Library in College Station, another stop on our tour, the President acknowledged the Prime Minister by assuring him, "This time, dinner is on *me!*" Humor transcends politics. If we laughed more often with our neighbors, either those across the aisle, the street, or the planet, we'd be a lot less likely to puke on them, literally or figuratively. And God would be a whole lot more pleased.

Liz Carpenter made some profound patriotic observations on life in America. She said that she learned from her four decades in D.C. that one person really *can* make a difference. If one person can make a difference in Washington, imagine what we could accomplish in our own towns. Saint Liz from Salado proclaimed that there were three keys to a meaning-ful life—a sense of purpose, a sense of humor, and a sense of curiosity. If each American developed all three, we would be a whole lot smarter, and the world a whole lot safer. She seemed to understand that might does not make right and power does not make mighty, but compassion does make us great, and kindness can overcome even the most formidable obstacle. Liz said, "If we can't turn the world around, we can at least bolster the victims." Sounds like Jesus' beatitude: "Blessed are the bolsters of the victims, for they shall be bolstered by God." She was fearless in her approach to change, calling on her fellow Americans to "charge hell with a bucket of water." Perhaps if enough of us grabbed a bucket and charged, cooler heads might prevail more often, and possibly dampen the fiery rhetoric that seeks to stoke the flames of intolerance and misunderstanding.

Liz is best remembered for the fifty-eight words she wrote for Lyndon Johnson just after President John F. Kennedy was pronounced dead in Dallas—words he read, almost verbatim, to the nation and to the world. For a brief moment in time, a President's words sounded more like a gospel hymn than a stump speech and sought to bring us together rather than drive us apart. Johnson began the speech: "This is a sad day for all people," and ended with "I will do my best. This is all that I can do. I ask for your help and God's." Liz later admitted, "I can't really say that I wrote it. God was my ghostwriter."

I met her once at a formal dinner hosted by Lady Bird Johnson in the Presidential Dining Room of the LBJ Library in Austin. Despite my nervousness, I made it all the way through dinner without vomiting on anyone. I was too young and dumb to know to take notes in the presence of greatness, so I cannot recall her words with any sort of precision. But I do recall her kindness. She complimented my prayer, my hair, and my date—perhaps not in that order. And I recall, above all, her laugh. It filled the room. I have often thought that the louder the laugh, the more loving the person. In her case, I believe it to be true. We'd all be better off if the leaders of our nation recovered a sense of purpose, humor, and curiosity—not necessarily in that order. A true leader is as kind as she is funny. The more we cultivate those qualities in our political landscape, the more we improve the quality of our collective character. Perhaps even to the point of understanding that we need each other's help—and God's.

Liz was long gone from Salado by the time Wili and I showed up on July 4, 2017. Salado was our only stop that took us not to a church, bookstore, or restaurant, but to a brewery. As it happened, the Barrow Brewery felt as sacred to us as any of the churches. In some cases, the brewery was doing better work bringing people together and to God than many churches did. The story of how the Barrow Brewing Company came to be, and how Wili and I came to be invited there on the Fourth of July, is an American tale of fortitude, faith, following dreams, finding courage, and fostering community.

Graydon Hill had been home brewing only for a few months when he told his wife, K.D., that he was quitting his job as a commercial airline pilot to open up a brewery. I'm surprised she didn't tell him to take off (or feel free to move about a cabin—in the middle of the woods). For a year she tried to dissuade him. That same year, she also began to ramp up her prayer life, which is always a dangerous undertaking in which God changes our minds more often than we change God's. She admitted that this new idea seemed to spark new life within Graydon. New life is a core religious truth, and K.D. had grown up conservative Southern Baptist. Although Baptists might drink beer, thou shalt not admit it, much less brew it. At least that's what she remembered from the sermons of her childhood that seemed to suggest that consuming alcoholic beverages was a sinful stumbling block. If that's true, then the preacher must have conveniently forgotten that Jesus had turned the water into wine at the wedding reception in Cana of Galilee. Leave it to Jesus to take all our stumbling blocks and turn them into stepping stones. He took the walls of our resistance and dismantled them—one brix at a time.

After K.D.'s spiritual enlightenment, she switched to a different denomination—one a little more tolerant, not to mention thirsty. She would be the first to admit that just because something is different doesn't make it right or the other wrong. Her revelation is true not only of theological positions and denominational affiliations, but also of political viewpoints. For better or for worse, on her transitional spiritual journey, K.D. was somehow introduced to a "heretical" work that attempted to make a connection between God and beer that was written by a clergyperson of questionable moral character (me), who occasionally turned stumbling blocks into building blocks (me), and who was also quite fond of the brewing process (me). After reading *The Beer Drinker's Guide to God*, K.D. came to realize that not only was brewing allowed by God, it could be an actual calling *from* God. Sometimes the first call is not the last, and the last call is never the final call in the kingdom of God.

Late that afternoon, after our event at the brewery, Wili and

I sat on the banks of the creek and pondered Graydon and K.D.'s divinely inspired quest to find a suitable location for the brewery. Their discovery of the property upon which Barrow would eventually be situated proved to be another miracle in which Jesus had a hand. The space was less than a mile from their home and backed up to a beautiful creek that surely had served centuries of thirsty travelers as a watering hole for the weary. But the situation was complicated by a local law that didn't allow the sale of more potent beverages without also serving food. As a restaurant didn't seem to be a part of God's plan for them, they realized they'd have to change the law—something people of good conscience have had to do on both the national and local level throughout our nation's history. Just because it's in the law books doesn't mean it's corroborated by the Good Book. Just because it's in the Constitution doesn't mean it was divinely inspired. Believe it or not, it was the church ladies of St. Joseph's Episcopal Church in Salado, Texas who made the miracle happen. Contrary to certain custom, feminist spirituality has nothing to do with baking casseroles (although there's nothing wrong with that, especially if said casserole is placed on your priest's front porch). These women of faith backed up their talk with the walk and went door to door asking their neighbors to sign a petition to get the brewery initiative on the ballot. In only three days, the same amount of time it took Jesus to descend into hell and whip-up on the forces of evil, these ladies whipped a tiny Texas town into shape in the name of good. They got five hundred signatures on the ballot, including many Baptists.

Unfortunately, dogs aren't allowed to vote. If they were, we might elect more highly evolved candidates. But, the humans got it right on Election Day as the Yeast votes prevailed 784 to 229. It was a landslide of biblical proportions in a town that could *barley* contain its excitement. At the Grand Opening of Barrow Brewing Company, the local priest, a homebrewer named Father Bliss, blessed the brewery. True story. I couldn't make that up even had I'd finished off all the beer from Salado to Luckenbach.

When Graydon and K.D. heard about the Howlelujah Tour, they decided to open their brewery to the itinerant preacher and his inspiring pup on a day that they'd previously planned to be closed. Wili and I quickly recognized that we may not get any closer to heaven on earth than a dog-friendly brewery. As soon as we set foot and paw inside, it was immediately apparent that we had entered a holy place that was brewing a whole lot more than beer. *Communion* was happening. Whether it was represented by bread and wine, beer and pretzels, or treats and tacos wasn't so much the point. People were coming together, and not only getting to know their neighbors, but even beginning to *love* their neighbors as themselves. One customer revealed that she'd lived in Salado for more than twenty years, but she hadn't met her neighbors until she started frequenting the brewery. The Barrow Brewery was brewing more than beer; they were also brewing a community—a gathering place beyond home and work. This family-friendly, dog-friendly, faith-friendly hangout has hosted more birthday parties for seven-year-olds than for 21-year-olds.

K.D. told me that there were really no words to describe what was happening. When the spirit is present, one can't quite capture what is ineffable. But K.D. offered words like *holy* and *hard* and *grueling* and *good*. She said, "It's all been worth it because of the cosmic connections that continue to be made. This is the place where people find just the right person at the just the right time—a teacher, plumber, sage, or priest. In this space, songs are written, burdens are shared, and life's deepest mysteries are explored."

On the Fourth of July, in a small-town brewery in Texas, I saw how a vision of a great nation might further unfold—a nation that's kinder and gentler, that speaks softly and listens intently, and that labels beer, but doesn't label those who may disagree with us. In a country where the digging in of heels is becoming more common than the sharing of dreams, in which polarizing extremes are the norm rather than finding common ground, this "less travelled way" versus "my way or the highway," seemed like the *right way* at the right time. Our hosts observed over and over again, over a pint, how people's hearts would seem to soften, and they'd start listening to each other. Perhaps the most patriotic prescription we can offer for the American people is one that hardens resolve more than hearts and closes mouths and opens ears. On that most American day in the most American way, Wili and I looked out upon a gathering that reflected some of the diversity that makes us so rich. There were bikers, construction workers, retirees, hipsters, clergy, and church ladies. There were liberals, conservatives, and everything beyond and in-between. There were families, teenagers, young adults, parents, grandparents, and dogs of many breeds.

They were all talking to each other. They were all listening to each other. They were all appreciating each other. They were all learning from each other. Cheers to them and cheers to us.

While I'm not as gifted as my Boss was and, thus, unable to turn water into beer, I was able to pair a few stories with some of the flagship brews we'd shared that day. I wasn't sure whether to title my talk: "Toward a Better Theology of Beer" or "Toward a Theology of Better Beer." So, in an attempt to set an example for our country, I compromised and called it: "Toward a Better Theology of Better Beer." As we sipped the Ski Boat Blonde Ale, I didn't discuss any blondes I might have dated (as it was a family affair), but I did recall being a much younger man and floating down cool, Texas rivers on hot, summer days. There was an understanding on the river—when someone else's tube bumped into yours, you didn't pull their plug and attempt to sink them, you latched on, connected, and floated with them for a while, sharing stories, if not beers. Whether we're floating, talking, or walking our dogs, we need less pushing off in our country and more holding on. For the Evil Catfish IPA, I decided not to dwell on the obvious—the evil of cats and the fish that try to look and act like them. Instead, I shared how my fortune changed when I bet big on my ace of hearts—Nawiliwili Nelson. For the Tipsy Vicar Stout, I simply asked the question worn on the wrists of a million followers: *WWJD?* That is, *What Would Jesus Drink?* Tipsy Vicar Stout, of course! We ended with a powerful taste of what happens when enough folks say (and vote) yes: 784 Belgian Witte. Our taste buds were satisfied, satiated, and refreshed all at the same time. This is what happens whenever we come together and agree to work together in the name of a brewery, a dog, and any good cause. There's no need to drive wedges between us and those who don't see things in quite the same way—even if those wedges are orange, lemon, and lime.

On the tour, Wili and I met Americans that represented every position on the political spectrum. Yet, they all came together to rally around a good dog and to do good for other dogs. Dog and God came together to bring people together—a purpose as noble as any we might declare. Setting aside differences of opinion for more than a dog-gone minute and agreeing upon the value of making a difference, might be the balm in Gilead that's the salve and salvation of our nation. When we come together, miracles happen, doors open, hearts open, minds open, arms open, shelters open, and breweries open. Church ladies demand the right to drink and Baptists recognize each other at the brewery.

But sometimes our political leaders are the last to get onboard the positive change train. Wili and I began to have a running joke on the tour. Since Wili was stirring townsfolk to positive action wherever he went, many of our sponsoring organizations assumed that their civic leaders would be quick to offer him the key to the city. Perhaps these politicians were afraid that Wili might swallow the key or that their voting blocs might go immediately to the dogs. Whatever their reasons, it seemed that everywhere we went every mayor said NO to the *paw*some opportunity of giving Nawiliwili Nelson the key to their city: Austin, Houston, Dallas, Lubbock, Tulsa,

Oklahoma City, Albuquerque, Flagstaff, even Las Vegas—where rat packs seemed to take precedence over dog packs.

So Wili and I decided that, perhaps, on our next tour from New Orleans to Las Vegas, we'd stop at all off-the-beaten path destinations where elected officials wouldn't take Wili for granted and roll out the ruff carpet or name the local high school football championship the dog bowl to honor Wili as the visiting *dog*nitary he truly was. Next time, we'd start the tour in the small towns of Louisiana—Waggaman, Slongaloo, Gross Tête, Belcher, Mowata, and Coochie. In Texas, we'd no doubt be rousingly welcomed to such slumbering cities as Loco, Cut and Shoot, Ding Dong, Notrees, Jot 'Em Down, Cool, and even Barrel City. In Nevada, surely Wili would be treated like a rock star in Jackpot, Beowawe, Gabbs, Puckerbrush, Winnemucca, or Pahrump. We could end, not in Vegas, but in Lovelock—so named after a prison and a gun range. Surely a dog could get his due in such a spot.

Some folks were so disappointed when they heard Wili wasn't given a single key to the city that they acted immediately to rectify this wrong. One night in Dallas, the front desk clerk at the La Quinta asked Wili to step into the center of the hotel lobby so that she might make a formal presentation. There, in front of the Texas-shaped waffle machine, near the 20% off coupons to Six Flags, she took Wili's paw in hers and presented him the key to room 212. Wili was so thrilled that he asked her if it allowed him early access to the waffle machine. La Quinta, Spanish for *a fifth*, most likely refers to a rest stop every five days, but Wili and I chose to believe it complemented our brewery stop with something even more powerful. In our religious tradition, we have interpreted scripture to mean that where two or three are gathered, there's always a fifth. Even more important was the spirit of kindness the desk clerk showed to both of us.

As it turned out, Wili and I didn't need to detour at all to be honored with a real key to a real city; our event in Dallas had benefitted the largest no-kill animal shelter in North Texas. Operation Kindness is based in Carrollton, Texas, one town over, but still in Dallas County, and home to a whopping 140,000 humans and at least that many dogs. Carrollton has many claims to fame. This city gave the world the extraordinary musical talent and cutting-edge innovator Vanilla Ice (not to be confused with Vanilla Coke, which came from Atlanta, and was almost as short-lived a craze as the rapper). This musical "gift" is more than offset by the fact that the eighth largest employer in town is Rudy's Tortillas, home of the ultra-thin white corn tortilla, an unleavened flatbread that has brought the world almost as much joy as the communion wafer. And as the "wrapper" without equal, Rudy's tortilla has made brisket tacos the official food of the Howlelujah Tour.

While difficult to conceive, the political leadership of Carrollton is even more impressive than its tortillas or musicians. The mayor of Carrollton, Kevin Falconer, got wind of Wili's good deeds and how he'd been consistently denied symbolic keys to cities all across the country. Mayor Falconer understood the key to being a real leader, to recognize and honor those who make a *paw*sitive difference, even if they're from out of town.

Despite the fact that he may be the busiest man in America, he made room for me and Wili. Mayor Falconer has a spouse, three daughters, a grandson, and two rescue dogs. In addition to running a major city, he also works as a full time architect, and somehow manages to find time to coach and referee youth soccer, go on mission trips with his church, attend ladybug releases at local parks, and ride his bike to city functions. As a politically conservative Republican, he understands the importance of public safety, fiscal prudence, and economic development, as well as conserving the rights of all citizens, including those who may not agree with him. With Mayor Falconer's guidance, Carrollton recently created a city ordinance protecting people from discrimination based on sexual orientation or gender identity. Not only does this mayor understand what equality looks like, he's a deeply spiritual person who has also found a way to balance work and family. In other words, this guy *gets* it. Whatever my political affiliation might be, I'd vote for him. For above everything else, he's a good and decent man. And such people are exactly what our country needs more than ever.

Even though his to-do list is longer than that of the manager of Jerry Jones' ego, Mayor Falconer managed to call us while we were on tour. He said that he'd heard from a reporter about all of the good work Wili was doing for his animal and human friends, including his gift to Operation Kindness, and that he wanted to present Nawiliwili Nelson the key to the city of Carrollton. On our way back home to Louisiana, Wili and I stopped in Carrollton and met Mayor Falconer at City Hall. The three of us gathered in the council chambers under the city slogan that read *Carrollton, Texas: Where Connections Are Made*. Such a slogan in such a place, thanks to good leadership, goes deeper than politics and farther than civic duty. Of all the awards that Wili couldn't eat, the key to the city of Carrollton was his absolute favorite.

The City of Carrollton has a big fireworks display every Fourth of July. I'd read that just before the show, the Carrollton Fire Rescue will raise the American flag from the fire engine on site, and that the Carrollton Police Department connects with those in attendance by passing out glow sticks and earplugs. If Wili and I had been there, we would've been among the proudest Americans in attendance. Although, Wili would've tried to eat the glow stick as I tried stuffing earplugs in his ears. But, we would've shared in celebrating the gathering of a community that connected each and every person. Our calling as children of God goes beyond our cities, and even our country, to connect with all those loved and called by God. We were reminded of that calling in Carrollton, and we'll always treasure the kindness shown to us by their mayor.

As Wili and I got on the road again, our hearts were full and our hopes renewed. We felt pretty cool as we sang along with our new friend, Mr. Ice: "Alright stop, collaborate, and listen." Such sentiments may seem plain vanilla, but they speak to a richer, tastier truth. The time has come in our nation's history when we are each called to Stop. Collaborate. And Listen. Before the mayor presented the key to Wili, he didn't interrogate him about his political party or voting preferences. The labels we place on people, like the labels we place on beer, aren't nearly as important as what is found within the bottle and within the heart of the person. We need to be careful and take care of each other. We need to see beyond any issues that may separate and divide us, and come together to seek the common good. We are called to engage in the most patriotic act of all—the special, holy, hard, and grueling work of creating community, listening to each other, and exchanging the keys to our hearts with those who might be different than us. There's more than a beverage at stake here—the future of our nation depends on it.

The good news is that miracles can still happen in our cities, shelters, churches, synagogues, mosques, breweries, countries, and even ourselves. What is true in Luckenbach is true in Salado and Carrollton, and whichever town you call home. Wili, Willie, and Waylon all agree. Maybe it's time to get back to the basics of love.

LUBBOCK OR LEAVE IT

What we see depends mainly on what we look for.

John Lubbock

In 2014, the Movato Real Estate Blog named Lubbock, Texas the most boring city in America. I call bullshit, blogger. You can eat my high plains dust. You can take my tumbleweed and cram it up your mortgage calculator. Move on along, Movato—and your little prairie dog, too. A world without Lubbock, and Lubbockians, would be a poorer world indeed. When the Last Howlelujah Tour rolled into Lubbock on July 9, 2017, Wili and I were treated like the Second Coming of Buddy Holly. And Lubbock would know. They gave the world Buddy Holly—and a lot more like him.

Maybe it's the wide-open skies or the never-ending plains in Lubbock that stimulate the musical part of the soul so strikingly. Some naysayers insist it's simply because there's nothing else to do there except make music. Whatever the inspiration, Lubbock has produced some extraordinary music-makers: Terry Allen, Mac Davis, Joe Ely, Butch Hancock, Jimmie Dale Gilmore, Delbert McClinton, Lloyd Maines and his daughter, Natalie of The Dixie Chicks. The Greater Lubbock Metropolitan Region, or GLAMOR as the locals call it (and live it), has blessed our ears with the musical who's who of Waylon Jennings (Littlefield), Floyd Tillman (Post), Tanya Tucker (Seminole), and Don Williams (Floydada). It might be a stretch, 147 miles to be precise, to include Wink's Roy Orbison, but any town named Wink ought to be represented by GLAMOR. And Roy Orbison fits in better with the High Plains Pantheon than even Roy Rogers.

Add in John Denver attending Texas Tech and Meatloaf graduating from Lubbock Christian, home of the Happy Chaps, and Lubbock's lyrical lineage is undeniable. Anyone who can get a rocky mountain high out of the flatlands of Lubbock has to have a vivid imagination. And the very notion that conservative Lubbock Christian University gave the world Meatloaf makes me rethink my rejection of religious fundamentalism. Well, I'd do anything for love, but I won't do *that*. Meatloaf delivered the greatest performance in cinematic history as Eddie in *The Rocky Horror Picture Show*. His solo on "Hot Patootie, Bless My Soul" sounds like something a high plains church lady might say if someone added a habanero pepper to her casserole without her consent. Meatloaf (his real name is Ground Beef) recorded the theologically sensitive album *Bat Out of Hell* which included the doctrinally suspect song: "Good Girls Go to Heaven (Bad Girls Go Everywhere)." Although, by recording

Bat Out of Hell 2 and *3*, he seemed to return to his Trinitarian orthodoxy. LCU is the same religiously-oriented university where the dress code states that the entire upper torso must be covered at all times, which makes me wonder whether Meatloaf ever considered clothing worn from the waist down optional.

A few years back I owned a bar called Padre's in the tiny West Texas desert arts town of Marfa. Every New Year's Eve, we'd have the good fortune of featuring two-thirds of the Lubbock all-star band, The Flatlanders—Butch Hancock and Jimmie Dale Gilmore. The 225 folks who would faithfully squeeze into the space every New Year's Eve probably felt like I did—like I'd been to church on a high holy night. Both musicians were the real deal. Critics praised Butch Hancock as being "one the finest songwriters of our time," and Jimmie Dale Gilmore's voice was heralded as one that would "make Hank Williams cry." That's high praise for our high plains brothers.

They could've played any number of better-paying, larger-capacity venues in much larger towns on New Year's Eve, but they kept coming back to Padre's. Maybe they liked our down-to-earth appeal to the common patron. I believe it was Jimmie who once said of his hometown-on-the-plain that "plain is the opposite of fancy." Padre's wasn't fancy. There were no velvet ropes or VIP seating. Instead, it had a chapel pulpit from a funeral home repurposed as a doorman's stand, salvaged church pews as bar seating, vintage shuffleboard, affordable margaritas made with real lime juice and pure agave tequila, and a cowboy boot-wearing priest who greeted bar goers with the same enthusiasm he did parishioners on Christmas Eve.

But no place can garner all the Grammys—not even Texas. Amidst every velvety voice and symphonious serenade, there had to be an occasional clunker. There was apparently at least one humdrum hummer in their regional midst and folks still talk about him. Maybe someday they'll even sing about him— as long as he's not given the microphone. The name of this tuneless troubadour was Robin Dorsey, and he hailed from the lyrically named town of Matador, Texas. Matador was known as being the home of Bob's Oil Well, a gas station that drew tourists in by featuring live rattlesnakes. Eventually, Bob added lions and a rare white buffalo. You'd think such a place would inspire extraordinary creativity, but not in Robin Dorsey's case. He'd fallen in love with a woman named Patty from Muleshoe, Texas, so in an attempt to woo her, he wrote her a love song. While he should've considered the context and titled his ballad: "The Muleshoe Matador," Dorsey's lyrical creativity instead followed a less abstract, more obvious path. The title of his love song: "Her Teeth Are Stained but Her Heart is Pure," was, perhaps, not the worst thing one could say about the object of one's affection. Turns out, Dorsey had Patty's name tattooed on his arm, so after they broke up, his dating pool was limited to only girls named Patty. This predicament eventually inspired him to write one more tune: "I Don't Know Whether to Go Bowling or Kill Myself." Bowling was likely the better idea.

Some music conspiracy theorists posited that because Lubbock was the Brass Buckle of the Bible Belt, this more oppressive religious climate had unleashed the creative juices of those outside the fenced-in fold. That is, knowing exactly what religion *tries* to limit added fuel to the fires of those who refused to be limited. Rather than squelch the originality of those less concerned about original sin and more concerned with original ideas, the fire-and-brimstone breathers had breathed fresh life into such sinners, now empowered not so much to repent as to rebel. Being told what *not* to do was a sure-fire motivation for doing it all, such as drinking, dancing, and writing songs of which your Sunday school teacher might disapprove. Chasing loose women and losing chaste women sounds as much like a conversion experience as it does a well-pitched woebegone wail.

Perhaps the best description of this unintentional awakening of the spirit was captured by Butch Hancock. Growing up, sometimes surrounded by life-denying lunatics and their more priggish demands than even those of their puritanical forebears, Hancock provided this powerfully contradictory observation: "Life in Lubbock, Texas taught me two things: One is that God loves you and you're going straight to hell, and the other is that sex is the most awful, filthy thing on earth, and you should save it for someone you love." While such juxtapositions may twist your soul into knots, the good news is that it will damn sure hone your song-writing skills. When you grow up in such a place, your awareness of the unpolished irony of it all puts you light years ahead of all the slicker-than-thou songwriters at the top of the Billboard charts.

A town like Lubbock so steeped in metaphysical mysteries

should no doubt be named after a person possessing a real depth of intellectual and creative prowess. The namesake of such a luminous and liminal land should be more erudite than uptight—a man of letters and learned in the ways of the world. He should be well-read, and even better-written. The founding father of Lubbock should be someone like Sir John Lubbock, a multi-faceted genius who was a politician, philosopher, philanthropist, biologist, and anthropologist. In 1842, when John was just a boy, his dad came home early from work one day to proclaim to his son that he had good news. Little Johnny was hoping for a pony. Instead, his dad informed the family that the esteemed and brilliant evolutionary biologist, Charles Darwin, was moving in next door. This new neighbor, whose knowledge of species vastly exceeded that of folks who didn't know feces, turned out to be, for John, even better than a pony—although if the good news had been that he was getting a dog, it likely would've been a toss-up.

Darwin's influence on John Lubbock was undeniable. It awakened within him an extraordinary curiosity for the natural world. Darwin piqued Lubbock's interest in science when he hired him to illustrate barnacles for a textbook. That's right. This creative genius started out drawing barnacles for Charles Darwin—which sounds like a great opening for a country-western song written by a Lubbock songwriter. Whether it's shucking oysters, baling hay, plowing fields, counting tumbleweeds, or drawing barnacles, all are unanticipated opportunities to practice mindfulness, if you ask me. Though the well-educated reader may scoff at such an introduction to the scientific world, much like the well-traveled nomad might be suspicious of the charms of any small town in the Texas Panhandle—the truth is that both are underrated. Barnacles are exceptional arthropods, as well as encrusters; meaning that, like some folks who frequent West Texas bars, they get attached rather easily. I can imagine John Lubbock in the context of Victorian England, having as much fun illustrating a barnacle appendage, with its largest to body size ratio in the entire animal kingdom, as the Lubbock gyrators did with their suggestive lyrics and hip-swaying beats in the realm of the religiously repressed. Many years later, after Darwin died, it was John Lubbock who led the campaign to have him buried at Westminster Abbey. I'll bet there were some Anglicans in England who objected to the evolutionist's interment, just like I'll bet there were some Baptists in Lubbock who took issue with a rock-n-roller's elevation to a status higher than a holy-roller.

Even though John Lubbock was never awarded a Ph.D. at Texas Tech, he was a very smart fellow. He went on from the barnacle-busting days of his youth to research and write all about this wonderful world God has made. One of his more formidable explorations into the natural world became a book titled *On the Senses, Instincts, and Intelligence of Animals, With Special Reference to Insects*. Wili would've loved this guy. As would have Wili's fleas. Perhaps Lubbock's most timeless work was *The Pleasures of Life*. Between the covers, he revealed all those aspects of life that enrich the human experience, that make us more complete, whole and happy—books, friends, health, love, art, poetry, music, nature, work, rest, and even religion. While the particular place people live cannot be found on that list, there's a higher plane of being expressed in Lubbock's thoughts that seems to parallel the higher plain of living in the town by the same name.

How I wish upon a fully-functioning, barrel-gushing oil well that the city of Lubbock *had* been named in honor of Sir John Lubbock. But it wasn't. It was named for a Texas Ranger by the name of Thomas Saltus "Salty" Lubbock, a soldier in the Texas revolution. As disappointed as I was to learn this, a disappointment no doubt shared by you, let us recall that in addition to the euphonious troubadours previously mentioned, Lubbock has also given the world the non-phony and unpretentious football coaches, Spike Dykes and Mike Leach. My favorite Spike Dykes story is how he would illustrate the difference between being *involved* versus being totally *committed*. Dykes said it was as simple as understanding the difference between bacon and eggs on your breakfast plate. The chicken is involved. But the hog is totally committed. That will preach! Leach, on the other hand, was well-known for giving his team three-hour lectures on pirates after losing a big game. He was also known to have written a book titled *Swing Your Sword*, and an entire collection of 700 of his most memorable quotes gathered in single volume titled *Squib-Kick it to a Fat Guy*. It's also important to mention that during Texas Tech football games, the fans would toss tortillas on to the field as a show of support. Furthermore, before each home game, Masked Rider, formerly called Ghost Rider, would ride a black horse the entire length of the football field wearing a mask and a scarlet cape.

So perhaps a Salty Soldier turned Renegade Ranger is not such a bad role-model. All I know is Lubbock is my kind of town.

If you'd told me before the tour that I'd develop a deep love for Lubbock, I would've howled in protest. I might have quoted Lubbock's favorite son and said, "That'll be the day." But that would've been before Wili and I wandered into St. Stephen's Church for a sold-out Howlelujah event. Nawiliwili Nelson is a big deal in Lubbock, Texas. Perhaps he's the dog version of a band hitting it big in Japan. There was no detail that this committee had overlooked. They weren't only involved; they were committed—to Wili, sure—but also to each other and to their town. There was Texas barbecue, of course, and Three Dog Bakery had provided tasty treats that Wili devoured in a millisecond. But, beyond a checklist, the divine seemed to be in the details that night. There was a sense of something sacred happening. People seemed to be lending, not just a hand, but a heart.

I found out later that St. Stephen's, like a lot of communities, faith-based or otherwise, had experienced its unfair share of conflict and schism. I know it's hard to believe, but you put together even the best group of human beings, and there's bound to be disagreement and misunderstanding. Add in things that folks are passionate about such as God, belief, salsa, or football, and it's liable to get ugly fast. It's the nature of groups that people will duke it out over who's going to be the top dog, or whose opinion more fully reflects that of the Almighty. But in seeking to win as individuals, the group usually loses. The single issue may trump the greater good in many disagreements, but the greater good is much more important than the single issue, whether we're talking politics or theology. Put people together, and being right often becomes more important than being loving. And that ain't right. You can gather together the finest group of dogs on earth, and the chances are good that somebody is going to growl. Barking is bad enough, but in some places, some folks can't wait to sink their teeth into someone who holds an opposing viewpoint.

Whatever the divisive issues were, this community was blessed to have folks that were committed for the long-haul. They'd reached a higher plane of understanding that the place to which God calls us completely transcends our opinions on particular issues. It also transcends the time limits we place on each other to "get it together" or come around to seeing things "my way." Such enlightened ones are the enlivened ones who aren't going anywhere. As Willie Nelson once sang, "I didn't come here. And I ain't leavin'." These are the ones who stake their claim, not on turf or territory, but on the grace of God, and on our capacity to forgive each other. They value their friends more than they value their feelings. They value their dogs more than they value their dogma. The writer James Thurber once observed that love is what you've been through with someone. When you love as God has loved us, you get through it together—whatever *it* is. Wili and I experienced such love and acceptance at a church named after a saint who was stoned to death because he proclaimed that people can change their minds and their ways and still be faithful. Stephen challenged the "stiff-necked" (not to be confused with "rednecked"), dig-in-your-heels crowd to understand that

God would not be confined to your way of believing *or* behaving. The awesome organizer of the Howlelujah Tour event at St. Stephen's, Maggie, told me later, "I love this community so much. We all truly love and care for each other, despite our differences. We're focused on reaching out to our town and our world. This community reminds me every day how much God loves us."

There will always be those who, in every country, city, church, and community, will adopt an attitude that goes something like this: *Love it or leave it.* But if you really love it, you're not going to leave it, and you're not asking anyone else to leave it, either. You won't be focused on ways of separating people—the walls, barricades, and keep out signs—these are clueless constrictions that are not for the benefit of anybody. You'll focus on opening and enlarging doors, building longer bridges, and obliterating every barrier that might prevent us from committing and connecting to each other in community. If we love our communities, we may criticize them constructively, but we'll not deconstruct, demolish, or tear down what others have built. We will not show folks the front door—although we may help folks on the outside find the front door to come inside if they are in need of a community that's willing to move on, pick you up, and take you with them. Relationships matter more than anything. *People* make the place. As Buddy Holly noted about the connections that move us: "I've got to play in front of *people*. If I'm not moved, how can they be moved?" In other words, we're all in this together. Such places filled with such people do exist. One of them is in Lubbock, Texas.

That place and those people on that night set a fundraising record for the Howlelujah Tour. It's a record that would be broken by only one much larger town—Las Vegas. The good folks who gathered in Lubbock raised $2,300 for a new rescue organization called Four-Legged Friends, whose philosophy is not to criticize any other group doing the best they can. They simply want to offer a constructive alternative, to make the difference they're able to make, and to do their own job by abiding to their own calling well. For the folks at St. Stephens, true community means that their concern extends well past the front door and into the greater community, and reaches out beyond the bipeds to include even their quadruped friends. That's what I call an inclusive community—a place where the horizons have no borders and God's love has no limits.

At the end of our event, Wili led me beyond that front door and outside toward a sacred space that showed just how far the loving reach of this community extended. Wili took me to a special site that celebrated the well-lived lives of their non-human family members. To some, at first glance, the St. Stephen's Pet Columbarium might look like nothing more than an uneven field of strewn rocks. But for people who see with eyes of appreciation, piles of rocks and barren plains reveal much more than what comes immediately into view. Scattered among the more jagged specimens were larger, smoother stones each bearing a simple cross and the name of a celebrated canine, a beloved beast, whose ashes were buried beneath. Wili and I wandered among the stones and paid our respects. Stones, like every other gift entrusted to us on earth, can be used for good or ill. We can see them as witnesses of wasteland or objects of rare beauty. They were used to take the life of Saint Stephen. But here, they affirmed life rather than destroyed it. They were an offering of unconditional, rock-solid, unwavering love. Plain ol' rocks remind us that we can use everything the Creator has given us to either bless or to harm. These objects can either help us cherish and honor our fellow creatures or repudiate and reject them.

I thought I might have to warn Wili not to mark any territory while we were out there and tell him that these spots were hallowed and had already been claimed for all eternity, but he seemed to already understand. He stopped to sniff repeatedly, but not once did he pee on anybody. Would that we humans be as restrained as Wili. I'm sure the dogs buried there wouldn't have minded because it's what dogs do. But Wili held it in for, perhaps, the first time in his life. He must've known something was different about these rough-hewn markers. Perhaps it reminded him of another whose song would also be *Howlelujah*, but without the howl. I stooped down and traced some of the names of the canine congregants: Lady, Charles, Checkers, Captain, Big Mama, Wolf, and Gracie. There was a large quarried bench on which one family had celebrated the lives of the entire family, including their best beasties: Rusty, Small Fry, Tiki, Cocoa, Cricket, Pocus, Boomer, Mr. Magoo, Scooter, Chichi, Macavity, Crash, Willie, Lola, Bob, Bird, Kitty, and Moose. On the wall keeping watch over all was St. Francis. There was a critter on his left and another on his right—one more reminder that whichever side you're on, you belong.

Exactly two years to the day that Wili and I were graced with the presence of our good and faithful friends in Lubbock, on July 9, 2019, I was asked to preside at my first official dog funeral. The dog's name was Klunk. He was one of two hundred dogs rescued by my local humane society during the Louisiana floods in 2016. He was only six months old at the time and was adopted immediately. But six months later, Klunk was returned to the shelter because he started fighting with other dogs. Unfortunately, fighting with other dogs, getting adopted, and then returned would become recurring themes for Klunk. But the staff and volunteers of the humane society fell in love with him. They recognized that he had some behavior issues, and after one particularly bad fight, he was given a "potentially aggressive" classification by Animal Control, but they never gave up on him. Klunk became part of their family, a member of their community, and it seemed as though they would do anything and everything for Klunk. They took him to a mega-adoption event in Florida where Klunk was the only dog among all twenty-seven dogs that didn't get adopted. Then they went the extra mile and stepped up to pay for training for Klunk. When Klunk was returned after another adoption didn't work out, he became sick. But the staff nursed him back to health. Indeed, they loved him unconditionally. Eventually they thought they had found a perfect foster-based rescue out-of-state that included training. He'd been doing well. But then Klunk got in another fight and was immediately euthanized. The staff and volunteers who loved Klunk were completely devastated.

Klunk's funeral was at high noon in the blazing Louisiana sun. The oppressive conditions didn't stop those who loved him from coming to be there with him, and for him, one last time. He was the first dog buried at the new pet cemetery, not unlike the pet cemetery created by our friends in Lubbock. The entire staff and a host of volunteers showed up. It was obvious that Klunk meant a great deal to many. There were a lot of broken hearts gathered together in that place. We read three passages from scripture, including Psalm 104 which speaks of God's love for all God's critters: "In wisdom you have made them all. The earth is full of your creatures. When you open your hand, they are filled with good things. When you hide your face, they are dismayed; when you take away their breath, they die and return to their dust." We also read Romans 8, a passage that reminds us that nothing can separate us from God's love—not any of life's greatest challenges, not fights with other dogs or other people, not even death. And finally, we read Jesus' observation from the Gospel of Matthew—when a small sparrow falls to the ground, God knows about it. And God cares about it. Because God loves every creature, even the smallest and most challenging among us, God's heart breaks when we are hurt or when we hurt others. I asked those gathered to share favorite memories and stories about Klunk, and the emotion in their voices spoke of their deep affection for him. Then I quoted the old hymn: "He Looked beyond My Fault." It seemed to express the sorrowful yet sacred sentiment I was feeling as I came to know Klunk's story and how an entire community embraced him with unconditional love. "For it was grace that brought my liberty. I do not know just why he came to love me so."

I had trouble getting the words out. I was moved so much by their deep love for Klunk. As one employee said, "Behind all of Klunk's challenges, we saw the sweet boy that he was." I believe the way they loved Klunk—to the very end—is the way that God loves each of us. We are given so many chances by God. God sees beyond our faults and knows our deepest needs. God sees our spirits, our potential, our beauty, and our goodness. God will go the extra mile and give everything so that we might be saved from our most dismal deeds. God will do anything and everything so that we might live more fully into his desires for each of us. An indestructible love like that seems rare in this world. I witnessed it at a dog funeral in Louisiana, and I witnessed it at dog fundraiser in Lubbock. I experience it every time I fall in my own life. God shows up to rescue me. God never gives up on me, even if my teeth are stained and my heart is impure. I'm grateful to Klunk and all who loved him in Louisiana. And I'm grateful for Wili and all who loved him in Lubbock. And for reminding us just how amazing grace can be.

Sometimes life goes *klunk,* and sometimes we are the clunker. In those times, we look beyond the surface of beauty toward the depth of grace. In those times, we look past the deficiencies of a place, to find the first-class heroics of a people. In those times, we come to understand just how important it is to have a community comprised of those who will surround you, forgive you, uphold you, never give up on you, and stay the course to the very end. It is special people that are capable of creating such a special place.

In Lubbock, at the end to the night, the good people of St. Stephen's Church presented Wili and me with a heart-shaped basket as big as Texas. Within it was an assortment of specialized gifts that would allow us to take some of Lubbock with us—brochures that extolled the virtues of their town, a corkscrew and fine bottle of Cabernet Sauvignon from the excellent wine-growing region nearby (who knew?), some Texas Tech cozies to keep our beer cold, a Chuckit! tennis ball chucker capable of tossing a tennis ball all the way to Muleshoe, Airedale notecards, chocolate candy, a beautiful hand-painted portrait of Wili, and a dog pillow with the hashtag: #LOVE. But even if they'd given us no gifts, we would've come. For Wili and for me, their presence mattered more than their presents.

I once saw a bumper sticker that read: "Happiness is Lubbock in your rear-view mirror." As we left Lubbock the next day, Wili and I were happy, alright. But we weren't happy about leaving. We were happy we'd found a place where people lived with hearts as wide-open and expansive as the plains on which they resided. On the frontiers of faith we'd found some true pioneers. We'd encountered a community that welcomed anybody and everybody—in life and in death. I suppose it's true that some joy did fill our hearts as we saw Lubbock in our rear-view mirror. But only because we knew that we could always return—and would always be welcomed back.

BIGGER THAN ELVIS

I never expected to be anybody important. Maybe I'm not now.
But whatever I am and whatever I will become
will be what God has chosen for me.

Elvis Presley

Wili stole the show wherever we went. Our first Sunday on the tour, we made a serendipitous stop at St. Francis Church in College Station, Texas, home of Wili's favorite Italian saint not named Prosciutto, and host of the most beautiful canine mascot in all of sports—Reveille the Collie. Wili described her as hotter than Lassie and even tried to date her while we were there. But she rebuffed and ruffed that she didn't date mutts with no papers—especially those who might keep questionable company with Tigers or Longhorns. For the Sunday service at St. Francis, I'd prepared an appropriate sermon based on the ancient hymn: "Proud to be a Sissy from Assisi" by Saint Merleton of Haggardo, while Wili had been instructed to stay put, keep quiet, and remain inconspicuously tethered to a table leg at the back of the sanctuary during the Mass. I reminded him that after the service he'd be allowed to greet his admirers, as well as receive offerings from the brisket feast to follow.

The organ bellowed as the congregation rose to sing the opening hymn. At the back of the church, the worship leaders composed themselves and lined up before parading down the center aisle in a stately procession of solemnity. The crucifer held the cross aloft between white-gloved hands and prepared to march forward, followed by choir, acolytes, clergy, and the Texas A&M yell leaders. Perhaps Wili must have seen St. Francis towering above the altar, beckoning to him to "come" just as he had to so many animal friends over the centuries, and just as Jesus had done so often whenever there were children in his midst. Whatever his motivation, the hairy Houdini somehow untied his leash and darted in front of the cross to saunter down the aisle in the pole position ahead of the scheduled servers. He pranced all the way up to the altar where I could've sworn he genuflected in front of Francis. Perhaps he was hoping he might snag an early communion wafer. He appeared so confident that I half expected him to stand up on his hind legs and start blessing the congregation, making a canine sign of the cross with his front paws. I was grateful that he didn't start sprinkling holy water on the gathered assembly by peeing on a pew. The joy on the faces of all in attendance as Wili led the procession that Sunday revealed their appreciation for his role as icon of creation, representing the Creator's best and most *howly* work.

On the second Sunday of the tour we found ourselves at a more formal location—the Cathedral of Saint Paul in Oklahoma City.

Perhaps they'd heard about Wili's liturgical prank the previous
Sunday, but they were kind enough to allow Wili to participate
in the opening procession, escorted by his father, until he was
handed off to the verger and taken through the side doors to the
parish hall to be supervised by the kids. The children of the parish
had been granted permission to watch Wili as their Sunday school
lesson for the day. I cannot imagine a more profound teaching
on God's goodness. But the children were so taken by Wili that
they fell in love with him. This condition of unconditional love
for and from Wili seemed to afflict everyone who met him.

When the verger went back into the parish hall to fetch the
Wili-watchers in time for the children's sermon, the children
would not be moved. They rallied around a revolution of dog
love and told the verger to send word to the Dean that they
wouldn't set foot in the worship space without their new friend,
Nawiliwili Nelson. On Wili's behalf, the children staged a
Sunday morning coup at the cathedral. If only the adults of our
worshipping communities were as firm in their convictions of
inclusivity—if we bid more strays *come on in*, the world might
not *go to the dogs* quite so quickly. As long as faith communities
are more concerned about who *doesn't* belong rather than who
does belong, the tail of intolerance will continue to wag the body
of Christ. But the children had the right, and the righteous, idea.

Their coup was successful. Wili accompanied the children
back into the church and to their places at the base of the
chancel steps. It might be the most cherished memory that I
held in my heart after the tour. As the children's eyes and

attention were focused on the Dean and his sermon, the eyes and attention of most everyone else in attendance focused on the giant dog head that towered above them and from among them. While the Dean's sermon was on point, it was Wili's presence that was on paw—and the children's insistence that he be present brought home both the Howlelujah *and* the Amen.

Wili's popularity had only increased by the time we got to our third Sunday stop, our final event on the Howlelujah Tour. It's a long way from New Orleans to Las Vegas, especially the way I drive. Having Wili as Navigator didn't expedite our arrival, either (we sometimes followed our noses and our hearts more than our GPS). Like most paths that unfold in God's time and in God's way, we didn't travel in a straight line from point A to point B—from N.O. to L.V.—that wasn't how we did things. Instead, we went where we were called. We followed where we were led (and fed). So, we zagged, zigged, zigzagged, and veered off course. We also backtracked, got lost, found, and then lost again. We managed to turn a 3,400-mile journey into a 5,000-mile journey. In other words, we traveled a truly spiritual track.

Lots of people were pulling for Wili to make it all the way to Las Vegas. Wili's vet had given no guarantees about Wili surviving beyond three months, and since he'd already made it to eight, we couldn't be certain he would make it to the end of the trail. A reporter asked me point blank before we left home: "What if Wili doesn't survive the trip?" He'd even interviewed Wili's veterinarian to be sure that doctor's orders didn't preclude a road trip to Vegas. The vet and I concurred—what could possibly be more healing, make us feel better, and enrich and prolong our lives more than a road trip with our best buddy, especially if it led all the way to Sin (Scent) City? Besides, there's an unavoidable truth for all creatures that walk or wag on this earth, about which every Las Vegas odds-maker agrees—all of our days are numbered. *No one* gets out of here alive. And if Wili's time came while on the tour, then what a way to go! We would know that he died doing what dogs love to do—traveling with their person, whiffing unknown aromas, making new friends, sticking their heads out the window while driving fast, sleeping in the back of the car, tapping their tails to the sounds of the Highwaymen, and eating barbecue so plentiful it's even available at drive-thrus. Why not go out with a bark and a bang?

I won't say that I didn't worry about Wili. I did worry. I worried about him every single day, hoping and praying that he would make it to the end. So when we drove into Las Vegas on the afternoon of July 15th, we headed straight for the historic Las Vegas sign on the south end of the strip to create photographic evidence that we had achieved our hoped-and-prayed-for feat, to show the world that this miracle was no mirage. A few years later, I'd return to Las Vegas to lead an Elvis Mass at the same church where Wili had his last hurrah. After the service, I'd have a celebratory meal at a restaurant just down the street from that very same sign, and I'd eat in the same booth in which Elvis sat when he had a *hunka hunka hankering* for Italian. During that trip, I'd return to this fabulously illuminated spot and give thanks again for both Wili and Elvis while savoring the delicious possibility the *Elvis Was Here* sign might be supplanted with one of even more spiritual significance—*Wili Was Here.*

When Wili and I arrived at the world's most recognized and fabulous welcome sign, there was a line that stretched all the way to the Hoover Dam. But nobody complained about the wait. Everybody was patient, cooperative, respectful, and happily waiting their turn. Perhaps none of them had come from a casino, or perhaps they simply sensed that they were in the company of greatness. Just ahead of us in line was a bachelorette party of a dozen California beauties, and they were all fawning over Wili. I used to think that dogs were chick magnets and that I could depend on Wili to be my wingdog. But from that moment forward it became apparent that our roles would be reversed. Wili wasn't *my* wing*dog*. I was *his* wing*dad*. The girls couldn't keep their eyes—or their paws—off of him. They patted his bottom, squeezed his cheeks, scratched his chin, hugged his head, and kissed his nose. Wili's tongue saw more action that afternoon than mine had seen since that high school church retreat where we were forbidden to engage in anything that even resembled heavy petting. Assuming that I was Wili's official spokeshuman, they shouted questions at me like they were reporters at the press conference just before Elvis's comeback concert in Vegas in 1969. *What's his name? What kind of dog is he? What does he like to eat? How long is his tail? Are those eyebrows real? Does he enjoy snuggling? Does he still have his balls? Who is his girlfriend? Will he marry me?* Apparently, not only am I chopped liver—I'm chopped liver served in a dog bowl.

As the professional photographer gathered the girls in front of the sign, placing them in order from hot to hottest, one girl yelled, "Wait! We want Wili!" Then, as if on cue, right there in front of God, Wayne Newton, Steve Wynn, Bugsy Siegel, Oscar Goodman, Oscar Goodman's martini, Siegfried, Roy, and the Tigers they rode in on, the bachelorettes began to chant, *WI-LI! WI-LI! WI-LI! WI-LI!* They upped their volume and more fervently pleaded their case: *WI-LI! WI-LI! WI-LI! WI-LI!* Their chorus rang louder than all the showgirls who'd ever sung in all the showrooms on the strip. They were completely oblivious to the Elvis impersonator silently sulking nearby and hoping to cash in on some photo ops. The girls (as well as the entire crowd) completely ignored him in favor of the celebrity who was so much more than a hound dog. Not only was Wili now the center of attention for all the *pup*arrazi, the young ladies wouldn't be silenced until their newly crowned King Wili joined them. Wili broke away from me and headed right for them—so much for having no sense of direction. I'd never seen Wili so aware of his surroundings or so happy to be in them. His smile stretched to the stratosphere, which is just about how high he must have felt being completely surrounded by a pack of pretties. He was floating on an oasis of admiration in a sea of affection. While Wili didn't end up with any phone numbers, he was most assuredly channeling the spirit of Elvis. Or perhaps, years earlier, Elvis was channeling the future spirit of Wili. All I know is that I was all shook up, and the girls couldn't help falling in love with him. Wili and Elvis had a lot in common—Wili wouldn't be the first (or last) improbable star to headline in Vegas.

Elvis Presley never imagined he'd hear screaming girls chanting *EL-VIS! EL-VIS! EL-VIS!* He never dreamed he would be famous. He never claimed to be a king. In fact, during his Vegas comeback concert in 1969, a reporter asked him how it felt to be "The King of Rock-n-Roll." Elvis pointed to a New Orleans musician who was standing nearby and said, "I don't know. You'll have to ask Fats Domino." Countless times when Elvis was greeted by admirers bearing signs that read: "Elvis—The King," he would correct them saying, "There is only one King, and that's Jesus Christ. I'm just a singer." He was a singer, alright. He could howl like no one before—or after.

Perhaps such awareness is what made Elvis great. He understood who he was in relation to God. He understood the particular gift with which he'd been blessed. He wasn't called to be a composer. He wasn't called to perform with the Royal Shakespeare Company. He wasn't called to preach. He wasn't called to be a hound dog. He was called to be Elvis. While Wili would have never claimed royalty, it was suggested by many of his admirers that his antics made him worthy of a place in the court of jesters. But, in the end, he was just a dog in the same way that Elvis was just a singer. No one can copy that. There'll never be another Elvis and there'll never be another Wili.

Anyone who does what God calls him to do, especially if no one has dared to do it quite so boldly or uniquely before, will always come under intense criticism from those who are suspicious of mind, not to mention heart, and soul. Elvis' mom,

Gladys, recalled that Elvis behaved like an unruly puppy during the first church services he attended where he began to explore his true life calling. Elvis would squirm right out of her lap and run down the center aisle, creating a procession of one. He would end up in the front of the First Assembly of God Church in Tupelo, Mississippi, right next to the choir. Little Elvis would match their voices and move to their groove. So, for those who find his shaking and grooving offensive and suggestive, blame it on the church—or the Holy Spirit. If either is doing its job, we'll *all* find ourselves on the move.

Considering the countless criticisms Elvis received from an early age, it's a wonder he ever found his voice or felt comfortable enough in his own blue suede shoes to contort freely in front of the world. When he was ten years old, he entered a singing contest in his grammar school, where the competition wasn't quite American Idol caliber. Elvis placed fifth. At twelve, he started bringing his guitar to school so he could strum and sing during lunchtime. His fellow students began referring to him as the "trashy kid who played hillbilly music." In his later teens, he auditioned for a gospel quartet. Surely those who sang for the Lord would recognize a God-given talent when they heard it—nope. Elvis was shown the door for the simple reason that, according to their ears, he couldn't sing. Riiight. And Wili can't wag, eat, sleep, or bark. Later, Elvis tried out as lead singer for a popular Memphis band. The bandleader gave him the benefit of the blues without the rhythm, telling him not to quit his day job of truck-driving, since he would never make it as a singer.

Even in Las Vegas (where he would someday be as popular as Wili), Elvis faced criticism after his very first gig at the New Frontier Hotel. An unnamed Newsweek critic, who was apparently uncomfortable with anything cutting edge, panned Elvis' performance as sounding like a "jug of corn liquor at a champagne reception." Pass the jug and let's all dance a jig in honor of all the critics who shall forever be ignored. Thank God that Elvis was aware that just as there is only one King, there is only one Judge, and the rest of the critics don't count whether they are musical, ministerial, or moral.

When Elvis began to sing a tune written for Willie Mae "Big Mama" Thornton called *Hound Dog,* he did it his way—a way that no one else could mimic. Big Mama sang it as a bluesy, burlesque ballad. Elvis sang it with an up-tempo canine cadence, and he changed the lyrics from "Quit snoopin' round my door / You can wag your tail, But I ain't gonna feed you no more" to the more Elvis-esque: "Cryin' all the time / Well you ain't never caught a rabbit and you ain't no friend of mine." Maybe Elvis couldn't write like Shakespeare, but Shakespeare couldn't move like Elvis. And neither of them could wag like Wili! The world is better for having all three, as long as they remained true to their God, to their gifts, and to themselves.

Elvis enjoyed who he was and what he did enough to be able to poke fun, even at himself. In Las Vegas, after he'd sung the dog song a thousand times (which felt like 7,000 times to Wili), he introduced "Hound Dog" by saying facetiously and definitely not philosophically, "Friends, as a great philosopher once said."

Apparently, the guardians of anti-groove felt that Elvis's moves, while performing this particular tune, reminded them of a dog chasing his tail. Certain members of the media were displeased with his contortionist capabilities, labeling his provocative gyrations "animalistic" and "vulgar." And the national Jesuit magazine, *America*, reinforced the Catholic Church's position warning all those who might fall under his spell to: "Beware Elvis Presley." While Elvis was hardly the Second Coming, the criticisms leveled at him sounded somewhat familiar to any who have read the story of a certain Savior who tended to hang out with the unsavory of his day and moved about freely in his own skin. Those who criticize are usually the ones who are trying to deflect their own guilt and project their own shortcomings onto others. By the grace of God, Elvis continued to be Elvis. After splitting his pants at a show in Las Vegas, Elvis didn't tone it down, calm down, or slow down. He simply changed into a one-piece jumpsuit. Hey haters—*Split This!*

One of the reasons Wili was so beloved is the same reason dogs are always the most popular guests at any party—they are unashamed of their animalistic tendencies. Dogs come to us just as they are and just as God made them. Wili was as uninhibited as Elvis. He never split a crotch, but he sure sniffed more than his fair share. If he was happy to see you he'd shake his tail uncontrollably, whether on stage or off. If anyone ever accused Wili of being "just a dog" he would respond just like Elvis: *Thank you. Thank you very much.* Wili knew that he was one-of-a-kind. So did Elvis. Don't ever let anyone suggest otherwise. In God's eyes each one of us is as fabulous as a city of light in the middle of the darkest desert.

When Wili and I walked into the Mountain View Presbyterian Church on July 16, 2017 for the last event on Wili's Comeback from Cancer Tour, we were mobbed by our fans. Let me rephrase that. Wili was mobbed by *his* fans. That hound dog had somehow managed to get his mutt of a mugshot prominently featured in the Las Vegas Review Journal with a spread that rivaled Elvis's legs on stage. Before we could even get inside the church auditorium, a lady came running up excitedly clutching her newspaper and demanded to know, "Where is he?! Where is WILI! Where is he?!" For a moment, Wili must have understood how Elvis felt in the 1950s when his adoring fans rushed him at his concerts. And Wili and I'd both soon feel the rush of overwhelming love and adoration shown by an entire community of the faithful who'd gone way out of their ways to make us feel right at home.

In some ways Wili saved the best for last—in life and on the tour. There was no detail that this group of people, who collectively formed the brightest beacon in the city of light, hadn't thought of. As we drove into the church parking lot we were greeted by a Hawaiian Shave Ice truck distributing Wili's favorite frozen treat to all who'd ventured forth in the heat to see him. Wili asked if the "Bacon and Butt" flavor was available, but he had to settle for pineapple. The congregation had another sweet surprise, two giant, specially-baked cakes that featured a favorite photo of Wili on top—talk about icing on the cake! I'd heard rumors there was a bidding war over who got to eat our faces—the winning bid for Wili's kisser exceeding mine by more than a nose. There were gifts galore for us that had been lovingly displayed on the altar next to where the more priceless gifts are displayed and served each Sunday. There was a tee shirt with an image of the Las Vegas welcome sign where Wili had been propositioned, if not proposed to. As Wili would later reflect, *what happens in Vegas...* There was a bag of Dingo Goof Ball chews that encouraged us to "rip into flavor," in this case, chicken. My good friend and the pastor of Mountain View Presbyterian, David Dendy, pointed out that this choice reminded him of the way that I lived my faith—goofy and flavorful. I was so grateful for that compliment I considered trying out one of those chews. The congregation also presented Wili with a giant, green stuffed frog that represented the message that Wili always took to heart: ***Fully Rely on God!*** The Frog of Dog object lesson was taken to heart by me and to mouth by Wili. It's not easy being green, being a priest, or having cancer. But having something fun to chew on and toss into the air helps. Finally, there was the True Touch Five Finger DeShedding Glove that empowered the wearer to "pet the hair away." This handheld, magic dog wand was able to massage a pet at the same time it removed hair from the undercoat and the topcoat—in Las Vegas that would be called the over and under coat. Pastor David delighted in telling the assembly that when he first laid eyes on the glove in the pet store, he immediately thought of me because "he likes to touch things." I was deeply touched. It's nice to be known—and loved anyway. Obviously, we were predestined to become friends.

This is the same pastor who, after the Medical marijuana

initiative was approved by the state legislature in Nevada, distributed snacks the following Sunday in case his flock got the munchies. Now there's a man of God who is in *touch* with the needs of the world! No wonder I love this guy. You can tell a lot about pastors just by visiting their offices. Is it dog friendly? Is there beer in the fridge? Are there photos of children and loved ones? Are there offensive signs displayed in neon? In David's office, looming over everything are two giant signs. One reads *PRAY BIG*, and the other reads *LAUGH*. In fact, his life motto is LOAFN. But it doesn't mean he spends all day just lying around— it stands for *Laugh Often and Fear Not*. Now there's some sound theology from a stand-up guy. If you're not convinced he's in on the joke, also in his office he has a pretend newspaper featuring a photo of him on the front cover and extolling the virtues of Pastor Dendy's Butterfinger Diet and the Proverb of the Day— *Replace Thy Socks If They Become Holier Than Thou*. David's sense of humor is almost as well-developed as Wili's. I have a photo of Wili lying on the floor of the church on that special day and he's all ears and all smiles and listening to the words of Pastor Dendy. He must have felt loved that night in Las Vegas. I know I did.

Authenticity in a spiritual community can't be taught as much as it's caught. When leaders are in it for the love, you can feel it—and you begin to believe it and to live it. When you laugh often and fear not, everything changes. You begin to realize that nothing can separate us from God's love—not miles, not disease, not criticism, not those who don't get you or your jokes. Even if those at the sign don't chant your name, you become aware that God knows your name, and such knowledge is so wonderful that it makes all the difference. People who laugh often and fear not tend to love deeply and give generously. It wasn't our first priority, but it was important to me, and to Wili, that we raise funds for our animal friends everywhere we went. The entire offering that night went to Las Vegas Animal Foundation. There was no pressure to give, but Pastor David is the kind of minister who will never ask his people to do anything that he's not willing to do himself. So he made the first pledge of $500 publicly and out of his own pocket. Before we knew it more than $3,000 had been raised that night—a record for the Howlelujah Tour. Because of the graciousness of the people of that community, every penny of it went to animals in need.

Wili and I still had a lot to learn by the end of the tour, but we'd come to know these truths: Generosity begets generosity. Authenticity encourages authenticity. Kindness creates more kindness. Love empowers a greater love. And when people go deep, they tend to dig deeper—into their hearts, souls, resources, and even their dog treat canisters. We will overcome evil only with good. We will destroy hatred only by compassion. We will conquer selfishness by being truly selfless. We will find true riches when we learn how to give more away. Wili taught me most of that. The people in Las Vegas confirmed it.

The next day the Howlelujah Tour officially ended. Wili spent the day hanging out at the church office doing what he did so well—greeting people in God's name. I was told that a dozen new people joined the church because of the warm welcome they received. And Pastor David and I went on a hike. One of the most important points of the tour was placing a priority on friendships, so hanging out with my friend was just as important to me as the events of the previous day. We shared as many laughs that day as we did the day before. I believe that's how God wants it to be—laugh often and fear not—every single day. David and I drove just outside the city to Mount Charleston and climbed to the top of Cathedral Rock. Most visitors to Las Vegas likely have no idea that there's a mountain so close and that it's twenty-five degrees cooler than the strip (and not just in temperature). The mountain is covered with bristlecone pines and one is thought to be 3,000 years old. I'm always amazed at how much we miss in this life, even when it's within driving distance—or right in front of our eyes and noses. But, most of us are too afraid, or maybe too comfortable, to venture off the well-worn strip to get beyond the beaten path.

I doubt that most of those who visit Las Vegas would know anything about a dying dog who stole not only the show, but lots of hearts in the summer of 2017. I can tell you this—he was more than just a hound dog. Some say he was bigger than Elvis. *Ladies and gentlemen: Wili has left Las Vegas.* But he's not forgotten. Perhaps his name will never appear on the marquee lights in Glitter Gulch. But then again, I'd never bet against Wili—*especially* in Las Vegas.

Third Paw:

HOWLELUJAH!
HE IS RISEN! (INDEED)

Only connect, and the beast and the monk,
robbed of the isolation
that is life to either, will die.

E.M. Forster

THE DOG DAYS OF SUMMER

For you I know I'd even try to turn the tide.

Johnny Cash

Exactly fifty years after the Summer of Love, Wili staged his own alterna-dog demonstration of flower power. Donning his Hawaiian lei for every Howlelujah Tour event, Wili's themes—*Make Woof, Not War; One Bark, No Bite; More Treat, Less Tweet*—resonated within the hearts of all those who longed to break on through to the other side. On the other side of the fence, as well as the ocean, we may discover that common ground can be found and our foes can become our friends. We need not suffer through another season dominated by winters of discontent caused by splinters of disconnect, or storms of malcontent brought on by fronts of frigid isolation. It's easy to growl menacingly at what's next door if you can't see it, sniff it, or watch which way its tail wags. While more difficult to consider, alternative viewpoints make for a fuller picture of the way forward—a way that welcomes everyone to come with us. No dude, no dame, and no dog left behind. The object of the game is not to drive people apart and hope that those who see things differently will simply tuck their tails and run. Good riddance is not such a good thing in the grand scheme. Discord and disunion aren't automatic by-products of differences of opinion. If we listen long enough and contemplate deeply enough we may find that our own lives are enriched and renewed. Opposites can not only attract, but they can come together and become much more whole, not to mention holy. Our narrowly-defined certainties can finally give way to broadly imagined possibilities. Wili reminded us that we are all in this together, even if we belong to different breeds, profess divergent creeds, or have conflicting needs. In the words of Mother Teresa: "If we have no peace, perhaps it's because we have forgotten that we belong to each other."

In 1967, a younger generation questioned the road more traveled and whether the destination to which it led was really the direction they wanted to travel at all. In many ways they were wiser than their elders. They offered an alternative to conformist consumerism, self-righteous rigidity, and waging war on people who did things differently. Timothy Leary's prophetic plea to "turn on, tune in, and drop out" was heard, but not heeded—at least not as he meant it. Like most audiences listening to most preachers, the hearers adapted it to fit their own easier way *out* rather than the more challenging way *through*. Leary was hoping people might *turn on* by exploring the depths of their divine being, *tune in* by connecting more harmoniously with the world around them, and *drop out* in the sense of detachment from what didn't offer ultimate meaning or satisfying purpose. Some thought this mystical mantra was simply an excuse to smoke a lot of dope and have more sex. While getting laid and getting high may have kept people out of trouble and incited less violence, there were other, more productive, ways to display a kind of love and a kind of high that could create a more sustainable transformation. Some flower children chose the constructive alternatives of political activism, art, music, and meditation. In its time, the Howlelujah Tour offered a different way, one that might bring people together in a more modern summer of love. Wili's wish was to replace barking up wrong trees with planting right, and righteous seeds—seeds that could eventually provide shade for all. It's more trouble to come together and work together for a common purpose than it is to keep our distance and crate ourselves from the cares of the world. But the community we create by mutual caring ends up being far greater than the sum of its parts, and far more pleasing to the Creator of all. The way of love is the way of Christ. Catholic curmudgeon and prince of paradox, G.K. Chesterton, once observed that "my dog knows that I'm a man, and you will not find the meaning of that word written in any book as clearly as it's written in his soul." He also said of a religion that hasn't already gone to the dogs: "Christianity has not been tried and found wanting; it has been found difficult and not tried." The best things in life require our best efforts. Dogs, for example, are a lot of trouble, but Wili barks, and I agree, they are worth it. So is a faith that requires commitment, sacrifice, and even a bit of chaos, so that a dancing star might be born. If it's difficult, it might be more likely to be good and true—and definitely worth trying.

Whether it has been challenging or comforting, on the trail or off, Wili devoted his life to loving others and trying to make a difference. Wili's summer of love continued long after we arrived back home in Louisiana. The miracle mutt had done much good out on the trail, but he wasn't done. He continued to inspire good works in others and helped people imagine even more ways to help those in need. Our friend Saint Francis once said, "All the darkness in the world cannot extinguish the light of a single candle." Wili's little light was dog-sized, and it rose no more than two feet above the ground, but the light of that single candle continues to overcome the darkness. The Howlelujah Tour lasted just over two weeks. That's not a long time, but the good that was set in motion in those two weeks continued to resonate long after we'd returned home. I believe Wili helped people think more intentionally about being kind, being aware, and being available for others in their time of need. Such a time for our neighbors in Texas would arrive just a few weeks after our return when Hurricane Harvey stalled out and caused catastrophic flooding over several days. Not since Katrina had there been such widespread displacement and destruction.

Wili sat next to me on our very comfortable, dog-friendly and above sea-level couch as we watched the initial news reports showing the murky waters of Harvey rise and threaten so many. We were stunned and experiencing the same feeling of helplessness that we'd felt when Hurricane Katrina devastated New Orleans ten years prior. When the news camera focused on a face we recognized, we both sat up. A minister friend, her children, and her dog were being rescued and loaded onto a small fishing boat from the second story of their mostly submerged home. They were being taken to a large, makeshift shelter in the downtown convention center. My friend is a confident leader and you could see it in the calm assurance on her face, a kind of demeanor that exemplifies the words spoken by St. Julian, "all shall be well." Rabbi Edwin Friedman helped me understand that when the shit hits the fan, floodwaters rise, chaos ensues, and all hell breaks loose, that true leaders will maintain a non-anxious presence. Change will happen. Sometimes it's good. Sometimes it's shitty. But leaders can look at a situation, regardless of where it falls on the panic scale, not with blame and despair, but with hope and concern. My friend didn't curse the floodwaters; she instead blessed the boat and its captain and gave thanks for their ability to deliver friends and neighbors to safety.

Wili and I kept watching. I was so nervous for my hometown that I was in desperate need of a chew toy. I drank a beer instead. Wili seemed concerned too. He kept watch from on top of his special blanket that he always chose over every other surface. Wili's blanket was the one that had accompanied us on the tour. It had a kind of snow leopard pattern, and its softness had to rival that of the behind of newborn leopard—although I cannot, and will not, speak from experience. Putting a hand on a baby leopard's butt would likely result in the same fate as attempting to separate Wili's teeth from a filet mignon. Wili always chose to spread out on this particular blanket wherever we traveled, even if there was a hard surface underneath it. All of us, it seems, have a soft spot for soft spots. Blankets seem to be the superman capes of the forlorn, the swaddling cloth for anyone unsure about being born into a cold, glaring world, a warp and woof of comfort whenever we find ourselves uprooted and far from home. In the Peanuts cartoon, Linus' blanket becomes a kind of shroud of Turin for the small-fry faithful. It captures a comforting spiritual truth and feels like God's presence in our midst. Linus' blanket was a major character, and it had a life, personality, and a power all its own. The only time Linus let go of it was during the children's Christmas pageant when he quotes the most powerful religious words ever spoken: *Fear not*. These are the comforting, liberating, life-giving words that belong to the language of those closest to God—angels and dogs, to name just two. If you ever hear these words, you can be certain of two things—an angel is speaking to you and you are part of a story much bigger than yourself. In the Christmas story, Joseph, Mary, and the shepherds all hear these words. Knowing that God's spokesperson is telling you to not be afraid is perhaps as comforting as the most comfortable blanket in the world. And you can take that blanket to the bank.

In Peanuts, everybody wants a piece of the quilted cover-up— even Snoopy tries to steal the blanket for himself. I get it. Dogs love to hog the covers. They'll take any chance they get to retrieve your blanket and not give it back. Besides, as I recall, Snoopy's doghouse was sparsely furnished. And he also took most of his naps on the roof of his doghouse which is not nearly as comfort-able as a soft blanket on a cushy couch. But Snoopy eventually saved the day and redeemed himself. After Lucy buries the blanket, Charlie Brown's solution, like those of most folks who cannot empathize and often offers idle clichés, advises Linus to replace it with a dish towel. Linus asks Charlie if he would give a starving dog a rubber bone. Wili could answer that. Fortunately, Snoopy's digging skills are almost as developed as his smirk-ing skills. He digs up the blanket and returns it to the happy owner, which then returns the happy owner to his happy place. Snoopy's good deed makes his day and he feels like his existence is now justified. Such a purpose feels good—it even makes him want to do the happy dog dance. No one does the happy dog dance as well as Snoopy, although Wili comes close. Snoopy is on to something profound—that when we help others, we help ourselves. To do good is to feel good. Paraphrasing Descartes: *I help, therefore I am.* Linus sums up the superpowers of such sacred serapes: "Happiness is a warm blanket, Charlie Brown."

The news report showed thousands of people arriving at the cavernous shelter from their flooded homes, most of them with nothing but the wet clothes on their backs. The volunteers were doing the best they could, but it's hard to distribute what you don't have. Overwhelmed by the urgent needs of so many suddenly displaced folks, they ran out of blankets. I imagined my friend and her family, and so many others, arriving sopping wet, shivering, and cold. While a blanket may not be much, I knew that even a tiny piece of common cloth had the power to provide a small sense of protection, security, and comfort that things would be okay and happiness would eventually return. I looked at Wili and his eyes told me two things—1. You're not getting my blanket, and 2. Let's get to work Barking for Blankets.

I couldn't say no to Wili. I'm increasingly certain that whenever I feel like *someone* should do *something* about *that*—that someone is going to be me. So, I put the word out to everyone in Houston that I was looking for blankets. I had no money, but I felt certain we could raise enough to purchase at least a hundred blankets. A friend in Houston heard my plea. He was miraculously able to get to Costco (which was, miraculously open) and bought all the blankets they had, which happened to be exactly one hundred. Financial donations began to pour in. By 5:30 a.m. the next morning, a hundred blankets were paid for and delivered to the George R. Brown Convention Center. Linus would've been pleased. Snoopy, too. Wili sure was. I imagine a hundred people who'd suddenly found themselves stranded far away from a flooded home were pleased, as well. A blanket is not the sole solution to all our world's ills, but it was what I saw was needed at that time and in that place. And it's what Wili encouraged me to do without saying a word. When there's something you *can* do, do it. Don't worry about what you don't know and what you can't do. Act on what you do know and what you can do. We knew that they needed blankets. We knew our friend could buy them and deliver them. And we knew that good people would rally around to help us do a good deed. And indeed, they did not just one good deed, but an ever-flowing stream of many.

We had no idea that one gesture of comforting kindness would open up the floodgates of sacrificial service. I got a call the next day from the owner of a local construction company. He'd been in Louisiana during Katrina, but he'd been so preoccupied with his own challenges that he wasn't able to help others during that time. He said that he regretted that he missed the chance then and wanted to help. He didn't want to miss out on another opportunity to make a difference. He knew I had lots of connections in Houston. He trusted me to do the right thing and connect with the right people. He had access to large trucks and flatbed trailers and he had a budget he was willing to spend to help others. Within a matter of days, a church, a construction company, a community, and our friends across the country came together to provide $100,000 worth of relief supplies to those whose lives, homes, and livelihoods had been negatively affected by Harvey. And it all started with a blanket.

A key to helping others is to make sure you're clear on what is needed. There've been many disasters when people with good intentions collected or purchased items that ended up on the trash heap. We bought and brought water, non-perishable food, lots of household cleaning supplies, and thousands of gift cards so folks could buy exactly what they needed, which was a boost for the local economy when they needed it most. My good friend in Houston, Father Grace (yep, that's his name and that says it all), got someone to donate an entire warehouse that could serve as a distribution center. As an added bonus, several of the construction workers stayed up all night making jambalaya. In Louisiana, if there's one thing we are exceedingly good at it is feeding people well. We brought enough jambalaya to feed the entire state.

People appreciated and benefitted from all that we brought. Our Harvey Relief efforts were a tangible reminder that there will always be another chance to do the right thing and make a difference. Disasters happen. So does goodness. All that's needed is our desire to help and a willingness to start with one small gift—whether it's with a blanket or a dog bone. When you put the word out that you need help, others will rise up and join you. I cannot express how much joy it brought me to tell people that we'd brought jambalaya from New Orleans. Houston was there for New Orleans after Katrina. And now New Orleans was there for Houston after Harvey. If I could capture the light radiating from the faces that accepted a bowl of deliciousness, I could power the planet. Serendipitously, the warehouse that Father Grace had donated to us was right across from Gallery Furniture. Gallery Furniture is to furniture stores what the Vatican is to Catholicism. It's run by a goofy guy with a giant heart. No, not Pope Francis. He's got a good heart, but he's not particularly goofy. This guy's name is Jim McIngvale, A.K.A. Mattress Mack. Mattress Mack opened his furniture store to families who were displaced by Harvey so they could have a comfortable place to sleep—on the display beds in the show-room! He also cleared out his warehouse and began distributing cleaning supplies to anyone who showed up and asked. About 100,000 did. When I tracked him down he was directing cars in the parking lot like General Patton at the Battle of the Bulge.

"You can't park there—move it—NO! Hey YOU! Dammit, people! Shit! God bless!" At first, he wouldn't hear my question about feeding people who were in line for supplies. He kept running around and barking orders. But we kept following him and politely asking for his permission. When I addressed him as Mister Mattress, he stopped, put his hands on his hips and said, "Oh why the hell not? It's already f-in crazy out here. Let's add some more chaos!" I think all would agree after we fed them jambalaya that it was the best tasting chaos they'd ever had.

While I was spooning up our tasty Cajun culinary concoction, a young girl with physical disabilities stood watching nearby. Her mom, like so many others, was volunteering that day distributing cleaning supplies. The girl slowly made her way over to me and asked me if I needed her help. I told her, "Of course I do!" One always welcomes helpers. She stepped behind the serving table and stood beside me. She didn't have quite enough strength in her hands to scoop up the jambalaya, so I wrapped my hand around her smaller hand and we served the jambalaya together. While it meant that serving folks might take a little longer, it also meant that serving folks got better. Everyone was fed, not just food, but pure, heartfelt, innocent love. It made my summer, and it made it even more of a summer of love. I felt love in her hand as our hands worked together. I saw love in her face as she beamed with pride to be able to be of service. We serve, therefore we are. We are more human, Godly, and perhaps even more *Dogly* when we give of ourselves. I saw some tears in the eyes of many we served, and I'm certain it had nothing to do with the Louisiana hot sauce we'd brought with us. Helping, serving, dishing up whatever it is you have to share, and allowing others to help you share it—such opportunities make life worth living.

The city of Houston was devastated by Harvey, but my prayer is that we played a small part in lifting those who were most affected up from the mud and muck and helped them recover—one blanket, one sponge, one spoonful of rice and spice and sausage and chicken—at a time. But Wili was far from finished helping my former hometown shine. While his Barking for Blankets campaign had been a hit, his bark-ball team continued to hit it out of the park. While I won't say that he directly impacted the Houston Astros finally winning what he called the *Woof Series*, even overcoming the dreaded Sports Illustrated cover curse, I can say with certainty he impacted my ability to be there and cheer them on to victory.

I am painfully aware that many would argue that the Astros championship is tainted because of cheating allegations that were confirmed long after the trophy had been hoisted and my joy was complete. While I'm incredibly disappointed in my guys, I still believe that they are better players than cheaters, and that they were (and are) good enough to win it all using nothing but their own talent and determination. Not to excuse their stupidity, but in the end, we have all said, done (and banged) things for which we are deeply sorry. Even Wili occasionally pooped in my house, farted in my face, and stole a rib from my dinner plate. But despite the error of his wags, he's still my number one. Let the one who has never sinned, cast the first stone. And let the one who has never cheated, throw the first pitch. All others may go ahead and kiss my asterisk.

All I knew at the time was that having a perennial loser as your hometown team is not something I'd desire for any city. I'm looking at you, Cubs fans! Futility is not particularly fun, especially if it goes on for fifty years or more. After Hurricane Harvey, the city's team seemed to find its stride and started blowing through the opposition. The Astros channeled all their town's frustration into playing with a kind of fiery force that's usually reserved for a NASA spaceship re-entering the earth's atmosphere. Wili was with me every step of the way, hollering *Howlelujah* for every homerun and woofing like a mutt as the opponent's ball landed in an Astros mitt. Whenever I'd stand up and clap, Wili would rise up and wag. Whenever I'd eat a hotdog, Wili would try to eat my hot dog. Wili's favorite players were George Springer Spaniel, Alex Barkman, Carlos Corgie, and Justin Vetlander. He thought Orbit the mascot was out of this world. And don't get him started on Nolan Ryan—his fastball *or* his sausage.

Although Wili was an Astros fan because I was an Astros fan, he had many fans of his own—fans that followed him and supported him, locally and globally. One of them was a woman named Georgia. She was an avid St. Louis Cardinals fan. Cardinals fans are the best in baseball—knowledgeable, supportive, and friendly to the opposition. When it looked like the Astros might be going to the show, she emailed me and asked if I might want to go to the World Series. Does Wili love Dodger dogs? That is a resounding yes! She told me that a relative's friend's dog groomer's unicorn's Jedi's dragon's acquaintance who lived next door to the San Diego chicken, or something like that, had been able to secure World Series tickets for her back when the Cardinals were in it—which has been often. I said sure, giving such a far-fetched feat about the same odds as I gave the Astros to win it all—when you know too much about disappointment, it's hard to be optimistic. However, I did have a feeling about this team. Something special was happening with them—on *and* off the field. So, just in case, before the playoffs ever started, I played out the potential scenarios in my head and decided that *if* they made it all the way, they'd likely be playing the Dodgers in the World Series, which meant that games six and seven, assuming it went that long, would be in Los Angeles. So, I booked a random but centrally-located hotel in Los Angeles for those two nights. And I made sure it was refundable. After fifty years, I'd learned to have a healthy amount of doubt.

The Astros started winning and they kept winning. They defeated the Red Sox and the Yankees and went to the World Series. Games one through four were all anyone could hope for in a well-balanced slugfest between two great teams. Just before game five, a friend and parishioner emailed me. "Fr. Bill. You love the Astros. You've got to see a game in Houston. Game five is Sunday evening. I'm paying for your ticket, your airfare, your hotel, your beer, and your hotdogs." I'll be the first to admit that I didn't deserve such a kind gift. But I'll also say this—when you're involved in doing good things, even if your good dog motivates most of them, good things will happen. My friend,

Billy, made it possible for me to be in my hometown stadium for game five, one of the most exciting World Series games ever played. When Alex Bregman, a local hero who played for LSU and is so popular in Louisiana that kids dress up like him on Halloween, hit the walk-off winning single in the tenth inning giving the Astros a 13-12 win, the energy in the stadium was the most intense I've ever felt in one space in my life. Even though we knew it was far from over, there was a spirit present that was so powerful it felt like we could overcome any adversities this world might toss our way—disease, disaster, and hurricanes included.

Wili's wonderful supporter came through for us in Los Angeles. Why would I ever doubt Wili and anyone that loves him? The elusive mythical creature who was supposed to provide two tickets to the World Series turned out to be real. We met in the parking lot of Dodger Stadium before games six and seven. Dear Reader, at the risk of becoming the object of your hate after reading this, I need for you to know that I not only went to games five, six, and seven of the World Series. I also went for free. Thanks to Wili and by the grace and goodness of God.

I decided I'd wear my clerical collar with my Astros jersey to Dodger Stadium. I figured that it would not only remind me to pray throughout the game, but it might also get me a free beer and hopefully assure that my ass wouldn't get kicked by Dodger fans. My collar also garnered a few television interviews. But the most satisfying moment was when we entered the outfield gate into a sea of Dodger Blue. As we walked to our seats, a wave of hungry and thirsty fans who'd bellied up to the bar and who were anticipating their own hometown miracle started yelling "Boo!" when they saw orange invaders were entering their camp. But that booing suddenly shifted to gasps when they saw my clerical collar. And a cry went up that sounded less like a cheer and more like a plea. "That's not fair! They brought a PRIEST!" All's fair in love, life, and baseball—especially if you've known loss for far too long and if Wili the Miracle Dog happens to root for your team.

The Houston Astros, after Hurricane Harvey and after the Howlelujah Tour, finally won it all. But this amazing season didn't end even when the Astros won game seven or even when I got to high-five Kate Upton. Although I admit that it was brief, I will tell my granddogs that I once held hands with a supermodel. The hotel that I'd booked in Los Angeles weeks prior happened to be the one at which the Astros and their families were staying. I shared a beer with Jeff Bagwell in the lobby and an elevator with Jose Altuve. I got to say to catcher, Brian McCann, just before game seven: "You guys got this and we are pulling for you all the way." I doubt that word of encouragement was the determining factor in their ultimate victory, but McCann did tell me later that he remembered me saying those words to him. Because "it ain't over till it's over," the Astros victory party after the big win happened to be on the Penthouse level of that same hotel. In the parking lot of Dodger Stadium, as we made our long way back to the hotel, my friend, Michael happened to run into a friend from Houston who happened to be one of the owners of the team. Somehow we made the guest list. That's right! After game seven, in the Penthouse of our hotel in Los Angeles, the Astros players and their families, and the Astros owners and their families, and my three friends and their priest, partied like, well, World Series Champions.

My baseball idol, Craig Biggio, posed with me for a photograph, called me "Padre," and asked me about my parish. He may have been disappointed when he found out I wasn't Catholic, but that's okay. It's not like the Astros hadn't disappointed me many times before—yet, I still claimed them as my favorite. Relief pitcher, Chris Devinski, spotted me and said, "Hey Father, how 'bout having a Tequila shot with me." Apparently, tequila shots with priests after winning the World Series are a fairly uncommon occurrence. I was happy to make history one more time. All those years owning a bar had finally come in handy. Alex Bregman carried around the Championship Trophy like it was his newborn baby. Bregman and I hugged each other for a photo. Other than my photos with Wili, my photos with Biggio and Bregman after winning the World Series are the ones I will treasure the most for the rest of my life.

At the end of the night, Alex Bregman and I were among the last to leave the party. Just before we got on the elevator together his teammates teased him about partying with a priest, taunting him with, "Do you even go to church?" Bregman responded, "Of course I don't go to church. I'm Jewish. I go to Temple." I'm certain that's true.

There, at the end of the most amazing summer of my life, I was reminded one more time that we can have differences and still come together and celebrate. We can find common ground and share the common good. We can cheer for each other, support each other, and lift each other up. We can be Jewish or Christian, Astros or Dodgers, gay or straight, conservative or liberal, even dog people or cat people. It doesn't really matter what divides us. What matters is what unites us.

Ultimately, we are all on the same team.

DUPLICITOUS DOGMA

There are many ways to say I love you.

Mr. Rogers

Amos Muzyad Yaqoob Kairouz nearly got me killed when I was twelve years old. Amos, the son of Lebanese immigrants, had nine siblings and early on in his career as a struggling comedian in Detroit, made less money than a priest—or maybe even a priest's dog. Just before his first child was born, he did what any rational parent would do. He went to church to fervently pray. If there's any population that deserves our prayers, it's parents. It's a miracle that any child survives childhood and a greater miracle that any parent survives their child's adolescence. Down to his final seven bucks, Amos took out his wallet and put every last dollar he had in the offering plate. While it may seem counterintuitive to give sacrificially when we're broke, I've discovered over the years that he who *gives* the most *gets* the most out of the giving—as long as the

intent really is to *give* rather than to *get*. As he gave away all
that he had, he pleaded with Saint Thaddeus, the patron saint
of lost causes, dire straits, and sick people to help him get hired
for a position that might support his family. Soon thereafter, he
was booked for a gig that paid, not seven bucks, but seventy. He
immediately made a vow to his new best friend, Thaddeus, who
also goes by the stage name Jude the Apostle. "Hey Jude," he
said, before a band in England stole his prayer: "don't make it
bad. Please make it better." He promised Jude that someday he'd
build a shrine that would help heal sick children. Yaqoob was no
boob. He realized that if he was going to make it in show biz,
he might have to change his name— Muzyad the Magnificent
sounded like a circus side-show act and Kairouz the Comedian
wasn't likely to land a slot on Comedy Central. So, he changed
his stage and screen name to Danny Thomas, became a star,
founded the American Lebanese Syrian Associated Charities,
and eventually built St. Jude Children's Hospital in Memphis—
one of the greatest charitable institutions in America.

My first crush, other than the time my Sunday school teacher
described a naked Bathsheba, was Danny's daughter, the actress
Marlo Thomas. I used to watch her on television and imagined
"praying" with her. While crushes on Hollywood starlets have
occasionally gotten me in trouble, it wasn't my Marlo infatuation
that nearly led to my early demise. It was her dad's good deeds.
Adolescence morphed me into a kind of hormonally-driven
monster with self-assured, though seldom pure, intentions. But
the kind of holy terror I'd become was only slightly more terror

than holy, so most seventh-grade teachers merely prayed that I'd be assigned to someone else's classroom. Though my teachers would preface their phone calls to my parents by saying they found my hijinks somewhat entertaining, they would inevitably launch into a litany of potential penitence for sins that most seventh graders wouldn't even have considered, much less committed. Perhaps it was purely a personality flaw, but I appeared to be either possessed by Casper the Friendly Ghost—more goofy than spooky—or I was simply destined to embody the energy of a pit bull puppy receiving daily testosterone injections while subsisting solely on caffeinated cannabis nuggets. I'm pretty sure my seventh-grade math teacher, Mrs. Cox, once told me in front of the class that I put the *pube* in *pubescence*. And I may have responded that I also put the *noxious* in *obnoxious*. But I do remember clearly the time when Mrs. Cox deviated from her lesson plan to allow each student time to attempt to diagnose my disorder, or, as she put it: "what is *wrong* with him?!" I'm going to blame it on hormones, or a premature calling from God to help humankind take itself less seriously, but I ended up in the principal's office more often than other good Christian boys. This was the age of corporal punishment. I received swats so often in Junior High School that it was a minor miracle that I didn't become a masochist. Or should I say *more* of a masochist? After all, I did go into the ministry. And I'm fairly certain that the principal was a sadist, at least he was by the time he was finished with me. But as my mother once said of my decision to become a priest, "I suppose there are worse things." As bad as I was, I know there had to have been worse teenagers than me. I wasn't *all* bad.

I was a volunteer with my Junior High *Youth for Christ* organization—an extracurricular activity so uncool it came with eternal honors. One day I found myself going door-to-door in my middle-class neighborhood to raise funds for a worthwhile charity. The charity we chose was the St. Jude Children's Hospital. Most adolescents, while occasionally smelling like barnyard animals, have the superpower of consistently sensing the presence of bullshit before they step in it and being able to cut right through it to the truth. I could tell that St. Jude was the real deal. They provided quality medical care to children at no cost to their families, plus they engaged in cutting edge research that drastically improved the odds for kids with life-threatening illnesses. I'd never asked anyone for money before and I was stunned out of my shyness to see that most people were happy to be asked to donate to an organization that actually made a difference. Nobody shut the door in our faces and almost everyone we asked gave generously. One man gave five dollars which, calculated in Dairy Queen Dollars, would be at least three Beltbusters and three Dilly Bars. If the funds were rationed carefully, there could've even been Peanut Buster Parfaits in my future. Instead, I was so inspired by my neighbor's generosity that I put everything I had in my wallet into the St. Jude's bucket. That was the day I also came to know how dangerous it could be to do a good deed and that fundraising wasn't for the faint of heart.

Having spent most of the afternoon going door-to-door, our canisters becoming heavy with donations, my friends and

I rounded a corner and saw two men walking toward us. They stopped us and asked what charity we're collecting for. We proudly told them about St. Jude and then waited for them to put money in our canisters. They both reached into their pockets but instead of pulling out their wallets, one man pulled out a knife, and the other man, a gun. Then they said something that I'd never heard uttered in our Youth for Christ prayer meetings, although it did sound a bit like something you might hear at a traveling evangelist's tent revival. "We're not fucking around! Give us the money—NOW!" We quickly determined that we would not only *not* fuck around, but right then and there we would relinquish our perceived teenage invincibility and immediately revert to the accommodating actions of our childhood. We handed them the money. They told us to turn around and run without looking back or they'd blow our "fucking heads off." And for the first time since fourth grade, we did exactly what an adult told us to do. I was mostly mediocre in my short-lived track career running relays, but I'm reasonably certain that I broke the world record for the half-mile that day. We ran as fast as we could all the way to my friend's house. We told his dad what happened and he immediately called the police. The men were never caught, but I prayed that if they used any of our St. Jude donations to feast at the Dairy Queen, that they'd both choked on a peanut from a Peanut Buster Parfait. The experience left me shaken, and I felt a bit less confident in my identity as the indomitable showman. But mostly, I was happy to be alive. And I felt terrible for the kind people who'd so generously donated their hard-earned cash to help sick children. Later in life I'd come to understand that those who give blindly to certain unworthy charities may be just as unfortunate, and that it wouldn't be the first time somebody was robbed blind by those who lined their pockets under the guise of doing good. But I'd refuse to allow the actions of a few selfish stealers, the ones who think it's more blessed to take than to give, to deter me from soliciting supporters for worthy endeavors. And I wouldn't close my own heart, or wallet, to the opportunities to give cheerfully.

When Wili was diagnosed with cancer and it became necessary for him to receive treatment at a veterinary hospital, I never once debated whether or not I could afford it. When people ask me how much money I make, which doesn't happen often, I tell them that I do well—for a priest. That qualifying caveat sets me back a bit. But I recognize that despite my lagging behind both my childhood and adult friends on the income scale, I live in America and make a decent living. Therefore, in the grand scheme, and certainly compared to the rest of the world, I'm rich. I'm blessed beyond measure and I have everything I need. I mostly operate paycheck to paycheck. I live in a quaint, historic $265,000 home. It's small, yet big enough for my dogs who sometimes let me sleep with them. I drive a black Honda pickup truck that I'm quite fond of, I own about $400 worth of vintage Hawaiian shirts, and I have health insurance. I've been able to afford to turn my garage into a Tiki Bar and I'm able to stock my bar with all the ingredients needed to make a Mai Tai. I have two televisions, hot water, air conditioning, and heating. Sometimes

I go out to dinner at a nice restaurant. Living near New Orleans, it would be a sin *not* to. I've been known to travel to the other side of the planet, occasionally upgrade to business class, drink decent red wine, and sometimes splurge on a fine Cuban cigar. But I also try to give away about 20% of my income to charities I believe in, and I spend another 30% of income on my four dogs. I'm practically running a shelter out of my home. I don't regret spending one penny of that last 50%. It's the most fun my money has that isn't related to fried chicken, gravy, or Jell-O wrestling.

Besides, for Wili, I'd empty not only my wallet, but my checking account, savings account, and retirement fund. I'd give him my last dollar if I didn't think he would eat it. Trying to out-give Wili wouldn't be unlike trying to out-give God—it's impossible. How much is it worth to be created uniquely and unconditionally loved? What is the value of being the center of someone's universe? How do you calculate forgiveness, loyalty, closeness, affirmation, and dog saliva? Add in a tail that wags and a joyful being that stands and smiles every time you walk in the door, and we are talking seven or eight figures. And this doesn't include his entertaining juvenile antics, the ability to sit with perfect posture whenever the refrigerator door opens, his willingness to smother complete strangers with affection, and the rare talent of farting so lethally that any robber wouldn't dare threaten us. I'm thinking this transaction defies accountability and transcends appraisal. Here's a guy who would give you the fur off his back if you needed it. How do you spell p-r-i-c-e-l-e-s-s?

When Wili and I decided to set out on the Howlelujah Tour,

an important part of our efforts was to raise funds for animal friends in every city we visited. Some places where we held events even charged admission with the proceeds going to local shelters. Interestingly, the places that charged admission tended to have the largest crowds, sometimes sell-outs, and raised the most money for charity. There is a valuable lesson on value here. Perhaps the more that's asked of us, the more likely we are to appreciate and respond. If something is truly valuable to us, we'll be willing to pay the price, however steep. Generous people understand that true generosity creates joy, meaning, and purpose. Giving generates happiness at a rate proportionate to our willingness to give.

Henri Nouwen, one of the world's spiritual giants, understood the gift that is ours when we give, and the gift we give to others when we invite them to join us. After teaching at highly esteemed academic institutions, including Yale and Harvard, Nouwen moved on to work with people with intellectual disabilities and developmental challenges at the L'Arche Community in Canada whose motto is: "Changing the world, one heart at a time." Developing diverse communities, connecting with those who are different from us, providing hope, and being of service—these values motivated Nouwen to move from working with the brightest among us to helping to support those who struggled with intellectual challenges. Nouwen's values paralleled those of the kingdom of God. The Bible constantly reminds us of the great paradox of faith, that the more we give the more we have, that the last are first and the first are last, and that we find life by being willing to die. Nouwen wrote brilliantly about the privilege of asking others to give. One of his most powerful lectures was titled, *The Spirituality of Fundraising*. Nouwen had come to understand that providing others with an opportunity to participate sacrificially in the funding of something worthwhile wasn't an occasion for awkwardness, shyness, or embarrassment. It was a rare privilege and an opportunity to share something amazing and extraordinary, as well as give others the ability to access the joy that accompanies generosity. He understood how profoundly transformed we can be when we begin to relate to our resources as a pure gift, entrusted to us as good stewards. He insisted that fundraising from the point of view of the Gospel of Jesus Christ would always take the high road and the healthy perspective when he said, "I will take your money and invest it in this vision only if it's good for your spiritual journey, only if it's good for your spiritual health."

Wili and I believed in our cause—a cause that was good for our spiritual journey and our spiritual health, as well as for our canine companions. At each stop on the tour, we had a large dog-food canister that we placed on our meet-n-greet book table. We didn't insist that anyone donate to help animals, and Wili's kisses were given as freely as God's grace, with no strings attached or requirement for reciprocity. We also had a small dog biscuit jar in which we received gifts. We were surprised early on that several folks wanted to donate, not just to the local humane society, but also to help with Wili's medical care. At first I wasn't sure I wanted to accept such gifts. But because people insisted and truly wanted to help Wili—to prolong his life, his ability to do good and set an example—we began to designate the smaller jar for the Saint Nawiliwili Nelson Medical Care and Dog Treat Trust. At the end of our journey, Wili and I had given away far more than we had taken in. And that's exactly how we'd hoped it would be. We both believe that it's more blessed to give than to receive. We concurred with the Apostle Paul, known to Wili as the Apostle Paw, who wrote to the young Christians in Corinth: "You will be enriched in every way by your great generosity." We set out to *raise* money not to *make* money. Our spreadsheet totals at the end of the tour may not have pleased our accountant, but we believe it pleased our God. Wili and I were so pleased we could hardly contain our joy. We were enriched in every way. Giving to help others always instigated the happy dog dance.

One Saturday morning Wili made an appearance in Tulsa, Oklahoma at St. John's Church. The event had been added later in our schedule so there wasn't much time for them to promote it. Still, at that event, we had several folks drive for three hours from neighboring states just to see Wili. That day Wili raised $291 for the Animal Rescue Foundation of Tulsa (ARF!). For some, that may have seemed like an insignificant amount, but it wasn't insignificant for us. And I'll bet it wasn't insignificant for ARF, either. After the event Wili insisted we drive over to Oral Roberts University. You may recall that Oral Roberts was a popular television evangelist who promoted the intersection of faith and medicine. Lots of positive things happen at that intersection. I certainly believe in miracles and I've seen and known the power of prayer to heal. I also know that our own spirits and the supportive energy of those who love us combine to contribute to our well-being, recovery from illness, and overall physical health. However, that's where I get off the "Oral medication" train.

Although it's highly unlikely he had a Tiki Bar in his backyard, Mr. Roberts did enjoy a rather extravagant lifestyle. He wore Italian silk suits, diamond rings, and gold bracelets. He had vacation homes in Palm Springs and Beverly Hills and he owned three Mercedes Benz. I have no idea how much he spent on his dogs or if he even had dogs, but I do know that the owner of two dog tracks in Florida once gave him $1.3 million. In 1987, Roberts announced that if he didn't raise $8 million dollars, the Lord would "call him home." While this particular fundraising strategy (also known as extortion) did pay off for Mr. Roberts, I personally don't feel comfortable with its implementation. I do, however, derive a certain level of amusement imagining my own congregation's response to such a challenge. I can hear them now, shouting as they gleefully withhold their pledges. *Good luck in the afterlife! Tell Saint Peter I said hello! We'll miss you—NOT! Can I have your dog? Party at the Tiki Bar in ten!* Roberts raised tens of millions of dollars to fund his City of Faith Medical and Research Center. It opened in 1981 and it closed in 1989. I'd say that it was likely a poor choice for sustainable charitable giving.

You may also recall that earlier in his "ministry," Mr. Roberts claimed to see a 900-foot Jesus who assured him that he was on the right track and that he would indeed raise all the funds needed to build the City of Faith. Apparently, for every 100 feet of Jesus seen, the Medical Center managed to stay open for one year. It's a damn shame he didn't see a mile-high Jesus or a Satellite Jesus or even an Interstellar Jesus—the hospital might still be open. Then again, Jesus probably knows when to hold 'em and when to fold 'em better than your average television evangelist—and those who support them. By the time Wili and I got to the university, the "World's Largest Praying Hands" that had originally stood in front of the City of Faith had been moved to the campus entrance. This thirty ton bronze sculpture is certainly, uh, large. Personally I prefer the much smaller Praying Hands of the artist Durer's simple, eleven by seven inch pen-and-ink drawing displayed in a museum in Vienna. It's not that Vienna necessarily has anything on Tulsa, which is quite a lovely town; it's just that the truly good and beautiful often come to us in the small and subtle ways and not so much the overpowering and in-your-face ways. While Wili didn't seem particularly thrilled to get his photo taken in front of the Giant Hands, especially after it became clear they weren't going to scratch his butt, he did tell me, once we got back into the car, that he'd seen a vision. He claimed that a 900-foot Airedale had appeared to him and told him that unless he raised $10,000 on the Howlelujah Tour, the Airedale would pull his tail. Or it might have been his leg. It didn't matter. Wili raised more than $14,000 on the tour for his animal friends. Those aren't Oral Roberts kind of numbers but, in the end, they may have accomplished more lasting benefits for the "least of these," especially for our faithful friends of the four-footed variety.

Even though the tour eventually ended, Wili wouldn't be

done raising funds and doing good. Wili and I love living in Louisiana, a state that has given the world some extraordinary gifts—Louis Armstrong, Mahalia Jackson, and Dr. John, to name three. But, it has also given the world its unfair share of television evangelists: Jimmy Swaggart and Jesse Duplantis, to name two. Jimmy Swaggart gets special dispensation because his cousins are the musicians Jerry Lee Lewis and Mickey Gilley. Although Swaggart didn't write the songs "Whole Lotta Shakin' Goin' On" (Lewis) or "A Headache Tomorrow or a Heartache Tonight" (Gilley), he managed to illustrate them with his two confirmed dalliances with prostitutes. After the first one came the well-publicized: "I have sinned" teary-eyed televised confession, but after the second he told his congregation: "The Lord told me it's flat none of your business!" I'm not sure which response was more pleasing to the Lord, but any television evangelist who can inspire a country-western song will be tolerated, if not celebrated, in my household.

Jesse Duplantis, however, is likely my favorite television evangelist. I find his sermonic hijinks more entertaining than the Geico Airedale and perhaps right up there with the Geico gecko. He tells funny stories, engages his audience, and has very white teeth, well-coiffed hair, a Cajun accent, and his books have clever titles such as: *Jambalaya for the Soul*, *What in Hell Do You Want*, and *One More Night with the Frogs*. He once received an honorary doctorate from Oral Roberts University, which would be much like Nawiliwili Nelson receiving an honorary doctorate from the Academy of Wiener Eaters—takes

one to know one. Brother Duplantis is one of the rare minis-
ters who does as *well* as he claims to do *good*. He has a net
worth of $40 million and lives in a home valued at $3 million,
tax-free. He's owned three private jets since 2006, which he
claims he's been "burning up for our Lord." It's good work if
you can get it. I'm not certain our Lord is particularly pleased
with the pollution implications for our planet, but I'm not blam-
ing any televangelist for his lifestyle as long as his supporters
are willing to fund it. Now, taxpayers may be another story.

Even after Wili and I had returned home and Wili had
passed on to his Eternal Home, he wasn't done making a positive difference. About the time Wili was lifted by angels to the
heavenly realm, Brother Duplantis must have wanted to follow
him upward, as he asked his followers to contribute $54 million
for a new private jet. He had his eyes on a Dassault Falcon 7X,
which I understand is slightly faster and more luxurious than
my Honda truck. After a bit of an uproar over his request, the
evangelist clarified that he wasn't asking his viewers to *pay* for
the jet, just to *pray* for it. Wasting God's time in prayer when
there are so many critical needs in the world might be a greater
sin than simply asking for donations. When we got a tail wind
of what was happening in the name of God, I got inspired by
Wili and decided that in the name of Dog *and* God, we would
together initiate what we would call the 54 Campaign. We
would ask Wili's followers, much fewer in number than those
of a TV preacher, to contribute not $54 million, but $54 dollars
to the worthwhile charity of their choice. We encouraged folks

to fund service, relief, health, environmental, animal, or human rights organizations that were benefitting our planet and those who lived upon her. Neither Wili nor I believe that one should criticize what someone else is doing unless one is able to offer a constructive alternative. It's easy to look down on the efforts of a televangelist to raise funds for a private jet and assert that we are against it. But what's better and more pleasing to God is to engage in something positive and constructive—funding and fundraising for what you're *for* and not simply declare what you oppose. It's important to identify initiatives that align with God's loving purposes and priorities for the world, and once we have done so, to invite others to participate. There's a particular heresy that's popular right now among some evangelical Christians and one that's promoted by Brother Duplantis—the "Prosperity Gospel." It basically goes like this: God's primary concern is to make me, I mean you, I mean me, rich. Wili and I find such dogma duplicitous and self-serving, and we believe in something quite different—the Generosity Gospel. It basically goes like this: God's primary concern is to make you and me more generous and loving. A big heart is more important to God than a big bank account. With both, you can make an even bigger difference. But if we *believe* only to *receive*, I'd say our faith is stuck in early adolescence. Spiritually mature people (such as Wili) know that it's more about what we give than what we get.

Our initial goal of the 54 Campaign was to get ten people to donate $54 dollars each, thereby sending a simple and subtle message that there are positive and sustainable charitable alternatives that are improving lives. Apparently, there were many others who shared our vision. We blew past that goal in a couple of hours. Some super generous folks gave $540 to a variety of organizations. While Wili hadn't outraised any television evangelists, within a matter of days he raised more than $20,000 that would help fund real mission and outreach to real people (and animals) in real need. It brought such joy to receive the notification letters from so many well-deserving organizations stating that "$54 dollars had been donated in honor of Nawiliwili Nelson." Even now, when I read through even a partial list, I break out in a smile and shout "Howlelujah! And thank you Jesus—for Wili and for those who love like him." Wili's campaign benefitted all sorts of good works, including but not limited to:

St. Jude Children's Hospital, The Salvation Army, The American Red Cross, Episcopal Relief and Development, Fairhaven Children's Home, Christian Health Center, Greater Fortress Baptist Church Day Camp, Refugee Ministries, Honduras Children, Northshore Humane Society, Promised Land Dachshund Sanctuary, The Hub, City of Refuge, Louisiana Boxer Rescue, Kindness for Everybody, St. Vincent's House, Pennies for Bread, Meals on Wheels, Operation Kindness, ASPCA New Orleans, Dolls for All, Everyone for Gun Safety, Molokai Humane Society, Long Way Home Rescue, Canadian Primates World Relief, Animal Care League Medical Fund, Animal Rescue of New Orleans, 4-Legged Friends, Bishop's Mission Appeal, Flood Relief, Cat Rescue, ECHO Foundation, World Vision, Coonhound Rescue, Church World Service,

Humane Society of Utah, Palm Springs Animal Shelter, Open Gate Homeless Youth, W.I.N.N. Academy, Doberman Rescue, Patriot Paws, America's Vet Dogs, Second Harvest Food Bank, Together Rising, HART Homeless Animal Rescue Teams, Cast Your Nets, Texas Great Pyrenees Rescue, Luke's House, Haiti Projects, Florida Humane Society, Disabled American Veterans, Juvenile Diabetes Fund, Venezuela Medical Care, Tangipahoa Humane Society, Sheltering Arms, Love for the Least, Haiti Neo-Natal Clinic, Magnolia Humane, St. James Storehouse, Paws and Stripes, New Orleans Musicians Clinic, Boys and Girls Club Indianapolis, Dream Dachshund Rescue, Catholic Charities, Puerto Rico Relief, Almost Home Dog Rescue, Fort Davis Humane Society, Lifeline Animal Project, New York Bully Crew, Abundant Harvest, Lumberjack Animal Rescue, Doctors Without Borders, Bridge House, Rock City Rescue, Clear Creek Abbey, Second Hand Pets, Dog Rescue Austin, Allen Animal Shelter, One Dog at a Time, Austin Humane Society, Friends Closet Homeless Shelter, Humane Society International, Friends for Life Animal Rescue, Zeus Rescues, Central Oklahoma Humane Society, Feeding Center, Crossroads NOLA, Illinois Raptor Center, NAMI, Flying Fur Rescue, Houston Women's Center, Hope for Paws, Austin Eldercare Summer Fan Drive, Donate Life, Christian House Sitters of Kenya, Paws in the City, Feeding America, North Texas Food Bank, Hungry Dog Rescue, Paws in Peril, Sweet Pups Sanctuary, Noah's Animal House, International Rescue Committee, St. Tammany Serving Animals Together,

Wounded Warrior Project, Sugarloaf Mountain Ranch, Pets for the Homeless, Houston Doberman Rescue, World Central Kitchen, Christ Church Garden Fund, Bread for the World, Innocence Project New Orleans, Humane Society of Corsicana, Free to Live No-Kill Animal Sanctuary, Safe Haven Animal Rescue, Louie's Legacy, Houston Food Bank, PBS, Christ Church Summer Enrichment Program for At-Risk Children...

...and that's when I stopped taking notes and went back to my day job! God bless you, Wili, for inspiring so much good in the world. And thank you, Brother Duplantis, for being the inspiration to motivate so many to help.

Thank God there are still people in the world who *get* the gospel and who *give* accordingly. They, like Wili, continue to inspire. The first person to donate to Wili's Fund, and who'll most likely be the last, knowing her ongoing commitment to compassion, is our friend Sallie. Sallie lives in Dallas. Her theology and understanding of God's call on her life are, shall we say, a bit different than that of your average television preacher. She exemplifies the deeply spiritual observation of Rabbi Harold Kushner who said, "You don't become happy by pursuing happiness. You become happy by living a life that means something." Sallie holds a PhD in Neurobiology and Behavioral Science specializing in PTSD. She's worked in refugee camps in Ethiopia, Tanzania, Sudan, Somalia, and Rwanda. Recently she started commuting to Reynosa, a Mexican town on the border with Texas. She works with nuns to help refugee families who've been victims of unimaginable cruelties. She's there because she's not willing to close her eyes, her heart, or her wallet to help mothers who walk two hundred miles with their babies because they have no other choice and they have no other options. While it's likely the Holy Spirit who empowers Sallie to make a difference, it certainly didn't hurt that she grew up around lots of animals: dogs, cats, rabbits, ducks, turtles, and horses. Her Golden Retriever, Hogan Bear (Hogie), a breed which I consider to be the Spiritual Gurus of dogs, was her version of my Wili. He lived for thirteen years. Sallie will tell you that Hogie made both the good and bad times of her life a lot more bearable. Over the years, she has taken in Kandace Ann, Mama Dog, Nugget, Belle, Teddy (Miss Barks-a-lot), and two cats, Beau and Tillie. The newest family member, Slate the Phantom Feral Cat, came to live with her after her longtime friend, Shelly died from cancer.

Sallie's life has not been a bed of roses or even a cushy dog bed. Her only child, JD, is the love of her life. When JD was ten, Sallie began taking him with her on her many trips around the world and JD began to share Sallie's love of helping communities in need and giving back to the world. JD was a brilliant student. He graduated from the University of Texas with a triple major in economics, political science, and Spanish. He immediately took a volunteer position with UNICEF to teach English in Paraguay and he eventually earned an MBA with honors from the esteemed Wharton School of Business in Pennsylvania. Every spring break and summer, JD would volunteer somewhere in the world. He had internships with the World Health Organization and the World Food Program. His plan was to create a more equal and sustainable world feeding program. He was working on completing an International Law degree at SMU and had already been accepted into the London School of Economics when tragedy struck.

JD suffered a seizure after contracting a viral infection. He was transported to the hospital and placed in ICU. JD's seizure resulted in him falling and hitting his head. Because the resident in ICU was focusing on too many things at once he ordered a blood thinner be given to JD. By the time they discovered their error in administering blood thinner, JD suffered a catastrophic brain bleed and lapsed into a coma. It wasn't until the next day that they contacted his mother. JD had several lengthy brain surgeries to try and repair the damage. He was in the ICU for twenty-two days and Sallie was told three times that he wouldn't make it through the night—even being given last rites. But JD hung in there. Although he was paralyzed on his right side, he worked with therapy dogs, and was eventually able to walk. But cognitively, he'll remain a neuro-atypical ten-year-old. There've been seizures, defibrillators, medication trials, trainers, and Neuro Feedback sessions. He has dyscalculia and is dyslexic. The laid-back kid with a servant's heart became controlled by fear and anger. Things are a bit more stable now and he lives with a caretaker in a home near Sallie, but his days are spent building Legos, playing video games, and watching comedies. I really don't know how Sallie is able to cope. One person who has greatly helped her and JD and is the greatest and most real television evangelist in the history of the world is Mr. Fred Rogers.

Mr. Rogers was an important influence in JD's young life.

It was Mr. Rogers who helped Sallie explain the deaths of both Chuck the Cat and his beloved nanny, Bertha. Years prior to JD's experience in the hospital, Sallie was flying home from a board meeting for Feeding America in Chicago and seated across the aisle was none other than Mr. Rogers. Between sobs, Sallie shared with him how important he'd been to their lives. Even though he'd just announced his retirement, Fred Rogers said that he'd write JD a letter and proceeded to do so right then and there. Sallie framed it and hung it in a place of honor where JD would be able to see it. Three months after his devastating stroke, JD was able to come home from the hospital. He'd not spoken more than a few words, but when he saw the letter from Mr. Rogers, he said clear as a bell, "He likes me just the way I am." Sallie said it was a stunning and significant moment in his tragically altered life because there was a glimpse of hope. She believes, even now, that Mr. Rogers is watching over JD.

I met Sallie briefly on the island of Kauai when she and her friend Rachel came to visit my church. It was a wonderful faith community, and Sallie remembers the service being lively with guitars, ukuleles, and brief glimpses of a black dog named Wili who emerged from the Priest's office just in time to chow down on some Lau Lau—Hawaiian pork wrapped in Taro leaf—one of Wili's favorite Hawaiian dishes. Three months later they were in the bookstore at St. Michael and All Angels Church in Dallas when they spotted my book, *The Gospel According to Sam*. So thanks to my dog, Sam, and his gospel, she started following my social media. When she saw that the Howlelujah

Tour was taking us to Dallas, she put it on her calendar. I didn't know Sallie's story at the time. It would be months later that I'd fully recognize how much she loved Wili and the extent of her extraordinary generosity and kindness. But I do remember her being there. Being there is perhaps the most important memory we'll have of all those who love us. It's what they do—they show up. Sallie not only showed up, but she also helped out by taking Wili for a walk. They slowly made their way around the grounds and stopped for a few minutes to rest. It was very hot outside. Sallie sat on the curb and Wili leaned in and put his paw on her hand. She says it was a healing moment for her. For her, she says, Wili is very much the Mr. Rogers of the canine world. She told Wili to remind me that she'd included some cash for us to stop at Dairy Queen on our trip so he could have some soft serve ice cream. Wili would never forget such a thing. One of my favorite photos from the Howlelujah Tour is Wili enjoying a DQ soft serve cone on the way home. Sallie recently said to me, "Our physical time together was short, but Wili will always have a place in my heart. Thinking of Wili always makes me smile. You are his person and that makes you special because he thought so."

According to a favorite Mr. Rogers song: "There are many ways to say I love you…Singing, cleaning, drawing, being understanding." Wili would add *caring, giving, loving, and licking*. There are also many ways to share God's love with the world: putting a paw on someone's hand, putting a hand on someone's shoulder, writing a check to St. Jude Children's Hospital, sharing a soft serve ice cream with a dog.

God's love never stops giving.
And neither should we.

APRIL FOOLS

Beware by whom you are called sane.

Walter Inglis Anderson

Easter should always fall on April 1st. One should not need graduate degrees in Astrophysics and Systematic Theology to be able to calculate when the first Sunday will occur after the ecclesiastical full moon following the vernal equinox. Add in a parade of moving parts—the Jewish Passover, colorful bonnets, dyed eggs, and silly rabbits, and it makes me want to go directly to brunch.

It makes much more sense to reserve April 1st for such an Easter parade of perceived foolishness. It's more of a feast fit for a fool. Considering the contextual chaos and liturgical levity of rocks that roll and basket-bearing bunnies perhaps the only appropriate celebration would be a Disco Mass—*Sunday Morning Fever*! It could begin with an Easter acclamation common in parts of Africa. "Alleluia! Christ is Risen! Ha! Ha! Ha! Ha!"

There could be heavenly disco balls like a constellation of mirrored orbs hanging from the apse just above the altar, illuminating the nave with a million dancing points of reflected light.

The chosen processional hymn could be "Stayin' Alive" by the Bee Gees, and would include the seasonally appropriate lyrics: "Stayin' alive! Stayin' alive! Ha! Ha! Ha! Ha!" Just imagine how enthusiastically the congregation would sing "How Deep Is Your Love!" They could sway to and fro while singing, "I believe in you. You're my savior when I fall." They could groove to a rousing chorus of "we're living in a world of fools." Can I get an A-M-E-N? Or at least a Y-M-C-A?

The Choral Anthem might feature Gloria Gaynor's "I Will Survive." The altos and sopranos could form a madrigal group and call themselves *Women at the Tomb*. I can hear Mary Magdalene utter the words, "At first I was afraid. I was petrified. Kept thinking I could never live without you by my side."

Who needs Handel or his Hallelujah Chorus when you have disco! The foolishness of April Fool's Day and the exuberance of disco may express the spirit and sentiment of the day better than any previous pairing. When I discovered that Easter 2018 would fall on April Fool's Day, the first such occurrence since 1956, I playfully posted such a plan on social media. I got dozens of messages asking me what time the Disco Service was. Knowing that folks think we might actually *do* such a thing makes something as far-fetched as resurrection so much more believable. For this day is all about believing the unbelievable.

Just before The Great Easter Disco of 2018, Wili celebrated

seventeen months of staying alive—much longer than the three months he'd been given. But Wili the Miracle Boy had finally begun to slow down. His breathing had become more labored, his appetite a bit diminished, his struggles more manifest. Even though the week before Easter is my busiest of the year, with more services than a priest can say mass over, I decided that Wili and I should take one more road trip together. Given those extenuating circumstances, it seemed a foolish thing to do, but thank God foolishness has never stopped either one of us before. I'm not sure it has ever stopped God, either—the One who keeps taking chances on the likes of us. I didn't know how long I had with Wili and wanted no regrets when the end came.

I knew we didn't have time to head west toward the wide-open skies and glittered gulches of Nevada like we did on the Howlelujah Tour. But I recalled that I'd taken my chances at the Blackjack table in Biloxi, Mississippi almost as often as I had in Las Vegas, and knew Wili could easily make the ninety-minute journey east. I'd also heard that just beyond Biloxi was a cool little coastal town called Ocean Springs. I'd always been too busy doubling down on tens and splitting aces to venture the few miles further down the road. How often we are so close to transformation, but the allure of an entertaining "get spiritual quick" religion keeps us from getting up from the table and venturing outside for some fresh air and toward a more authentic and sustaining spirituality. But this time I was going all-in with Wili—and only with Wili. I found a dog-friendly hotel online that was called The Roost. Any place frequented by chickens or roosters in need of a good perch, or a nice nap, seemed just right for Wili and me. Back on the island of Kauai, where Wili was born and raised, roosters roamed free and were among his best friends. I also remembered Walter Anderson, an artist from Ocean Springs, who'd derived most of his inspiration from the natural world. I didn't know much about him and certainly didn't realize when Wili and I headed that direction that Anderson had once written: "dogs, cats, and birds are holes in heaven through which man may pass." I knew at least one dog that was my personal opening to the God above *and* my ace in the hole. All bets were off when Wili was around. There was no more heavenly experience than hanging out with him.

I really don't know why we chose to go to Ocean Springs during Holy Week, but deep down, I knew why *we* were chosen to go *there*. Like all of the most profound things in life, there's no rational proof I can offer as evidence. I only know that springs have naturally been sites of healing in every spiritual tradition from the Ganges and Jordan Rivers to the Pool of Siloam. The Native Americans considered the springs where Ocean Springs was founded to have restorative powers, as did the European settlers who came after them. The springs may not be able to bubble all the way to the surface these days, but they are still there and available if you're willing to dig a little deeper. The same can be said of the Living Water of the Spirit—it refreshes and renews, but it's often found deep beneath the surface. Ocean Springs is also the place where the French explorer, Pierre Le Moyne d'Iberville first came ashore. D'Iberville apparently was, at one time, destined for the priesthood, but instead chose a life of adventure. It's possible that I was, at one time, destined for adventure, but instead chose a life of the priesthood. Then again, maybe the two will someday meet. Given its history, there's an element of adventuring toward a new world in Ocean Springs. Perhaps Wili's transition was supposed to play out there—in a place that would sustain his own transformation toward a different state, while also providing healing for his dad who would mourn his loss and begin anew without him. Maybe it was there that I'd come to recognize that I could survive—that as long as I knew how to love as he did, I'd be able to stay alive.

Most of Holy Week, the week leading up to Easter, is just plain hard. The beginning of Palm Sunday and the joyous wagging of palms quickly gives way to the solemnity of Jesus carrying a cross. The donkey who leads the celebratory procession goes home early and with him all hope for levity and lightheartedness. The Passion is not for sissies. The Last Supper, the Agony in the Garden, the abandonment of the disciples, the betrayal of best friends, the carrying of the cross, the crucifixion—these aren't trite, lightweight clichés—they are tough truths that, like all meaningful transformation, hurt like hell. Pain and sacrifice aren't for the faint of heart, or skin, or soul for that matter.

Our first night in Ocean Springs, Wili struggled to climb the stairs to our room. But, proving he had more wagging to do, he decided to visit the cute girl in the room next to ours. She'd arrived at her room at the exact same time we did, so while I was wrestling with our suitcases, Wili decided to pay her a visit. He was sick, but he wasn't dead yet! He always assumed that any open door should be walked through—a spiritual lesson his dad is still learning. I raced in, grabbed the errant beast, and apologized profusely. She didn't seem to mind his presence, but I quickly removed the criminal from the scene of his crime and escorted him back into our cell. "He sure is cute," she told me on our way out. *So are you,* I thought, but I quickly remembered that we were here on official God/Dog business. The Holy Spirit must grow weary of opening doors for me through my dog, only to have me race in and right back out before the magic has a chance to happen. Most of us close doors faster than God can open them.

Our first night felt very much like Good Friday was drawing near. Wili was restless and couldn't get comfortable enough to sleep. He needed to go out repeatedly, so I'd roust myself from my roost, bleary and weary, throw on some clothes, grab his leash, and slowly lead him down the stairs to a patch of grass. He would wander around, sniff, squat, and pant, but with nothing to show for his efforts. He would look at me like I was a fool for thinking that a trip outside was going to cure him of his ills. I thought about my father, just before he died from cancer, telling me that if he could just go to the bathroom he knew he would feel like a new man. Maybe that's what Wili thought. Too bad we can't just poop out all disease, evil, and ill-will. Maybe most of our troubles are exacerbated because we hold them all in. Maybe my dad—and Wili—were on to something. Letting go of our shit, literally and metaphorically, might solve a load of problems. But as Wili led me up and down the stairs all night, all

I could think at the time was that this trip was a very bad idea.

But the next morning, Wili seemed to be a new dog. He was suddenly filled with life and curiosity (which are the same). He reminded me again, as we began to explore this creative small town that it's not so much about getting to the destination we desire, as it is about recognizing who walks with us. It's about taking our time to pay attention along the way, about being keenly aware that revelation, and maybe even resurrection, are just ahead of our eyes or nose, and that if we seek the lively among the living, we'll always be surprised by joy. The lessons on Easter Day often include a prophetic description of a sumptuous and scrumptious Easter feast with rich food and well-aged wine. While Wili and I didn't stumble upon an all-you-can-eat buffet or a wine-tasting, he did lead me to a place called The Greenhouse, just up the road from our hotel. It was a real greenhouse with real plants, real flowers, and real people. They served only three things: coffee, biscuits, and beer, which aren't only representative of all the major food groups, but also could be the title of my autobiography. And they welcomed dogs—which tells you everything you need to know about a place. Wili was even given his own cheese biscuit. Their biscuit selection was simple, but included both a sweet and a savory option—which is the kind of balance an authentic spirituality must maintain. A musician was there picking up biscuits for his co-workers. When I introduced Wili to him (using his Christian name, of course), he patted Wili on the head, paused for a second and said, "I've heard of you! Aren't you the dog who's supposed to be dead?" That was our first clue we were hot on the Easter trail. Our second was when the owner told me that any future plans for the place would definitely include community, music, food, and magic. Sounds like church—especially on Easter Day.

After Wili had devoured his biscuit, what was left of mine, and at least one bite of everyone else's in the establishment, he led me down the street toward the cobblestone labyrinth at St. John's Episcopal Church. He wasn't stumped by the circular meditation maze; he simply sauntered right across it. Perhaps there's a spiritual lesson there, too. Maybe we aren't as trapped as we think we are and that the path is only as limiting as our perception dictates. While stopping to wander, wonder, ponder, and pray is always a good thing, at some point we need to move on. Wili kept on walking. We walked past the Moon Pie Cottage, which made us crave the southern version of Holy Communion—a Royal Crown Cola and a Moon Pie. As we approached the funeral home, Wili stopped, lifted his back leg, and peed. I swear I saw him smile and I'm almost certain I heard him quote I Corinthians 15: "Oh death, where is thy sting? Oh grave, where is thy victory? Thanks be to God which giveth us the victory through our Lord Jesus Christ." Because I knew how much he liked the British poets, and that Wili longed to play catch with elegant phrases, I tossed out a passage from one of John Donne's Holy Sonnets: "Death, be not proud, though some have called thee mighty and dreadful, for thou art not so." Wili always loved Elizabethan English and theological banter. Although my canine can be rusty, so it's possible that he simply said, "Bow wow wow yippie yo yippie yay!" And I responded, "Where my dogs at? Bark with me now!" Either way, death ain't nothin' for this hound dog.

Wili took a right on Washington Avenue and appeared to be heading straight toward the beach. You can take the poi dog out of Hawaii, but you can't make him go inland. He stopped right in front of the Walter Anderson Art Museum. Neither of us could believe that on the large exterior sign was a giant cat face that read, *CATS! Thou who carriest the sun: The Feline in Walter Anderson's Art*. Wili looked at me grinning like a Cheshire as if to suggest that he was in on this Easter April Fool's joke that celebrated cats on this last leg of his Divine Dog's journey. Walter Anderson, we would come to discover, loved all living things. He believed that the natural world communicated all the truth that any seeker of spiritual wisdom might hope to find, and that his goal was to become one with creation, realizing that "humanity has a relation to nature as close as a dog or a cat." But his cat-centric-ness could not be denied. In his book, *Robinson: The Pleasant History of an Unusual Cat*, Anderson describes a cat's head as being the sun, its tail as a serpent, and its four feet as flowers. His loyalty to the feline is undeniable. His daughter, Leif, believed as a child that her father would've paid her more attention if she were a cat.

Wili waited patiently for me as I wandered inside the museum to see what sort of holy inspiration I might find. I wasn't disappointed. While there was no stone impeding access to the entrance, an inner sanctum conveying the brilliance and splendor of life was to be found. After Walter died, his wife, Sissy, decided to see what was in the "Little Room" that Walter used as an art studio. Built as an addition to their small cottage in the woods, the Little Room was off limits to everyone but Walter and his cats. Sissy had never been allowed to enter, so after Walter's death, she cut the padlock, opened the door, and stepped inside. We often encounter such secret rooms of resurrection and revelation whenever we seek to know God. Such sacred places may be entered only by those who are persistent enough to look for them, curious enough to open the door, and courageous enough to walk right on through to the other side. What we find inside may change us from the inside out, emerging transformed into someone completely different.

Before entering the Little Room, now residing inside the museum, you pass under a powerful quote written just above the door: *Beware by whom you are called sane.* I paused and pondered that statement. And I prayed. I prayed that I was foolish enough to be labeled as such by a world gone mad—a world too engaged in what Walter called, "the sordid thing most people call reality." Although debated, some suggest that Walter may have struggled with mental illness. He was definitely quirky, offbeat, and unusual, but he was gifted beyond measure. He knew what his calling was, and when he finally embraced that calling and all the idiosyncratic behaviors that seem to accompany creative genius, he found some peace. He contributed to the beauty of the creative world by first noticing and appreciating God's creation, and then moved to interpreting and recreating it. His words ring true today when our entire planet seems hell-bent on destroying itself. The more "normal" we behave in a world marked by materialism, destruction, violence, dishonesty, hatred, exclusion, injustice, anxiety, and dysfunction, the less spiritually sane we are. Unless we choose to be a bit "different" we'll march right on through the hell that we helped create. Perhaps it's a *narrow* way to which God calls us—a road less traveled, a canvas less painted, and a life rarely lived, but it's most certainly a kinder world. God calls us to co-create a new world in which reality is tested, trusted animals speak to us, and we are completely transformed—simply by paying attention.

When Sissy, and her sister Pat, first entered the Little Room, it must've felt somewhat like Adam and Eve when they first opened their eyes to the Garden of Eden. Pat said, "It's the creation at sunrise!" It's that and so much more. It's been called "The Sistine Chapel of the South," and I think I prefer it to Rome's version. It's an explosion of vibrant color radiating the warmth of God's love. Walter painted a flight of Sandhill cranes at dawn. He painted soaring birds, blooming flowers, colorful moths, and brilliant butterflies. He painted a watchful fawn, a curious raccoon, a playful rabbit, a crowing rooster, and of course—a wise and knowing cat strutting its stuff. He painted a rainbow, an earth mother with antlers, and on the ceiling, a zinnia unfolding into a mandala. It was Psalm 104 brought to life. It was God breathing life, feeding, and caring for all creation—especially God's animals. The room was more radiant than a disco ball on Easter day. I felt like I'd entered the holiest of holies, the empty tomb, and Wili's favorite doghouse all at once. In this tiny room, only about ten square feet, Walter had created a masterpiece according to the vision and gifts given to him by God. Just imagine if each of us beautified the small spaces entrusted to us using the gifts given to us by God. The whole world would be museum quality. Actually, the world would revert to being what God originally envisioned and created.

Not far from the Little Room, sat a sacred relic that was striking in size and profound in its spiritual message—the large skull of a giant sea turtle. Like all of us, Walter had important lessons to learn. He struggled between being good and being less than good. He wasn't always as appreciative of the natural world and all of God's creatures as he eventually became. As a young man, he was once out in a fishing boat in the Gulf of Mexico with his brothers when they stopped at Horn Island, an Island which, later in life would reveal life's deepest mysteries to him. While on the island they saw a giant sea turtle that had come onshore to lay her eggs. Without provocation Walter killed this innocent creature. He's immediately filled with remorse for committing this evil deed. Years later, after he married, he fell at Sissy's feet and confessed his sin. He began to weep openly and begged her forgiveness for taking the life of an innocent animal. He kept the skull and displayed it prominently because he wanted to honor the memory of this majestic sea sojourner. Perhaps he also needed to remind himself of ´ ˉ ˉ ˉ of penitence and the possibility of change. Ne′ for each of us, even when we do stupid thin reasons. Easter comes each year to remind u⁺ finished with us and that it's never too late t

Next to the museum is another of Walter's masterpieces. To say that it was originally underappreciated would be overly generous to the people of Ocean Springs, who taunted him so much, that he eventually left his masterpiece unfinished. In 1950, Walter agreed to paint murals on the walls of the community center as a gift to the community. The art he lovingly created celebrates d'Iberville's landing and the flora and fauna of the Mississippi Gulf Coast. The mural is a whimsical collection of Native Americans making music with flute and drum, a French priest carrying a cross and leading French soldiers onshore, happy-go-lucky gators, and bears climbing trees. Anderson was sometimes ridiculed and avoided in his hometown. He was an eccentric character who wore a floppy hat, paint-spattered shirts, and rode a rickety bicycle barefooted. On occasion, even his children would walk to the other side of the street when they saw him coming. His family loved him and thought him to be extraordinary, but sometimes guilt by association can be overpowering, even to those with the best of intentions.

Many of the townspeople were embarrassed that Anderson's artwork was featured so prominently in their town. A mayoral candidate ran on the sole platform of whitewashing his murals. Thank God the candidate lost. The murals are now valued at well over $30 million and have been called by more recent city leaders the most valuable cultural asset in the region. When I gazed upon the beauty of the walls of the community center, a ___ce of derision and criticism from a majority of local citizens, ___t of the words of Mother Teresa when she said, "Give the world your best and it may never be enough. Give your best anyway. For in the end, it's between you and God." Inspired by creation, he kept creating, offering his unique gift to the Creator, and making beauty in the midst of a world accustomed to, if not committed to, all things ugly and offensive. Whatever master-piece each of us might offer to the world, it's always possible someone will come behind us and try to whitewash it. According to Walter, Wili, and the wisest among us—create it anyway.

I would later meet and become friends with Walter's grand-daughter, Moira, a yoga teacher in Ocean Springs. Since she's a private person I'll not mention that she's the greatest hula hoop artist I've ever known. What she's able to convey with a hoop is not unlike what the hula dancers in Hawaii convey with their graceful movements. She gladly shares her joy in all creation—a gift she believes was cultivated by her grand-parents. Her mother was a professional ballerina and modern dancer and her dad was an artist in New Orleans. She remem-bers going to the community center as a young girl to watch her mother dance. In her eyes, the community center was the biggest, most beautiful room in the world—despite what those naysayers might have said. Moira is especially grateful to her grandmother for helping her see the natural world in a way that loves and appreciates creation. She fondly recalls that whenever her grandmother would go outside and look up into a tree, she'd clap her hands and call to songbirds, "I hear you, you beauty!" Her grandmother took delight in God's creation, whether it was a bird or a blossom—a gift that she imparted to Moira.

Walter was just as interested in things that were dead as he was in things that were alive. He was fascinated by the mystery of what comes next—curious about where the life went once it left our bodies. When his mother died, he stayed at her bedside for hours and sketched her over and over again, hoping to see and sense clues about the next chapter of our existence. Once, Walter saw a bird fly from inside a dead, hollowed-out tree. That became a powerful symbol for him that from the tree's exhausted life something new and liberated had emerged. Perhaps it sounds foolish, but I believe in such symbols—in Death and Resurrection, in Good Friday and Easter, in Earth and in Heaven.

Walter wrote as beautifully as he painted. After spending so much time on Horn Island, he began to see the pelican as the creature that somehow represented the whole of creation. The medieval Christians also revered the pelican, thinking that, perhaps, the pelican would wound her own breast and provide her own blood for her brood if no other food source was available. Pelicans came to symbolize the Passion and the Holy Eucharist—the Body and Blood of Christ, sacrificially given. For Walter, the Pelican represented all the best qualities of both man and bird—song, understanding, gentleness, mystery, and potential. As I read his description of the pelican, I recognized that Wili was my pelican—my all in all. He represented Christ and his unconditional love, the farthest reaches of forgiveness, and the nurturing sustenance of pure affection. He also represented the best of creation—its playfulness, uniqueness, tenderness, and mystery.

Even though I spent a longer time in the museum than I'd

anticipated, Wili was still outside waiting for me when I returned. He always was. As I approached, he stood up and wagged his tail—another sign of the Spirit's presence. He'd made a new friend while I'd been inside. Apparently a cat had come calling. And Wili had answered. Perhaps the cat had been sent by Walter or maybe by God, or possibly by both. It was slow going, but Wili and I eventually made it all the way to the beach. The beach in Mississippi is not quite Hawaii-caliber, but Wili didn't seem to mind. On that special day, the sound of the waves, the scent of the salt air, and sense of the ocean breeze all took us back home to Kauai where we'd begun this journey of faith and faithfulness, so many years before. The best part of the day, as usual, was right at the end. Just like on the tour, we ended up in our little room with the door shut and locked, sharing snacks and enjoying each other's company. It was just the two of us there together, creating some magic, even if Wili snored right through it. Call me a fool, but that moment was pure art—an Easter miracle. It was a moment as beautiful and life-giving as the dawn of creation.

HE WAITS FOR ME

This is the waiting time; I wait for you.
Willie Nelson

Wili was fast when he was young. He could have gone for the gold in the Dog Olympics, setting records with his fleet-footed paws. Wili could sprint faster than a sailfish could swim away from a ravenous shark. In an instant he'd be off—out of site quicker than a coconut's meteoric plunge over Waimea Falls. Wili was to hard surfaces what spinner dolphins were to the sea—an acrobatic, head-turning, gravity-defying expression of joy. And don't get me started on his Michael Thomas-like start-and-stop-NFL-wide-receiver maneuvers. He could leave an All-Pro cornerback in the red Kauai dust. One of the reasons I selected the house I did on Kauai was because it had nice grass. Who am I kidding? The only reason I bought the house was so Wili could have a yard. Part of the backyard was long and narrow like a dog run. The side yard opened up into a wider, roomier space that felt more like a dog wrestling ring. Whether he ran the straight line or the circle, chose drag racing or Formula Woof, he blinded with his blazing speed. Whirlwind Wili was so swift I'd frequently invite guests into the side yard to watch him run circles around them. They were so impressed they would often shout, "Hey Bartender Bill, how fast can you mix me a greyhound?" I'm reasonably sure that the Abita Brewing Company named their Turbo Dog Beer after my favorite speedster. He was known island wide and even across New Orleans as the "lap-dog," as in, my dog can lap your dog.

He slowed down quite a bit when he got older. Being sick didn't help. Although he was wrestling stuffed gators until the end—his walking pace only slightly exceeded that of a high church snail. He would often have to stop and sprawl out on the grass to catch his breath. But, I'm not one to throw bones. My stamina was not what it used to be, either. I'd sometimes get winded after drinking a beer. Of course, it might have been smarter not to try to lift kegs directly to my lips. Wili had always been the hare to my tortoise. Now he was nothin' but my hairy tortoise. But our relationship didn't depend on his ability to chase anything. My chasing days were numbered as well, yet he still loved me. After walking only a short distance from home, Wili would put on the brakes and crumple into a gangly sprawl of sweaty, panting fur on the nearest patch of grass. I never grew impatient with him. In fact his periodic breathers were good reminders for me to stop and breathe—something I'd forgotten to do with increasing regularity. I never minded

waiting for Wili. It gave me great joy just to be there for him
and with him. Whenever he'd stop he'd look up at me, directly
in the eye, as if seeking permission, if not support and understanding. I always reassured him with my eyes and my voice
that he could take all the time in the world—however much he
needed. It brings a smile to my face to recall all those times Wili
waited for me, some of which may have felt like an eternity to
him. And now that the end was drawing near, I waited however
long he needed me to wait. I would've waited forever for Wili.

While his physical prowess diminished over the years,
his relational capacities only increased. While his walks grew
shorter and slower, his love grew larger and greater. When
there were finally four of us—Wili, Lili, Sinbad, and I—the
dogs no longer had free range status in the house. In case an
unannounced guest came a knockin,' I didn't want every surface
in my home to be covered in dog hair. I'm hairy enough. But
don't feel sorry for the banished beasts—they had the entire back
third of the house, including the kitchen, dining room, hang-out
room, couch, big screen television, and most importantly—the
refrigerator. There were also six dog beds back there, just in
case anyone got lucky and had a canine sleep-over. But I still
let the three of them sleep in my bedroom every night. We had
a ritual—a kind of preparatory sacramental process for slum-
ber. They would watch the clock (and my movements) and the
minute I reached to remove the dog gate and said, "Let's go to
bed," the race was on. Lili would dart like a freight train through
the living room, a blur crossing the length of the house, and go

flying into my bed. I think she realized how lucky I was to have any girl in my bed—and thought of herself as the "passion pit" bull. Even slow Sinbad would leap and bound like a bunny at full speed all the way onto his special *paws*turepedic mattress on the bedroom floor. But not Wili. Wili always waited for me. He'd walk slowly to the living room and then stop. He'd move no further. He'd turn around and look for me, and only when he saw that I'd caught up with him, would he walk alongside me to the bedroom. If I was ever delayed, Wili would still stay put and wait. He'd never go on without me. Wili always waited.

There is a powerful story that Jesus told about how God waits for each of us, regardless of how long we take. While some call it the parable of the prodigal son, I think of it as the parable of the waiting father. There was once a young pup of a son who didn't realize how good he had it at home with his dad. He felt like obedience school was beneath him, and that he could handle commands all on his own. He desperately wanted to experience life on the other side of the fence and venture into unknown backyards—places previously considered off-limits. He just knew the grass was greener, the walks more interesting, the scents more scintillating, and the company more exciting. So he handed his collar, his tags, and his leash to his dad and asked him for his share of the inheritance. His dad, who was as accommodating and loving as he was wise, gave in and gave him what he had coming, even though he knew the story might not end well. The boy bolted out the door and never looked back. He set off for an alluring far-away land and once he got there, he found himself surrounded by exotic species and erotic enticements. He picked his own bones and barked his own commands. The people, who didn't care about him and only wanted his money, obeyed and played along for a while. He drank his beer by the barrel and spared no expense having a good time. His life, without boundaries, curfews, expectations or commitments, felt like a never-ending play date with a pack of poodles—that is, until his resources ran out. He got so hungry he found himself craving the treats the pigs were eating. He thought about home. He imagined his father's walkers and groomers and sitters and feeders—all of them paid, fed, and content. He decided that he would return home, plead his case, and ask his dad to put him to work as a pooper-scooper, or perhaps a trainer. Maybe his story could help those who are too stupid to realize how blessed they were. He wanted no special treatment, he just wanted to be treated as a hired hand and a penitent pup that'd learned his lesson the hard and expensive way.

What the son didn't know was that his father had been waiting for him at the front door from the moment he'd left. All day, every day, his dad would look out into the distance to see if his beloved son might be returning home. The loving father, like my loving dog, and like our loving God, didn't keep track of the time. Every moment he was separated from the object of his affection was an eternity to him. He waited. And he waited. And he waited. Until one day, while the son was still far off, just a tiny speck in the distance, not even within sniffing distance, the father saw him. He flung open the front door and he ran to greet his son as fast and as joyfully as Wili would run to greet me, no matter how long I'd been gone. The son had rehearsed his speech. He would sit, stay, and obey from here on out. He would be happy with table scraps for the rest of his days. He would never growl, bite, or hog the couch. The son fell to his knees to beg forgiveness, but the father lifted him up and took him in his arms, just as he'd done when he was little. His father embraced him and kissed him. He brought out the special studded collar of unconditional love and called on his servants to barbecue an entire cow. To be reunited with the one who loves us, who waits for us, and who calls us home always calls for a feast. The hymn "Softly and Tenderly Jesus is Calling" still gets me misty-eyed when I hear it calling me back to where I know I belong. "See on the portals he's waiting and watching, watching for you and for me. Come home. Ye who are weary come home." The prophet concurs that our God always waits. "Therefore the Lord waits to be gracious to you; therefore, he will rise up to show mercy to you...blessed are all those who wait for him." Waiting is what Wili did best. It spoke of a love that never gives up and that's longing for our return—a love by which God calls each of us home.

Even at the end, Wili waited for me. After our road trip to Ocean Springs and my Easter Disco sermon, I had to leave him again to lead a pilgrimage to the sacred island of Molokai. When I told Wili where I was going, he told me that he would stay alive and be waiting for me when I returned, but only *if* I'd bring him back some delicious kalua pig (that's smoked pork for those of you who don't know a luau from a loo). I knew that our time was limited, and Wili was on my heart every moment of every day that I was in Hawaii. But I also realized that, like Wili's home island of Kauai, Molokai always had a spiritually transformative message to impart. From the beginning, Molokai's animals welcomed me with open paws. I might have never gone back with groups of pilgrims had it not been for one special dog. Years prior, when I first wandered into the Kalele Bookstore and Divine Expressions, a dog named RC greeted me. He was so named because of his resemblance to Nipper, the RCA Victrola dog of international fame. He was quite the handsome fellow. His mom, Teri Waros, was the owner of the shop and committed to her small island community. When she lost her job years ago, back when the last resort on the island closed, rather than seek to make a living somewhere else, she decided to make a life right there where her heart was. Her dogs RC and Honey Girl would often spend their days in her shop greeting customers and making them feel right at home. I've been friends with Teri and her dogs from the moment I met them. I couldn't lead my special pilgrimage without her help and support.

Every morning at dawn, Teri would walk along the Kalaupapa Lookout with her dogs to watch the sun rise and give thanks for all the blessings of life. Above some of the tallest sea cliffs in the world, the lookout offers a glorious site, even if its power wasn't reinforced by looking down at the Peninsula where Father Damien gave his life in service to others. It is a gratifying and edifying way that Teri chose to begin each day. One morning, after Teri had been confined to her home for a few days during an illness and really needed to get out of the house, she, RC and Honey Girl went for their usual walk. RC was not a young pup anymore, so he'd become a bit unsteady on his feet and would sometimes get disoriented. That day, RC got a little too close to the cliff's edge and pulled Teri off balance. She lost her footing, slipped off the trail, and tumbled 150 feet. Careening off of vegetation and rocks, she was finally able to grab ahold of the very last tree root before reaching the sheer 2,500 foot drop into the sea and its rocky shore. Teri was severely injured, but she held on for dear life. Honey Girl immediately made her way down the steep embankment, found Teri, and stayed by her side. Even though Teri would be there for almost eight hours, Honey Girl sat next to her the entire time. In the meantime, RC had walked back to the parking lot and waited by her car. Waiting there, where he could be seen, turned out to be a very good move.

Teri's friend, PF, a renowned photographer of presidents and rock gods, was on his way to Kauai for a photo shoot, but he first wanted to check in on Teri to see if she was feeling better. He stopped by her house, but seeing she wasn't there he assumed she and the dogs had gone to the Lookout. As he pulled up next to Teri's car, he saw RC patiently waiting all by himself. PF knew something was wrong. His dog, Ehu Girl, was with him. And as soon as he was able to get the leash on her, she started pulling him to the edge of the trail. When she came to the spot where Terri had fallen, she sat down and wouldn't budge. She stayed there and waited. And waited. PF got the message. Serendipitously, and perhaps miraculously, the retired fire chief was driving into the parking lot to show a visiting friend the Lookout. Once the chief heard that Teri was missing, he drove back up the hill to get a better cell signal and called the local EMT. It took hours for two firemen to repel down the cliff, load Teri in a basket, pull her up to the top, and get her medevacked to Honolulu. Only then did Honey Girl make her way back up to the trail to join RC. How do you spell love? W-A-I-T. How do you spell miracle? D-O-G. True love waits. A truly loving miracle dog waits even longer.

Wili was alive and waiting for me when I returned from Molokai. The very next day I'd promised to visit the Angola Prison with my good friend who's also the Chief Public Defender for our parish. He wanted me to learn about a community-based release program that was making justice reform a reality in Louisiana (speaking of miracles). People from across the political spectrum, Republicans and Democrats, who want to make lasting change that would benefit their communities, had come together to create this purposeful initiative—one that gives those released from prison tools to aid in their re-entry, empowering them to become more productive members of society. Seeing such a positive unifying undertaking gave me hope that people can come together for a good cause, joining hands, minds, and hearts to work together, much like they did on the Howlelujah Tour. These are the political initiatives that will start to create change and that are worth the wait.

So, Wili waited once again. Then I had to give my undivided attention to preparing a sermon for the celebration of the 300th Anniversary of New Orleans that would be held on the following

Sunday, May 6, 2018. Featuring music from Louisiana legends like Jimmie Davis, it was called *Spiritual Roots: A Tricentennial Celebration in Song.* We sang the state song—a song I sang to Wili when we lived in Hawaii: "You Are My Sunshine." My sermon was titled, *God's Gumbo.* Having just returned from Molokai, our group had managed to entice our Hawaiian chef, Kay, to come visit us in Louisiana by promising her that if she came, one of our pilgrims would make his world-famous gumbo. There is no greater gift a Louisianan can give a visitor than a delicious bowl of homemade gumbo. While researching in preparation for my sermon, I went straight to the goddess of gumbo, New Orleans chef, Leah Chase. She revealed the secrets to good gumbo—1. *You've got to go all in with your heart, soul, and mind.* If you aren't wholly dedicated, you will be entirely disappointed. 2. *You cannot be in a hurry.* You've got to be willing to work, watch, and wait as the magic happens—being mindful, aware, present, and willing to stir slowly and consistently. 3. *You start with the hot stuff.* In this case, Leah would start with hot sausage grease. If it's not spicy then it's not special. Leah's Holy Trinity sounded like an approach to a feast that would be pleasing to God. Hearing her describe the process of beginning a gumbo was like hearing of someone being born again. It starts simple. It takes time. But the result is nothing short of miraculous. Making roux, it turned out, is a lot like making faith. If you're overzealous, you will burn it. If you are impatient and unwilling to hang in there for the long haul, you will undercook it and end up with a kind of lumpy gruel or what Leah called "gummy goo." If you want your gumbo fast, cheap, and easy, the result would be bland, tasteless and unappetizing. As with gumbo, so it is with God. As with cooking, so it is with faith. As Leah said, "You can't do anything well if you're in a hurry." Wili would agree. He would certainly wait for a good gumbo. Of course, he would likely also wait for a bad gumbo. But in his new home, there's no such thing.

Wili waited until I returned from Molokai after leading a pilgrimage in the footsteps of a saint. Wili waited until I returned from the notorious and currently-being-redeemed Angola prison with hope that when good people come together and work together, things can change for the better. Wili waited until I'd prepared and preached my sermon for the 300th Anniversary of New Orleans, not just once, but four times on Sunday. I finally got home from church about 7:30 that night and at long last exhaled. Wili could always tell when my work was done for the day. I'd plop myself down on the couch and Wili would plop himself right on top of me. It was the best moment of every day.

Later that night, the pups and I observed our usual pre-so-matic ceremony—removal of the dog gate, two dogs racing to the bedroom, one dog waiting. Wili, as always, waited for me. But that night, he was restless. He kept standing up, pacing, and panting. I gently picked him up and put him in my bed to see if that would calm him. He stayed put for a short time, but then jumped out again. I got down on the floor and lay down alongside him. I surrounded him with pillows and began to stroke his fur and reassure him. I told him he meant everything to me—everything in the whole wide world. He looked at me appreciatively, but I could tell he was very uncomfortable. His demeanor had an urgency like there was somewhere he needed to be—and soon. He finally indicated that he needed to go outside, which on occasion he had to do during the night—but not often. Wili always communicated well with me. He would consistently convey what he wanted or needed. Sometimes I felt like we communicated telepathically. Or maybe the Holy Spirit served as our facilitator. I opened the back door and let him go outside. I waited for him to return. And I waited. And I waited. Finally, I went to look for him and found him hiding in the farthest corner of the backyard, as far as he could go. He had burrowed under some shrubs as if he was trying to return to the earth. It's what dogs do when they are ready to die. It's an instinct that I don't really understand. Perhaps when they are weakened, frail, and ill, they'll hide to protect themselves. Or maybe they go as far off as they can to spare their humans the pain of seeing them die. It was against all my instincts, but I knew what he was telling me. Still, I wanted to be sure. I led him back to my room and got back on the floor with him. He continued to get up, pace, and pant and look me right in the eye, telling me it was time. I could barely see through my tears. I could barely breathe through my sobs. I could barely think through my sorrow. But I knew what the loving thing would be to do. As painful as it was for me, I didn't want him to be in pain. I tried to give him some pain medication, but he wouldn't take it, even if wrapped in the most delicious morsel. I'd always known that if Wili ever turned up his nose at the tastiest treat that meant his time had come.

I would've waited longer but I didn't want my boy to suffer.

It was almost 4:00 a.m. and neither of us had slept a wink. I led him out the front door for the last time, picked him up, and put him in the back seat. We drove to the 24-hour veterinary clinic where he had first been diagnosed with cancer, where he'd had surgery to remove his tumor and lymph nodes, and where he was given chemotherapy. Eighteen months had passed since then—they said he'd only live for three. I was so grateful that he'd outlived the odds. Our instinct as humans is to prolong life—to put off death as long as possible. So even after Wili and I arrived at the clinic, I asked the doctor on duty repeatedly for reassurance. "Is this the right time?" "Are we doing the right thing?" "How can I know for sure?" There aren't many things of which we can be certain. But two things I knew to be true: Wili loved me and Wili would always wait for me. My inclination would always be to wait for him, too. But Wili's time had come. The decision had been made. There was a special room where we waited. It reminded me of the rooms in funeral homes where people would spend time with their loved ones. It reminded me of all those times I'd been with families as they said goodbye—and all the times I've had to say goodbye. The room was softly lit and comfortable. The veterinarian told me to take as much time as I needed with Wili and that she'd come back and administer the injection when I was ready. Of course, the time I needed with Wili was eternal. Anything less than forever wouldn't be nearly enough.

Wili sprawled out on the floor with me right next to him.

I remembered the extraordinary journey we had shared. I told him that he was the most special critter in the world—a one-in-a-million dog—and that there would never be another like him. I'm pretty sure I heard him say, *you're not bad for a human. Shorten your sermons and all is forgiven.* I told him how much I loved him. He told me how much he loved barbecue. I cried. He yawned. I prayed. He farted. I sobbed. He sighed. It all seemed so beautiful and just right. I wanted desperately to hold onto that moment forever. But time disappoints. Even in this most solemn moment, Wili made me smile. When the vet came back in the room, he stood up and wagged his tail. Of course he did. She told me that he could get on the couch with me—like he didn't already know that. Was there ever a couch that Wili considered off-limits? I'd already heard that heaven had just ordered another dozen couches in anticipation of his arrival, all of them sleeper sofas. She said that she'd first administer a drug that would totally relax him and make him sleepy. I'd taken that drug before—it was called Sprawling Wili. Those moments when he would lie down on top of me and sprawl across me were the moments that I felt closest to God. Or was that Dog? Or did one exist for the sole purpose of communicating with the other?

I picked him up and put him on the couch next to me with his head in my lap. The vet asked me if I was ready. I'd never be ready. I held him close. I squeezed him tightly. "I love you buddy," I said over and over again. As she was leaving the room I said to her, "He's still warm." Maybe that was a silly thing to say. None of us knows what to say in a moment like that.

There are no words that make any real sense. But it was true. And it is still true. I feel his warmth even now, and so do many others. The warmth of Wili's love is still felt in the world.

I waited with him a long time. I felt like the sun had set. But the sun was actually just starting to rise. Day was breaking just outside. My favorite photo of Wili is the one where he's lying in the grass and wearing his cowboy hat. Wili in his cowboy hat and wearing a lei became the prayerful icon of our Last Howlelujah Tour. That was the image I had of him there at the end—my cowboy riding off into the sunset. I kept hearing a George Strait song in my head: "And my heart is sinking like the setting sun...Oh, the last goodbye's the hardest one to say. This is where the cowboy rides away."

As it turned out, Wili had left what he called a *Last Wili and Testament.* True to form, it was short and sweet: *Help animals. Love people. Work together. Make a difference. Pass out treats to all.* He added at the end: *don't give away any dog beds. You will need them. I'm sending you two special ones.*

Dammit, Wili.

I'm still sad when I think about him. I know that someday my own time will come. And that I will pass on to the Great Beyond. I don't know exactly what eternity will be like, but of one thing I'm absolutely certain—on the other side someone I love will be waiting for me.

WAYLON AND WILI
(AND THE BOY)

Nothing catches Jesus by surprise.
Waylon Jennings

Wili was gone. But he wasn't done. Maybe that whole "Howlelujah! He is Risen!" acclamation is just believers actually barking up the right tree. Although Wili had left the building, there continued to be sightings.

A few months before Wili died, I received a text from my friend Ranaella, a good-hearted veterinarian who rescues animals on Kauai. She'd discovered a young dog that had been abused and spent his entire life chained to a tree. It bites to be chained to any tree. But to be surrounded by all that beauty and be chained to the point of not being able to see it, sniff it, or mark it, would bite big time. Chains, of whatever variety, that bind us—addictions, anxiety, fear, greed, prejudice—tend to do that. They keep us from seeing the big picture and from finding true freedom in that place to which God calls us. This dog not only looked a lot like Wili, he was a Catahoula, the state dog of Louisiana. Catahoulas have kept some good human company over the years including Jim Bowie (thanks for the knife), Teddy Roosevelt (thanks for the parks), and Louisiana Governor "Uncle" Earl Long (thanks for the stories). While Long was best-known for cavorting with the famous stripper, Blaze Starr, whom he met at the Sho-Bar on Bourbon Street, I doubt Earl would've traded his Catahoula for all the strippers in the world. There is still a famous festival held every year in Winnfield, Louisiana called "Uncle Earl's Hog Dog Trials," a competition to see which dog can best bay a hog. While the Kauai critter was likely part mutt, he was mostly the blue leopard version of a Catahoula—one brown eye and one blue eye. The Native Americans would say, given such vision, that he was able to perceive both heaven and earth, keeping an eye on both at the same time. So maybe he could see things that most of us would miss, even while chained to a tree. That sounds a lot like Wili. It also sounds like good spirituality—a way of seeing that keeps looking straight ahead *and* above, and understanding that if we focus on only one, that we miss the big picture, the dimension that's divine. Before my friend could comfort the Catahoula, the Catahoula ran up to comfort her. While the "nice gentlemen" who kept him chained may have hoped he'd help hunt hogs, this pup was definitely more lover than fighter. The only bay he would've been good at was sunbaying at Anini Bay just down the road, or maybe corralling by howling at the Hanelei Moon. Ranaella claimed that he whispered in her ear that he was my dog, and he had a Cajun accent! If he did, I'm certain Wili had somehow woofed those words in his mouth. She texted me and asked if she could get him to Louisiana, would I adopt him? I showed Wili the photo of the "'Catahoula hula" dog, and he told me, with a Cajun accent, *Ca C'est Bon* (that's good), *Laissez les bon temps rouler* (let the good times roll), and *Ouaf Ouaf* (Woof Woof). He also requested, yet again, that the beast bring him back some kalua pig. You can take the dog out of Hawaii, but you can't make him become a pescatarian.

I told Ranaella that not only would I take him; I already knew what I'd name him. He would be called Waylon Jennings. He looked like Waylon Jennings in the same way that Wili looked like Willie Nelson. Plus, I always wanted to tell people that I was going on the road again with Waylon and Wili. In keeping with my psychiatric diagnosis of excessive canine nomenclature disorder, I couldn't have it be just a simple first and last name of an outlaw country singer. On Kauai, I lived near the Wailua River, which emptied into Wailua Bay. Wili and I would frequently walk there in the early morning and watch the sun rise over the bay. Wailua means "two waters" in Hawaiian, which made contextual sense given Waylon and Willie's tendency to let their lyrical abilities flow into each other. Plus, they each had a fondness for watering holes. So he would be christened Waylon Wailua Jennings. But that still seemed too short and sweet and without New Orleans representation. This new dog dude also looked a little bit like Ferdinand Joseph LaMothe—if Ferdinand had facial hair. Ferdinand a.k.a. Jelly Roll Morton, was one of the early jazz pioneers. He claims to have invented jazz, and most music historians have a hard time disputing it. Ferdinand was born in the Faubourg Marigny, which is still the best neighborhood in New Orleans to go for good music. But Ferdinand would be found most evenings playing in brothels where he got the nickname of Jelly Roll. It was the name of a dish that was only served in brothels (hint: it wasn't a pastry). But, Jelly Roll spent all of his time in those brothels playing jazz because they were the only places that offered paid gigs. Jelly Roll Morton composed tunes titled: "Pacific Rag" and "Pontchartrain"—two bodies of water associated with my former and present homes. Perhaps it's a stretch, but I liked the way it sounded when you put it all together. And since I was the one doing the baptizing, I could name this child whatever I pleased. He would henceforth be known as Waylon Wailua Jelly Roll Jennings. It rolls off the tongue like an outlaw country song.

Not long thereafter, Ranaella, with a small army of women as backup, returned to the tree where Waylon was chained to try to give him a new *leash* on life and set him free to tour with Wili in Louisiana. Apparently, the upstanding citizens who were holding Mr. Jennings captive had their graduate degrees in chemistry. In addition to the occasional pork processing at their canine-certified plant, they were also running a meth lab on their property and didn't want any do-gooders threatening their operation. So, they threatened to kill the animal ethics interlopers—with a weed eater. While such prospects may sound like fodder for some silly hillbilly lyrics, things could still have ended poorly for those who don't respect the power of gas-powered garden implements. While there may have also been a machete involved, it's the thought that counts. They made it perfectly clear that they intended to put a hurt on anyone who threatened to remove the appointed hooligan 'houla-guard. The chains of these fools would remain chained to my hoped-for companion for Wili. The kind and compassionate rescue squad returned home disappointed and defeated.

This whole scenario sounded like a sad country song. In fact, it sounds like a Waylon Jennings tune. The one that immediately came to mind, considering the goodness of the liberators and the meanness and cruelty of the oppressors was "Good-Hearted Woman." In 1969, Waylon Jennings was staying at the Fort Worther Motel in Fort Worth, Texas, home of my first dog, Sam Houston. Jennings had come across a newspaper article about the legendary singer, Tina Turner. She was originally from Nutbush, Tennessee and was known as Anna Mae Bullock. The article mentioned that Tina was a good-hearted woman who happened to be in love with a two-timing man. Inspiration comes from all kinds of sources—heartache, the newspaper, and even the neighborhood dog. Jennings was so inspired that he started writing a song. He went and found Willie Nelson, who was in the middle of a poker game, and asked him to help finish it. Between hands, Willie did just that and the rest is history. I'm surprised that "hold," "fold," "all-in," bluff," or "call" aren't in any of the verses. But this story about music-making brings me almost as much joy as the story of how the "Dogs Playing Poker" paintings came to be. Lots of art historians make fun of Cassius Coolidge's series depicting dogs engaging in different kinds of human activities, much the same way music critics and country purists, at first, dismissed this newfangled musical genre called outlaw country as downright criminal. While Coolidge was never financially rewarded or critically-acclaimed, he just kept painting dogs doing amusing things in provocative ways. If you look closely at his paintings, his attention to detail is exquisite, and the artwork is actually quite fine. But Coolidge got the last laugh—in the afterlife. Just a few years ago, one of the poker-playing dog paintings sold at Sotheby's for $658,000 dollars. Established art museums are now proud to have a Coolidge hanging in their collections.

Waylon Jennings faced the same kinds of challenges as he attempted to break away and do something different in a genre that didn't leave much room for creativity. He wanted to create something that not only spoke *to* him but spoke *through* him. At one point in his career, he was so broke that he lamented, "If I go on the road, I lose money. If I stay home, I lose even more." But he kept at his craft, doing it the best way he knew how to do it—or the way that he was learning to do it. His Nashville producers used to tell him that his sound was "not country enough." Jennings thought labels were pointless—in music and in life. Thinking about Waylon and Willie blazing new musical trails reminded me of another kind of troubadour who tried to live out his faith authentically, who walked to a different beat, and who shared a new tune emerging from the old traditions—one that was deep within his heart. It's important to remember that the "experts" in Jesus' day told him repeatedly that his teachings were "not religious enough." The producers and critics of his day preferred the "grand ole" lyrics of the "good ole" songs. Their ears hurt when they heard this lead teacher and his band of long-hairs proclaim an alternative sound. But even though Jerusalem (Nashville) never offered him a record deal, he kept right on singing until his followers were set free. The keepers of the charts did everything they could to keep him off the radio, having him convicted as a criminal and crucified, but even his death empowered a movement that rolled away stones and rocked the whole world. His song would be forever sung.

Eventually, Waylon and his fellow outlaws began to develop a passionate and loyal following. They had a string of albums that would become classics—*Ladies Love Outlaws*, *Lonesome, On'ry and Mean*, and *Honky Tonk Heroes*. But it was Waylon's album, *Good-Hearted Woman* that set everything in motion. That tribute to good women also featured the spiritually evocative "To Beat the Devil" by Kris Kristofferson, as well as "I Knew That You'd be Leavin'" and "One of My Bad Habits." And I hoped that Waylon the dog would be leavin' soon too, but it wasn't looking likely, or even possible. Even though a good-hearted woman had set a miracle in motion, it wouldn't be the first time in history that some bad people had tied things up. Ranaella told me that even though there were other dogs tied to different trees on the island, and more strays than you could shake a bamboo stick at, whenever there was a violent storm on the island, the one she worried about most was Waylon.

It wouldn't be entirely true to say that I'd forgotten about him. I knew that I'd never completely forget about him. It broke my heart to know that he was still chained to that tree—underfed, unloved, and unprotected from the elements. But I also knew that the chances of him ever coming to live with us in Louisiana were about as likely as Tina Turner becoming a Buddhist and moving to Switzerland (oops). Besides, Mano Professor Shorthair had come to live with us, no doubt sent by Wili, and we were back to our Holy Trinity of Almighty Mutts once again—Sinbad, Lili, and Mano. Three is a good, holy, and sufficient number.

Each December I go back to my former island home of Kauai. Typically, I tell no one that I'm coming because I'm there to stay focused and work in solitude on my Christmas Eve sermon and whatever Jazz Mass we might have coming up. In December of 2018, almost a year after I'd received Ranaella's text about Waylon, I went back to Kauai. As was my custom, I told no one that I was coming and no one knew that I was there. At least I assumed no one knew. I arrived on the island in the afternoon and drove to my temporary home on the sunny south shore, far from where Waylon was being kept captive on the north shore.

That evening, out of the pacific blue, I got a text from Ranaella who had no idea that I was on the island. *Hey Padre, are you still interested in Waylon? You're not gonna believe this but somehow, some way, he miraculously escaped, and he's at the humane society right now and we'll figure out a way to get him to you in New Orleans.* I texted her back that not only was I still interested, I was *on* the island and had arrived that afternoon. That afternoon, right about the time I was arriving, Waylon, who I believe sensed my presence, broke through his chains, set himself free, and ran away from his captors. In Hawaiian, there's a special and powerful word that means spiritual energy—*mana*. We might call it the Holy Spirit. It's that extraordinary and powerful force that empowers us to be set free and that connects us to our Creator and to each other. When there's good *mana* within you, others feel your love and want to share theirs with you—even if you are on the other side of the island, or the other side of the world.

Waylon broke free, ran to the paved road along the ocean front, and headed south. The humane society officer just happened to be driving down the road at precisely that moment. She saw Waylon running on the road just as they had found Wili fourteen years earlier. She picked him up and took him to the safety of the shelter. Knowing how Ranaella had longed to save him, she called her to tell her the good news. Then Ranaella immediately texted me. When she found out that I was on the island and that Waylon had cast off his chains about the same time I was arriving, she said, "Well that explains everything." It explains some things, I suppose. But some things still defy explanation.

The next morning I went to the humane society to meet Waylon. He'd ripped open his ear as he was freeing himself from his chains. When we are desperate to be free, an ear is the least of our worries. When I got there, his ear was still bloody, but his spirit was completely intact. And the miracle wasn't over. The humane society gives a name to every stray critter they take in.

But they had given this special guy a name I'd never ever heard given to a dog—Mana. They'd named him after that spiritual energy, the power of God, the Holy Spirit. They'd given him a name that expressed the extraordinary ability to connect us to our Creator and to each other. They'd named him after the life force that truly gives new life. What were the odds? Mana had brought us together. Mana had set him free. Mana was what we shared. Like the prophecies of old, his name would reveal a deeper spiritual truth. And they shall call him Mana, the Energy of the Good, the Dog of God. But I'd still call him Waylon.

A few days before Christmas, on one of the darkest days of the year, there was a light shining brightly in the cargo hold of Alaska Airlines. Mr. Mana, The Free Spirit, the Miracle Dog, the one and only Waylon Wailua Jelly Roll Jennings landed at Louis Armstrong Airport in New Orleans. I still wonder how that happened. But, as Louis Armstrong once said about jazz: "If you have to ask, you'll never know." My Christmas Eve sermon, which Waylon had already written my first day back on Kauai, was about the best gifts—the ones that love us back. The presents that are so present to us that they live, wag, move, and have their whole being in our homes and in our hearts. The best gifts are the ones about which we aren't certain if we are giving them or receiving them. Christmas, as Waylon would teach me, is more about opening our hearts than opening our presents, and conveys the ultimate spiritual truth that it really is more blessed to give than to receive. When we give—we receive even more.

Christmas, also called The Feast of the Incarnation, is when

God, wanting to communicate ultimate love to us, becomes one of us. And if God can become a creature with flesh surely God can speak through a critter with fur. Toward of the end of the Christmas Eve service, as we rose and sang, "Joy to the world, the Lord is come," the Lord's most recent representative came on in as well. Waylon, donning his dapper, gold tinsel collar adorned with jingle bells, pranced in the side door like a reindeer on a Christmas mission. He joined me as we processed down the center aisle, jingling with joy all the way out the back door. Waylon is the best Christmas gift I've ever been given. A home for Waylon is the best Christmas gift that I've ever given. That Christmas Pageant, with Wili directing from the Great Off-Stage above, whispering in the ear of Mary, Joseph, the shepherds, angels, sheep, camels, cows, Santa, the veterinarian, Rudolph, and the rest of the reindeer, was the best one ever. But it all began with a good-hearted woman, Mary, opening her womb to Jesus, which was not unlike Ranaella opening her heart to Waylon. Women like these have hearts, not just of gold, but also of frankincense and myrrh and all that's priceless.

Waylon's story was and is a miracle story. But miracle stories aren't the same as fairy tales. Perfection is not of this world. The kingdom has not yet come *completely*. Sometimes happy endings elude. Unlike fairy tales, these bona fide tails wag, sag, get mad, and get sad sometimes. It wouldn't be a true outlaw country album without a sad song or two, an obstacle to overcome, a disappointment or devastation to work through. As true stories unfold, the truth must always be told. Even though goodness will ultimately prevail while we dwell on earth, there will always be two-timing bad guys, choke-chains and their after-effects, weeds that threaten our yards, weed eaters that end up in the wrong hands, situations that bite, and dogs that bite because of their situations. While Waylon looks a lot like Wili and possesses certain similar charms, as well as a spirit of unconditional love, Waylon is not Wili. And Wili is not Waylon. We do each other (and our dogs) a great disservice by not allowing those we love to be their authentic selves. Too often we want them to be created in the image that we have chosen for them rather than the image that God chose for us. All of us come with quirks, baggage, issues, problems, fears, and challenges. But each of us also comes with a one-of-a-kind uniqueness that can help others, stories worth sharing, particular gifts and combinations thereof, and insights that no one else might perceive.

I wish Waylon could tell me about his past—his hurts and wounds and those things that still cause him to fear, and even to hurt, others. Waylon is a damn good dog. But he does have some issues. I suppose if I'd been chained to a tree most of my life with a meth-making daddy who didn't love me, I'd have issues, too. Hell, I didn't have any of those obstacles and I *still* have serious issues! Waylon is no outlaw. Ninety-nine percent of the time Waylon behaves like an angel. He's a lover—affectionate, shy, and sweet. But Waylon's fears sometimes cause him to come unleashed and lash out. The first time he was supposed to go into the mobile dog-grooming command vehicle, he balked. The generator was making a loud noise, so Waylon put the brakes on and cowered in fear. Waylon is terrified of loud noises—cars, thunder, fireworks, and fire-and-brimstone preachers. The groomer picked him up to carry him inside and Waylon bit him. It was quick and it was over. Waylon immediately recognized that he'd done a terrible thing, and he looked ashamed and penitent the whole time he was being bathed. That was a fear-based bite. Much of the violence in our world is a result of people's fears—or desperation that they have no other way out of a situation that seems bleak and hopeless. But Waylon's bad deeds weren't singular. Even though he has now come to an agreement with the groomer that involves me hand-delivering him straight to the grooming table, there was another incident. I blame this one on mob-mentality, the intense desire to protect those closest to us—and sharks. He and Mano, for a while, would get all worked up in the backyard over the appearance of any person showing up—they didn't even have to be a Jehovah's Witness. They would bark their heads off. One day Waylon, feeding off of Mano's shark-like barking frenzy, jumped over the fence, ran over to my sweet neighbor who was pulling weeds just next door, and bit her on the back of her leg. Oh, how I wished she'd had a weed eater to chase off the criminal. But this time, when I ran outside to apprehend the perp, he was already wagging his tail, as if to brag *look dad, I saved you from the evil intruder.* Mano and Waylon are now not even allowed to bark in a threatening manner. I'm working with Waylon to be more Christ-like and welcome the stranger in our midst. And I'm working with Mano to be less shark-like and not eat them. I believe we are making progress and Waylon's learning, like the psalmist, to fear no evil. He still has a lot to learn. He also has a lot to teach me—I'm sure. Perhaps that's why Wili sent him.

I wish Waylon could tell me when he's feeling threatened or afraid. Our world would be a whole lot kinder and safer if we were better able to tell each other what we need, instead of just acting out in defensive and harmful ways. There was a powerful incident on the Howlelujah Tour in which we experienced the healing power of asking for what you really need. Such a moment can raise us up and turn our lives around. When we are able to share our sadness, anger, hurt, and fear, the intensity of all that pain diminishes, and we are far less likely to inflict pain on others. Wili and I were appearing at the Cathedral in Oklahoma City on a Sunday morning. While I was signing books and Wili was *paw*tographing them, a lady came up to meet Wili and asked for an inscription and a prayer for her husband, who'd refused to get out of the car. While there are a few churches whose theology is so unhealthy that I'd recommend staying put in the parking lot, this wasn't one of those churches. After all, they welcomed Wili and me. This man's refusal to come inside had nothing to do with my theology, personality, or appearance (for a change). The man was devastated. His best friend and faithful dog had recently died unexpectedly. He was so sad that he just couldn't bring himself to come into the church. He'd read about Wili in the newspaper and really wanted to meet him, pet him, and shake his paw, but his grief was so intense he was paralyzed. Then a miracle happened. For a moment he let go of what held him down and held him back, and he got up and walked inside. He came directly to me, his eyes filled with tears, his voice quivering, his body shaking, and asked me one of life's most important questions. "Father Bill, may I have a hug?" He was a big bear of a man, no doubt formidable in much of his life, likely a force to be reckoned with on most days. But in that moment of openness, vulnerability, and the deepest connection, I was able to offer him just what he needed. I embraced him for a long time. We held on to each other right there in front of God and all those church ladies. No one was embarrassed. No one was ashamed. No one was uncomfortable. If only we could talk to each other, admit our pain, share our deepest worries and sorrows with each other, and ask for what we really need without fear of shame—the whole world would change for the better.

Many centuries ago there was a saint in Italy who loved animals more than he loved Chianti. His name was St. Francis. Several years ago, I knelt at his graveside in Assisi and prayed that he would help Wili and me help animals. I could swear on a pile of pasta that I heard him respond, instructing me to become an instrument of peace. Wili claims that what he really said was that we should become instruments of pizza. Either way, I love this guy. I'm sure he and Wili have already gotten acquainted up in heaven over a slice of Quattro Formaggi. I wouldn't be surprised if Wili shared his cheesy pie with the Wolf of Gubbio who will be the first creature I seek to meet in the afterlife, other than Waylon Jennings, Jelly Roll Morton, and Bathsheba (for purely biblical reasons). The Wolf of Gubbio

could teach my dog Waylon a thing or two. And his relationship with Saint Francis could teach the world multitudes.

Although dogs are simply wild wolves that became docile
after they discovered we had couches, their formerly more vicious
selves had more bite to their bark. The Latin word for wolf, *canis
lupus*, very loosely translated means "loopy canine." Trust me you
do not want to approach a loopy canine. Although not as famous
as the wolf who attempted to fool Little Red Riding Hood, the
Wolf of Gubbio has a profound lesson to teach us. By the way,
the wolf in the hood story does deserve commendation. Think
about it this way. The next time you feel stupid just remember
that Little Red Riding Hood couldn't figure out that a wolf in
drag wasn't her grandmother. Makes you feel smarter, doesn't it?

In 1220, Francis moved an hour north from Assisi to
Gubbio, whose local townspeople were called "Goobers" by
the more sophisticated residents of Assisi. The noble citizens
of Gubbio, not to be out-insulted, referred to their southern
rivals as "Assisiholes." Italy is a place where God has done
some good work starting with Sophia Lauren and continuing
with Prosecco. The patron saint of Gubbio, Saint Ubald, is also
the patron saint of men with hair loss. He was the first bishop
to wear a mitre, which served the same purpose as Dwight
Yoakum's cowboy hat for many years. Who ever knew what was
under there? Silliness aside, the Gubbians had a real problem
on their hands back when Francis first came to town. There
was a giant wolf who roamed the outskirts of the countryside.
The Wolf of Gubbio was so fierce he made Wolverine look as

threatening as Scooby Doo. Famished, the wolf began to eat his fill of local livestock. Still hungry, he moved on from his appetizer course and devoured several of the town's residents. The citizens couldn't decide whether to rise up, form a well-armed militia and attack the wolf, or to stay home, invest in walls and security systems, and cower in fear. Enter Saint Francis. Francis told the townsfolk he would approach the wolf and have a "come to Jesus" meeting with him. He also reminded them that violence rarely reduced violence and that building more walls wasn't exactly what God envisioned when creating the earth.

Francis was warned by the townspeople not to approach the wolf. He did anyway. As Francis got closer, the wolf began to charge. Francis didn't back down, but he also didn't threaten harm to the wolf. He made the sign of the cross, the universal sign of self-sacrificing love, and showed honor and respect to the beast by calling him "Brother Wolf." The wolf had never encountered respect or kindness, and he'd certainly been called many names, but never brother. The wolf knelt at Francis' feet. He told Francis—or maybe Francis just knew—that the cause of his violence wasn't hate, it was hunger. A wolf's gotta eat. Francis acknowledged that when we have needs that threaten our own viability as creatures, we'll do what we need to do to survive. Francis and the wolf negotiated a peace treaty. Francis promised the wolf that if he would be kind and gentle, the residents of Gubbio would feed him. The wolf promised he would become tame and docile if the residents of Gubbio fed him. Francis led the wolf, without a leash, back into the town as the terrified humans gasped and fell back. The wolf's demeanor became more dog-like when the citizens became more Christ-like. He became the town mascot going door to door seeking food. Everyone was kind to him and fed him. The wolf became the most beloved creature in the history of Italy.

Whether they are in sheep's clothing or appear as themselves, I believe that most wolves in our world would be subdued and transformed more by kindness than by violence. I believe that if we were able to understand the root causes of why creatures engage in harmful acts—to themselves and to others—it would be a much better world, for humans and animals, alike. Jesus showed us this different and better way long ago. He told us clearly that those who live by the sword will die by the sword (or the gun, or the bomb, or the fist). He said that the peacemakers were blessed and that those who turned the other cheek would be more powerful than those who strike back. Some of us are slow to catch on—most of our world leaders, I'm afraid. But there are still saints among us like Francis and like Wili, who remind us that we are called to replace hatred with love, injury with pardon, doubt with faith, despair with hope, darkness with light, and sadness with joy. Francis (and Jesus) was right—it's in giving that we receive, it's in pardoning that we are pardoned, and it's in dying that we are born to eternal life. It's the way of Jesus, the way of Francis, and the way of Wili. Someday, it might be the way of Waylon and, perhaps, even the way of the whole world.

Until that day comes, don't despair. Keep doing the good, right, and loving thing—for people *and* for animals. Some will say it's an exercise in futility. Some will tell you that the story of the Wolf of Gubbio is entirely fabricated, that it never happened and never could happen. But in 1872, as renovations were taking place at the Church of Saint Francis of Peace in Gubbio, workers uncovered a sarcophagus dating from the early Middle Ages. Underneath it was the buried skeleton of a giant wolf. Apparently, miracles happened back then. And they still do today. I know one of those miracles and his name is Waylon Wailua Jelly Roll Jennings.

My miracle boy has been with me now for eighteen months. That's the same amount of time I had with Wili after he was diagnosed with cancer and given only three months to live. Wili lived so much life in those eighteen months, and he accomplished so much good. I'd hoped that Waylon, Wili's heir apparent, would live a long life and accompany me on the road again on lots of Howlelujah Tours for many years to come. But as I was wrapping up this book, Waylon stopped eating. When you live in Louisiana and you stop eating, even if you're a dog, you know there's a problem. I took Waylon across Lake Pontchartrain into New Orleans to the same 24-hour veterinary clinic I took Wili that late night in November of 2016. When the vet told me that Waylon had a large, inoperable malignant mass in his heart and that he had only two weeks to live, I broke down and cried. I'd not cried with such deep sorrow since Wili's death. As I anguished over Waylon's heart, my own seemed to break. I'm praying for another miracle for Waylon, but if it doesn't come, it'll not diminish the beauty and power of the one we've already received. Every moment I had with Wili was a miracle. Every moment I've had with Waylon is a miracle, too. In the most holy sense of time and timelessness, this book ends where it began—not as a fairy tale but a faith tail—celebrating the precious gift of those we love who love us most.

Thomas Merton begins his famous prayer with these words: "My Lord God, I have no idea where I'm going. I do not see the road ahead of me." I've felt somewhat lost these last days. So I've been listening to a lot more Waylon and Willie to get me through to the other side. I believe with all of my heart that someday, someway, somehow, somewhere, Waylon and Wili will be on the road.

Again.

Fourth Paw:

ROOM AT THE END

But love is bigger than us all. The end is not the end at all.

Willie Nelson

FRIEND OF DOGS: AN EPILOGUE

You'll never walk alone.
Rogers and Hammerstein

Even after the last chapter is written, the book closed, the pen put away, and computer turned off, there's always more to the story. That's good news for anyone who thinks it's all over, the fat lady has sung, the dying dog has howled, and that's all she wrote. The addendums, epilogues, and postscripts are inexhaustible, if not eternal. And don't get me started on the ongoing reality of the revisions, re-writes, renewals, rebirths, and resurrections. At least I believe that to be true in Wili's case. Wili's good work will never end and he keeps showing up in the most unlikely places.

After the Last Howlelujah Tour, while Wili stayed back home in Louisiana, I ventured off to the land of terriers. I started in Wales, moved on to England, and finished up in Ireland. I thought of Wili often, but especially each evening in Wales when my teacher, Esther DeWaal, fed me delicious Welsh cheese! Esther, a scholar of the monastic and Celtic traditions, did her best to impart her wisdom to the student. But she had help. As the Great Airedale once said, "When the puppy is ready, the trainer will appear." Wili rephrased that to read: "When the mutt is hungry, the treat will appear." Either way, one morning an animal showed up inside the former pottery studio in Rowlestone where I was staying with Esther. It was a vole. A vole is really a Welsh version of a field mouse, the same way we might think of Tom Jones as a Welsh version of a singer—same thing, just a bit sexier. I'd never met a vole before. I'm not sure the vole had ever met a priest before either.

The vole was adorable. Esther seemed stunned when she walked into my cottage and saw it. She looked at the vole and then looked at me. Apparently it's not every day that a vole comes for a house call. She said, "This is quite extraordinary. You seem to attract this sort of thing, don't you?" Yes, I do, especially if the "sort of thing" is of the canine variety. Voles are rather remarkable rodents. Studies have shown that voles can exhibit empathic tendencies, giving more attention, for example, to another vole that's ill or has been mistreated. We underestimate the animal kingdom's capacity to out-compassion us. This vole, whom I named "Volley," seemed to be sick. I did my best to make the tiny creature comfortable. I made a bed of straw. I provided a small bowl with milk and water. I put a dollop of honey within tasting distance. The kind man next door, a doctor who'd taken to farming, came by and examined the vole. He, too, was perplexed as to why the vole had come inside to hang out with me. He didn't think the creature was long for this world. "But you've created a really nice place in which for him to die," he reassured me. Perhaps that's an ultimate gift we can give to each other. For the end will come for each of us. And in that moment, we want to be surrounded by things that comfort us—something that's soft and sweet or someone who loves us and will miss us terribly. The vole wasn't with me long enough, but I think I loved that vole. What is wrong with me? How can anyone be so tenderhearted to fall for a mouse? Did I learn that from Wili? I wonder if he would've eaten the vole. For some reason, in this instance, I don't think so. Still—it was becoming obvious that I needed therapy.

Esther made me write poetry about the vole. She wanted me to engage in "creativity within structure" which is a concept I've often contemplated. It's not a bad way to approach life. She instructed me to write Japanese Tanka poems which have a 5, 7, 5, 7, 7 syllable sequence. I dedicated my poems to Volley the Vole:

FIELD OF FORTUNE
Can I buy a vole?
With milk and honey and grass
Hoping to restore
Seeking your resurrection
Praying for a miracle

CONTROL

Why are you here?
Rodent reminder of There
Beyond my control
Unexpected and unknown
As is life and death and all

HA (BREATH OF LIFE)

You stirred this morning
Yet I knew it was not long
When I blew on you
You would not struggle for breath
You would not struggle at all

PSALM

You are resting now
Eternally in God's hands
So unlike your own
Tiny, uncertain, grasping
Gently cradling all of you

SALVATION

Could I have saved you?
Could I have done something more?
These questions I ask
Perhaps because of great love
Love for all God's creatures

TEACHER
Did you come to teach?
To remind me about death?
Death comes before life
The old passes before new
What shall I bury with you?

Esther appreciated my poetic passion, but encouraged me to keep my day job. Esther and I had wonderful discussions about all facets of life while I was with her. We often focused on the Celtic concept of thin places. The Celtic Christians believed that thin places are where the veil between the temporal and eternal is shear and transparent. Heaven is so close to earth that you can see it, feel it, and even sniff it. Esther had a beautiful way of expressing this creation-centered idea that God can be found surrounding us. She told me that the Celtic approach to God opens up a world in which nothing is too common to be exalted and nothing is so exalted that it cannot be made common. On earth, as it is in heaven, so to speak, as it is revealed on earth. I have found myself in thin places on numerous occasions: Patrick's Mountain and Skellig Michael in Ireland, the island of Iona in Scotland, the Kalaupapa peninsula on Molokai, the Napali Coast in Kauai, the Maple Leaf Bar in New Orleans on Monday nights when the George Porter Trio is playing, my lap when Wili would crawl into it. I felt God's immanent and immediate presence in those places and in those moments. But I had no idea I'd experience two unlikely thin places just after leaving Esther's home.

Although I'm more passionate about football and baseball, I have two favorite soccer teams in the world. One is in Glasgow and the other is in Liverpool. From Esther's place I traveled on to both towns. In Liverpool, I was preoccupied with all-things Beatles. I'm talkin' about a revolution. But while I love music the most, I also have a healthy appreciation for sports. While in Glasgow, a special field trip to Celtic Park was in order. What connects the Celtic and Liverpool Football Clubs is not just a devoted and passionate fan base, but both clubs have the same theme song: "You'll Never Walk Alone." Originally written by Rogers and Hammerstein for the musical, *Carousel*, it was the Gerry and the Pacemakers version that made it popular, topping the charts in Great Britain in 1963. And shortly after the song's popularity exploded, it was adopted as the anthem for both football clubs and their fans. It was likely that the Liverpool F.C. started using the song during matches first, and then Celtic F.C. followed shortly thereafter. But, Gerry and the Pacemakers were from Liverpool, so there's no more soul-stirring a moment in all of sports than to hear thousands of Liverpool fans sing these words with the passion of the most devoted of disciples: "When you walk through a storm hold your head up high and don't be afraid of the dark…And you'll never walk alone." Those aren't just good lyrics—that's good theology.

The Celtic Football Club was founded in 1887 by Brother Walfrid, a member of the Marist Brothers Teaching Order. Brother Walfrid started Celtic in St. Mary's Church Hall in order to fund charitable endeavors, mainly an organization that fed poor,

Irish immigrant children in the Glasgow Ghetto which led to the establishment of the charity, *The Poor Children's Dinner Table*. Now that's an organization I'd gladly cheer for. The club crest for Celtic was originally a Celtic cross, but in the 1930s, the crest was changed to an Irish Shamrock. But religious fervor has been a part of Celtic's tradition from the beginning. There's a stained-glass window that was moved from their first stadium and is now displayed near the player's locker room in the new stadium—a sacred site which is called Paradise by those who believe. The team is collectively known as *The Invincibles*. My nephew, who is not a soccer fan in the slightest, accompanied me on a tour of the new stadium that was more inspiring than it was informative.

Our guide was a kindly older gentleman who resembled Captain Kangaroo in both appearance and in demeanor. There was nothing flashy about the stadium or our tour. The tour began with Captain Kangaroo shoving a video tape into an old VCR, but that nine minute Celtic highlight tape gave me goosebumps. Our guide was accompanied by a young man with Down's syndrome named Peter. When we got to the trophy room, Peter took over the tour. He proudly pointed out the European Champions Cup that the Celtic team, the "Lions of Lisbon," had brought home fifty years earlier. He also showed us the Celtic cross made from the stone of St. Mary's Church where Brother Walfrid formally constituted the Celtic Football Club. It was a sweet and holy moment that showed us that this organization was about so much more than football. It began as an expression of God's love, and it continues to be the same today. As I walked out onto the field, I could almost hear the angels singing, "You'll never walk alone." It was at that moment that I felt like I was stepping into a Thin Place. If loyalty, dedication, and fervor, could manifest a Thin Place, then it would surely manifest here.

In the gift shop, I purchased a green and white Celtic soccer scarf which would become the stole I wear during St. Patrick's Day services. And I can never walk out of a gift shop without first visiting the dog section. I found Wili a dog bowl painted with two powerful symbols of God's presence—shamrocks and paws— and a green and white collar with a matching leash that read: "You'll Never Walk Alone." I couldn't promise Wili that I could heal him of his cancer, make him rich, or even feed him a filet at every meal, but I could promise him that he'd never walk alone. He would never be without me. Maybe that's what all of us really need to know. Regardless of our condition or prognosis, as long as we are with those who love us—we'll never be alone. Go Celtic or Go Home. Or that should be—Go Celtic and *Come* Home.

Eventually, during my tour of Celtic lands, I ended up with my family in the small town of Cobh in Ireland. That day, they all decided to go bend over backwards to kiss the Blarney Stone. There is nothing wrong with that, but I felt like I was already fluent in Blarney—some would say full of it—and I'd already kissed more than my fair share of hard, cold, unforgiving surfaces. Sometimes, I even bent over backwards to do so. I decided, instead, to wander around the charming town of Cobh to see what adventure might await me, which is my favorite traveling philosophy. Cobh, formerly called Queenstown, is an interesting place associated with both tragedy and hope. Tragically speaking, it was the final port of call for a ship called the Titanic on April 11, 1912. And then shortly after that, in 1915, the Lusitania was sunk by a German U-boat just off shore. Hopefully speaking, it was also the embarkation point for 2.5 million of the six million Irish people who, between 1848 and 1950, immigrated to North America seeking a better life. Along the waterfront there's a lovely statue of Annie Moore and her brothers looking longingly and hopefully to the West. She was the first person to be admitted to the United States through New York's Ellis Island on January 1, 1892.

As I strolled along the waterfront, I came across a couple of really nice, quasi-fancy pubs where I heard live Irish music pouring from their open doors. I usually can't resist the pull of live music of any kind, but none of them felt like what I was looking for, so I kept walking. And I kept walking. Far beyond where tourists fear to tread I finally found it. It would've been more accurate to say I felt it. The positive energy of *mana* was coming from that bar's open door. It reached out, embraced me, and pulled me in. It was a simple neighborhood pub, but I could tell immediately that it was the real deal. There was nothing prefabricated, contrived, or manufactured about it. On the side of the building, faded letters identified it as Connie Doulin's. But on the front, framed by cheap plastic banners resembling Irish flags, it read Danny's, with half the D worn away by the salty sea air. There was an old, yellowed photo of a toothy and grinning donkey with the words: "Get Your Ass in Here" taped to the window. I stopped and peered inside. It looked like I've always imagined heaven to look like—warm and comfortable. There were two men sitting at the bar who gave a welcoming nod in my direction. There was a dog I'd later learn was named Tamara stretched out on a plaid padded bench beneath a sign that read: "Warning: Pomeranian on Duty!" Next to her was a woman who was waving at me to come on in. I saw plush animal toys everywhere, some obviously set aside for dogs, others for children, and still more that I assumed must be for adults who might be in need of some comfort and reassurance. There was also the largest, stuffed Bengal tiger this side of LSU that sat in his own chair—a sure sign for this new Louisiana boy. Behind the bar was a notice that reminded me I was in Ireland. It read: "Good Morning. Let the Struggle Begin." Of the Irish, it has been said that they fight happy wars and sing sad songs. I looked around in awe at the simple, life-affirming surroundings—a Celtic cross (of course), a stuffed owl, a guitar, a drum, Titanic memorabilia, and a hurling stick and ball with an embossed Celtic knot. There was a framed photo of two golden retrievers with an inscription that read: "To the management, staff, and customers of Danny's Pub in recognition of your support of the Irish Guide Dogs for the Blind." There were explanations of important Irish curse words and a notice reading: "Friends Welcome, Relatives by Appointment Only." And there was a poster that was instantly my favorite that read: "Dogs aren't our whole life but make our lives whole." I will drink, and maybe even dance, to that.

Along the bar there were donation boxes and jars for every

charity imaginable, and many of them were almost full: The Irish Cancer Society, the Mercy Hospital, the "Please Help the Donkeys" Donkey Sanctuary, the Mission of Saint Anthony, and the Lifeboats Association. On an old glass vase, a hand-lettered sign read, *For Liam's Grave.* I'd find out later that Liam had been a customer here for many years, and the funds raised were to maintain his gravesite. The lady with the leg brace introduced herself as Monica and offered me my choice from a box of Mrs. Kipling's Fancy Cakes. I chose chocolate. Then vanilla. Then another chocolate. After a few moments of conversation, she wanted to know if the girls in Hawaii were "as pretty as the television makes them out to be." "Yes ma'am," I assured her. "They may be even prettier." For the next five hours, I became a part of their community as we shared stories of life, laughter, love, and loss. We talked about Ireland and Hawaii, Cobh and Covington, music and sports, soccer and hurling, and dogs and more dogs. There was no one there who wasn't a regular—and I was quickly becoming one, too. As the gathered group began to expand, good-natured insults began to be hurled. A debate broke out over which Irish beer was the best. There were votes for Beamish, Bulmer's, Murphy's, Guinness, and Smithwicks. Everyone had a definite dog in the fight—just like with other vitally important, turf-defending issues such as church music or the perfect temperature at any given time in any given room. When someone advocated for Beamish, a burly man drinking a Bulmers boomed, "I wouldn't wash my cow with that!" The cow might not have minded. Although

I recalled that Wili preferred his baths to be in Smithwicks.

There was a lovely gentleman seated in the corner of the bar who sat the whole afternoon sipping tea. He had warm eyes that crinkled when he smiled. His name was Connor, which he explained was Gaelic for "Lover of Dogs." He shared with me the story of his wife, Mary, and how, over the years, they'd rescued and taken in more than forty stray dogs. I realized I'd finally met my match. Connor may have actually loved dogs more than I do. As he reminisced about his wife, who had died not too many years before, his eyes grew misty and his voice quivered. "I miss her so," he told me. I knew that he did, and I told him that she must've been a very special person to take in forty dogs. "Aye, indeed, she was," he said. When I shared that I loved dogs too, and had a special type of terrier back home, the bartender, Noel, immediately walked the block home to fetch his dog, Tom the Terrier. Tom was a fine beast and well-named for Ireland. But Noel wasn't finished bestowing gifts upon the visitor from far away. He reached behind the bar and gave me his last copy of a CD he'd recorded with the local Quarry Cock Choir. It contained only one song to benefit the Marymount Hospice, a recording of the Ben E. King classic, *Stand by Me*. Featured on the CD were singers with names as Irish as Tom the Terrier— Paddy Kavanaugh, Duncan Gerrish, Pa McGrath, Paudie Cadogan, and Eamonn Britton. I told him I loved the song and counted the lyrics among my favorites. We recited them together. "When the night has come and the land is dark and the moon is the only light we'll see. No I won't be afraid, just as long as you stand by me." Along with "You'll Never Walk Alone," it could be Wili's Theme Song. As long as you stand, sit, and stay by my side, I will not fear. I'd experienced everything in that pub that a true community provides: genuine laughter, real compassion, authentic concern, the giving and receiving of gifts, the opportunity to make a difference, sweet treats, and potent beverages. That's a list that should describe every religious institution and faith community in existence—that's how it's supposed to be. We were missing only one thing—song. And before I knew it, Noel comes from behind the bar and announces that he would be singing a favorite Irish tune for the guest from America. He launched into the Irish classic, *The Town I Loved So Well*, a song that was written by Phil Coulter about his hometown of Derry in Northern Ireland. The first few verses speak of the simple joys of small-town life—playing ball, running in the rain, feeding kids, training dogs, and playing music, but then he returns later to discover how violence and the conflict called "The Troubles"—pitting north against south, Protestant against Catholic, and brother against brother—had turned the once calm haven into a furious hell. But he will not let the bad news be the final word. So, the song ends with a ray of hope for the future, that even though the music has faded, they will carry on. Their hearts are set on tomorrow and on peace once again. No one spoke while Noel sang. Everyone listened reverently to this sacred Irish tune, paying their respects. Truly, this was a sacred space, a thin place with a sheer veil. My initial assessment turned out to be right. This is what heaven surely looks like.

It was getting late, the bar was getting full, and my ship would soon sail. I knew the time for me to walk on had come. I'd noticed that next to Connor, the lover of dogs, there was an empty stool that no one sat in the entire afternoon. I wondered if there was some significance to the spot—if it belonged to someone special. Suddenly Monica shouted to the crowd, "Willie's comin!" Everyone applauded, perked up, and sat up. Connor's face lit up with joy as he turned to me and told me what was happening. "Aye, Willie is coming. He's one of our regulars. He's a good friend to us all. He may not be able to get out of the car though. You see, Willie's got cancer and we don't know how long he'll live. But this here is his stool. No one can fill it but him. We'll always save a spot for Willie—even when he's gone. We'll never forget Willie. We'll always love him."

I will always save a space in my heart for Wili.
I will never forget him.
I will love him forever.

Has not God sent us a good messenger?

ACKNOWLEDGEMENTS

"I know you are doing God's work." One of my amazing parishioners at historic Christ Church Covington made that comment to me during the time I took away from parish ministry to focus on the ministry of writing this book (and the tour that led up to it). Knowing that there are people in this world who perceive that what you're up to is God-blessed (and are even praying for you accordingly) makes all the difference. When Wili and I set off on our 5,000-mile Last Howlelujah Tour, we weren't sure how many folks would recognize that we were doing God's work or show up to support us and help animals in need. But they did—eventually by the thousands. There were so many who worked tirelessly to advance our *howly* cause that I can't name them all. To each person who helped organize a Howlelujah Tour event, welcomed Wili and me into your homes, churches, bookstores, breweries, and restaurants, prepared a meal or a doggie bag, bought a book or made a donation—words can't express the deep gratitude we feel. Just know that Wili wags eternally in thanksgiving for you.

The writer of a book is one of many who participate in its creation. I am grateful for a team of talented (and dog-loving) individuals. Tina Richardson's editing skills vastly improved my content and also kept me from saying things of which the Pup, I mean the Pope, might not approve. Plus, she let me make up words according to my own *dog*tionary. Diana Branton is not just great with text; she's also a genius with design. Her graphic art makes Wili come alive with the force of an Easter miracle. Melissa Rabidoux helps me make sense of life, work, ministry, communication, deadlines, and details—and does so with a sacrificial spirit and a heart-warming smile. As usual, Bill Broyles offered the insights only an extraordinary writer can, and Ron Starbuck and Robbin Brent provided publishing wisdom and guidance along the way. Ann Christian believed in both of us beasts and spread the word about the amazing Nawiliwili Nelson and his Howlelujah Tour all the way from New Orleans to Las Vegas—and far beyond.

Until recently, I had planned to grow old surrounded solely by my pack of canines. Human beings would be tolerated only on special occasions. While such a scenario is not so bad, everything changed for the better when God brought into my life a being more loving than a beast. Sandy Carter (soon to be Miller) is the human partner I had no idea could exist. She loves dogs, God, wine, and me—perhaps in that order. She brings a smile to my face and creates joy in my heart. She is the greatest blessing in my life. Her dogs Dash Riprock and Roscoe Worthington Jones now bring our pack to six, which must make us the "Brady Bunch of Bark." I can't wait to sniff out the trail of adventure that awaits us together.

Wili's work is not done. A portion of the proceeds of every book sold will go to his Howlelujah Foundation to help our animal friends. You can learn more about The Howlelujah Foundation at www.howlelujahfoundation.com. We are grateful to each and every one of you who loves dogs and works to make their lives better. While they make our lives better than we will ever make theirs, we are called to work, pray, and give on their behalf. To all who serve the canine creatures of this world: I know you are doing God's work.

August 26, 2020, The Feast Day of Sam (my first dog)

www.HowlelujahFoundation.com
Donate@HowlelujahFoundation.com

In Loving Memory

Nawiliwili "Wili" Nelson
February 14, 2005-May 6, 2018

CPSIA information can be obtained
at www.ICGtesting.com
Printed in the USA
LVHW091433201120
672144LV00005B/271

9 781735 7716